NEVADA
TRAVEL ✦ SMART®

VALLEY OF FIRE STATE PARK

NEVADA
TRAVEL ✦ SMART®

Carolyn Graham

John Muir Publications
A Division of Avalon Travel Publishing

John Muir Publications
A Division of Avalon Travel Publishing
5855 Beaudry Street
Emeryville, CA 94608

Printed in the United States of America.
First edition. First printing February 2000.

ISSN 1525-3791
ISBN 1-56261-434-7

Editors: Peg Goldstein, Lizann Flatt
Graphics Editor: Bunny Wong
Production: Scott Fowler
Design: Marie J.T. Vigil
Cover design: Janine Lehmann, Marie J.T. Vigil
Map style development: American Custom Maps—Jemez Springs, NM
Map illustration: Julie Felton
Printer: Publishers Press
Front cover photos: *small*—© Henryk Kaiser/Leo de Wys (Hoover Dam)
                    large—© John Elk III (Wheeler Peak, Great Basin National Park)
Back cover photo: © Henryk Kaiser/Leo de Wys (Reno, Nevada)

Distributed to the book trade by
Publishers Group West
Berkeley, California

2·22·00   ing   15 95

While every effort has been made to provide accurate, up-to-date information, the author and publisher accept no responsibility for loss, injury, or inconvenience sustained by any person using this book.

19080258

NEVADA TRAVEL•SMART: A GUIDE THAT GUIDES

Most guidebooks are primarily directories, providing information but very little help in making choices—you have to guess how to make the most of your time and money. *Nevada Travel•Smart* is different: By highlighting the very best of the state and offering various planning features, it acts like a personal tour guide rather than a directory.

TAKE THE STRESS OUT OF TRAVEL

Sometimes traveling causes more stress than it relieves. Sorting through information, figuring out the best routes, determining what to see and where to eat and stay, scheduling each day—all of this can make a vacation feel daunting rather than fun. Relax. We've done a lot of the legwork for you. This book will help you plan a trip that suits *you*—whatever your time frame, budget, and interests.

SEE THE BEST OF THE STATE

Author Carolyn Graham has lived in Nevada for 10 years. She has handpicked every listing in this book, and she gives you an insider's perspective on what makes each one worthwhile. So while you will find many of the big tourist attractions listed here, you'll also find lots of smaller, lesser-known treasures, such as the Berlin-Ichthyosaur State Park north of Tonopah and the Extraterrestrial Highway near Rachel. And each sight is described so you'll know what's most—and sometimes least—interesting about it.

In selecting the restaurants and accommodations for this book, the author sought out unusual spots with local flavor. While in some areas of the state chains are unavoidable, wherever possible the author directs you to one-of-a-kind places. We also know that you want a range of options: One day you may want a seven-course feast at Caesars Palace, while the next day you would be just as happy (as would your wallet) with a burger from a brewpub. Most of the restaurants and accommodations listed here are moderately priced, but the author also includes budget and splurge options, depending on the destination.

CREATE THE TRIP YOU WANT

We all have different travel styles. Some people like spontaneous weekend jaunts, while others plan longer, more leisurely trips. You may want to cover as much ground as possible, no matter how much time you have. Or maybe you prefer to focus your trip on one part of the state or on some special interest, such as history, nature, or art. We've taken these differences into account.

Though the individual chapters stand on their own, they are organized in a geographically logical sequence, so that you could conceivably fly into Las Vegas, drive chapter by chapter to each destination in the book, and end up close to where you started. Of course, you don't have to follow that sequence, but it's there if you want a complete picture of the state.

Each destination chapter offers ways of prioritizing when time is limited: In the Perfect Day section, the author suggests what to do if you have only one day to spend in the area. Also, every Sightseeing Highlight is rated, from one to four stars: ★★★★—or "must see" sights—first, followed by ★★★ sights, then ★★ sights, and finally ★—or "see if you have time" sights. At the end of each sight listing is a time recommendation in parentheses. User-friendly maps help you locate the sights, restaurants, and lodging of your choice.

And if you're in it for the ride, so to speak, you'll want to check out the Scenic Routes described at the end of several chapters. They take you through some of the most scenic parts of the state.

In addition to these special features, the appendix has other useful travel tools:

- The Planning Map and Mileage Chart help you determine your own route and calculate travel time.
- The Special Interest Tours show you how to design your trip around any of six favorite interests.
- The Calendar of Events provides an at-a-glance view of when and where major events occur throughout the state.
- The Resource Guide tells you where to go for more information about national and state parks, individual cities and counties, local bed-and-breakfasts, and more.

HAPPY TRAVELS

With this book in hand, you have many reliable recommendations and travel tools at your fingertips. Use it to make the most of your trip. And have a great time!

WHY VISIT NEVADA?

From sagebrush to neon, cowboys to showgirls, Nevada offers a diverse range of attractions to visit, places to see, and people to meet. Visitors often are drawn to Nevada for its gambling, nightlife, and 24-hour attractions and then discover its desert solitude and out-of-the-way places.

Nevada is the neon capital of the world whose lifeblood is centered in Las Vegas, a glittering outpost that continues to outdo itself with each new hotel. Las Vegas has a skyline that includes castles, pyramids, and pirate ships, and now also has an Eiffel Tower and a mini-Manhattan. In Reno and Lake Tahoe, the glitz is tightly concentrated in small pockets and surrounded by a playground of natural attractions.

But beyond the neon-splattered cities lie hundreds of miles of roads, rivers, and hiking trails that lead into an ocean of unspoiled wilderness. Even if you don't gamble, you'll find a jackpot of attractions and a wealth of wide-open spaces that will continue to lure you to the Silver State.

LAY OF THE LAND

When most people think of rural Nevada, they see images of a vast sea of sagebrush, covering a landscape of basin and range. But Nevada is a jagged, bumpy state with more than 300 mountain ranges. The tallest point in Nevada is Boundary Peak, 13,140 feet in elevation, and there are several other ranges with peaks that top out at more than 10,000 feet. Nevada's mountain ranges provide many different types of terrain (granite, limestone, volcanic rock, and sandstone) for visitors to explore.

Nevada is basin and range country, a fact that is especially noticeable to travelers heading east or west on U.S. 50. As you crest one summit, the next basin stretches out below—a pattern that repeats itself as you march toward either side of the state. The Great Basin Desert covers most of Nevada, which, thanks to the numerous mountain ranges, means that very few of Nevada's rivers ever see the ocean—most of them flow inward and feed lakes or sinks. The Mojave Desert creeps in at the southern tip of Nevada and is the lowest—and hottest—part of the state.

Nevada may be hot, dry, and landlocked, but that doesn't mean visitors won't find plenty of water—the state has several natural and man-made lakes and marshes. In southern Nevada, Lake Mead is the country's largest man-made lake, formed when the Colorado River was tamed by Hoover Dam. In northern Nevada, Lake Tahoe was formed millions of years ago when the mountains were pushed up, volcanoes sealed the outlets, and a glacier carved out the basin. Regardless of how they were formed, all of Nevada's lakes provide recreational opportunities for boaters, anglers, and sunbathers.

FLORA AND FAUNA

For a desert, Nevada has surprisingly diverse flora and fauna. Southern Nevada is part of the Mojave Desert, where Joshua trees, mesquite trees, creosote bushes, and yucca plants thrive. Sagebrush is Nevada's state flower, so it stands to reason that just about anywhere you travel in the state, you'll run across the pungent smelling bush. Several varieties of cacti, including beavertail and barrel, grow in southern Nevada and put on a brilliant show in the spring. Lake Mead and the surrounding desert are home to bighorn sheep, which like to clamber up the canyon walls above the Colorado River. The desert is also a haven for the endangered desert tortoise as well as jackrabbits, marmots, coyotes, rattlesnakes, and a host of lizards.

Eastern Nevada is far more mountainous, providing a suitable climate for piñon, juniper, bristlecones, and other evergreens. Near Elko, in the Ruby Mountains, you'll find some of the state's best wildflower watching—the lupines and mule's ears bloom in abundance. Deer, antelope, elk, squirrels, and bobcats roam this region, as do several species of raptors such as bald eagles and red-tailed hawks.

Northern Nevada is equally diverse. The valley floor is carpeted with sagebrush and occupied by desert animals such as jackrabbits and coyotes, but you'll also find wetland areas that offer spectacular animal- and bird-watching. Washoe Lake north of Carson City and Stillwater National Wildlife Refuge near Fallon are popular destinations for bird-watchers, who can expect to find great blue herons, egrets, pelicans, and other majestic waterfowl. Pyramid Lake is a nesting site for white pelicans as well as home to the endangered cui-ui, a prehistoric suckerfish that was a traditional food of the Paiute Indians.

Near Lake Tahoe, Carson City, and Reno, deer and bear forage among the pines and aspens. Near Virginia City the herds of mustangs that roam free in the desert are a spectacular sight. Lurking deep in Lake Tahoe are huge mackinaw trout—a prize among fishermen—as well as kokanee salmon, which spawn in the Truckee River as it flows out of the north end of Lake Tahoe.

HISTORY

In the beginning, Nevada was covered by a giant sea, evidence of which you'll still see in such areas as Berlin-Ichthyosaur State Park, where the remnants of prehistoric fish lizards were unearthed. It is estimated that the earliest humans began to occupy Nevada around 11,000 B.C. About 2500 B.C. Anasazi Indians are believed to have lived in Southern Nevada, although they disappeared without a trace in about A.D. 1150, leaving no sign of why they left or where they went. At the Lost City in Overton near Las Vegas, visitors can explore the remains of the Anasazi Indians' former dwellings (and re-creations of dwellings) and view their artifacts.

Later the Southern Paiutes came to occupy the Anasazi territory. The Paiutes were hunter-gatherers, and oddly, their civilization was not as advanced as the Anasazi. The Washo Indians occupied Northwestern Nevada while the Shoshone lived in central and eastern Nevada. For the next several hundred years, the Native Americans lived peacefully off the land, gathering pine nuts, weaving baskets and cradleboards from reeds and other plants, and using innovative hunting techniques for capturing rabbits and sagehen.

The first European explorers began to cross Nevada in the late 1700s, but it wasn't until 1843 that explorer John C. Frémont began to document Nevada's diverse geography. Frémont, while mapping the state, "discovered" and named the Great Basin as well as other places such as Pyramid Lake. By this time, folks back East had begun to migrate out West. One such group was the tragic Donner Party, whose members, in 1846, endured incredible hardships along their journey through Nevada. The journey resulted in cannibalism when the party became snowbound in the Sierra Nevada.

In 1848 and '49, gold was discovered in California, which set off a massive migration of people and instigated Nevada's own mining boom. The first major gold strike occurred in 1849 in Gold Canyon near Dayton. At Genoa, then called Mormon Station, a strong settlement had taken root. Industrious prospectors began to dig for gold in other areas of the state. Gold was the first precious metal discovered in nearby Virginia City, but a short time later the bustling Comstock Lode became the site of one of the world's biggest silver strikes. Other mining camps began to spring up throughout the state, and railroads, such as the Virginia and Truckee, soon followed.

Nevada became a state during a turbulent time in U.S. history. The Civil War was raging, and President Lincoln needed the new state to bring more electoral votes toward his reelection and money toward his plan to abolish slavery. On October 31, 1864, Lincoln signed the proclamation giving Nevada statehood.

At the turn of the century, the mines began to play out, and former boomtowns went bust and new towns appeared wherever gold or silver was found. Throughout the state you can still see remnants of Nevada's glory days, from ghost towns where only piles of rubble remain to towns like Virginia City, where the old buildings have survived and are filled with the spirits of the past.

In southern Nevada the Mormons were the first white settlers. But the colony that Brigham Young had established near present-day Las Vegas in 1855 proved to be troublesome. The desert climate took its toll, as did the isolation and problems with miners in the area. Within three years, the Mormons abandoned their fort. The arrival of the San Pedro, Los Angeles, and Salt Lake Railroad in 1905 formed the beginning of Las Vegas as a viable town, and soon saloons, banks, hotels, and schools began to appear in the dusty railroad stop. Thanks to the state's liberal laws on gambling and prostitution, as well as the construction of Hoover Dam in the midst of the Great Depression, Las Vegas began to take shape. In the 1940s, after a few Western-themed casinos had popped up, gangster Benjamin "Bugsy" Siegel appeared on the scene to build the Flamingo—and the rest is history.

CULTURES

Nevada has a rich cultural fabric. Nevada's Native Americans include the Paiutes, Shoshone, and Washo. Their influence can be seen and felt at such sacred sites as Pyramid Lake north of Reno and Cave Rock at Lake Tahoe. Throughout Nevada visitors can see petroglyphs etched by ancient tribes into the desert varnish on the rocks. The Native Americans drew animals, people, and archaic symbols that archaeologists are still deciphering. Some of the best places to see petroglyphs include Valley of Fire State Park in southern Nevada, the Hickison Petroglyph Recreation Area near Austin, and Grimes Point and Hidden Cave near Fallon.

Other ethnic groups have also left their influence on Nevada. In the late nineteenth and early twentieth centuries, Basques emigrated from their homeland (a tiny region bordering France and Spain) to herd sheep in the remote areas of Nevada. The Carson Valley, Elko, and Winnemucca were major concentration points for Basques, and their descendants still run Basque restaurants and hold annual festivals in honor of their heritage. The cowboy culture is also strong in Nevada. The spirit of life on the range—where the cattle roam and coffee is made over a campfire—is still alive and well in Nevada. In Elko, cowboy culture is celebrated annually during the Cowboy Poetry Gathering. Winnemucca is surrounded by ranch land and features the Cowboy Hall of Fame. Throughout the state, in big cities and small towns, you'll find community rodeos. The chaps-and-spurs set completely overtakes Las Vegas during the National Finals Rodeo and descends upon Reno during its Reno Rodeo.

THE ARTS

The arts are alive and well in Nevada despite the state's reputation for being a cultural desert. Artists can't help but become inspired by Nevada's wide-open spaces, majestic mountains, and pristine lakes.

In Reno, visitors are surprised to find several art galleries and community-theater houses. Reno has a renowned opera company, and the University of Nevada produces several orchestra, jazz, and choral groups. In July, "the Biggest Little City" puts on a monthlong celebration of the arts, with exhibits, performances, and workshops in parks, theaters, and galleries.

The arts scene in Las Vegas is a bit more scattered, but it is strong, nonetheless. The Nevada Ballet Theatre is based in Las Vegas, and several theater and musical groups from the University of Nevada-Las Vegas perform throughout the city. You'll also find an eclectic collection of visual arts in Las Vegas. Neon is an art form, and some of the more famous neon signs have been salvaged from casinos, preserved, and placed on display in an outdoor museum at the Fremont Street Experience. At the Charleston Heights Arts Center you'll find plays, musical performances, and even film festivals.

On the performing arts scene, casinos shouldn't be dismissed. Several hotel-casinos bring jazz greats, dance artists, and Broadway shows and musicals to their showrooms. Some of the long-running, elaborate production shows, such as *Jubilee!* at Bally's and *Enter the Night* are glamorous, and the showgirls are highly trained (sometimes classical) dancers.

Southern Nevada has proven that it is not particularly sentimental about its older architecture, but Hoover Dam's art deco design is worshipped among architects and art lovers. While it serves the important purpose of generating electricity from the Colorado River, the dam and its sculptures, mosaic floors, and other touches are a monument to the artistic eyes of its designers.

While the arts are thriving in both northern and southern Nevada, you'll also find pockets of eclectic arts and artists throughout the rural areas. In Beatty and the nearby ghost town of Rhyolite, a group of artists have developed surreal sculptures in the desert. The road to Great Basin National Park from Baker is an outdoor art gallery where visitors will see whimsical pieces made from discarded toys and junk. Look for an alien wearing a chef's hat and sculptures of bicyclists perched on fence posts.

In Eureka, don't be surprised to find well-known performers like Don Edwards, or obscure music, dance, and theater groups that come from as far away as New York and Africa. The town's performing arts headquarters is the Eureka Opera House, built in the 1880s and restored to its original glory in 1994. Today an eclectic lineup of performers attracts big audiences to the magnificent building. The opera house has its original stage curtain—signed by every performer who's ever played there—as well as an unusual horseshoe-shaped balcony.

Artists also seem drawn to Virginia City and the surrounding communities of Gold Hill and Silver City. You'll find this is an area where a disproportionate number of authors, poets, painters, and sculptors make their homes. Virginia City boasts a good art gallery as well as the newly restored Piper's Opera House, where you can see such performers as Michael Martin Murphey and Lacy J. Dalton.

One of the most bizarre artistic expressions is the Burning Man Festival held on the Black Rock Desert north of Reno. During the week prior to Labor Day, folks build a self-contained, surreal city and culminate the week with the fiery, symbolic destruction of the 40-foot Burning Man sculpture.

CUISINE

Those elaborate buffets where you can pile your plate to the ceiling with prime rib, crab legs, and every form of dessert imaginable were invented in Nevada. Originally a concept designed to keep gamblers in the casino late at night, the buffet is an enduring icon of Nevada's cuisine scene.

Today's buffets can range from simple spreads with meat and potatoes to elaborate affairs with several serving stations and "action" preparation where chefs cook up omelettes, steaks, and Mongolian barbecue while you wait and salivate. Most major casinos have buffets, and the spreads in big Las Vegas hotels tend to be very elaborate. Some offer serving stations from nearly every corner of the globe—it's not uncommon to find Mexican, Asian, Italian, and American all at one glorious buffet. The desserts are just as splendiferous. Carrot cake, chocolate cake, cream puffs, ice cream, and pies of every variety await the already overstuffed buffet connoisseur.

Nevada may be several hundred miles from the nearest ocean, but you wouldn't know it by visiting a buffet on a Friday night, when some of the state's most sumptuous seafood spreads are offered. There's peel-and-eat shrimp, all-you-can-eat crab legs, seafood salads, oysters on the half-shell, and clam chowder—seafood lovers are likely to never leave. The Rio Suite Hotel in Las Vegas even opened a separate buffet dedicated solely to serving seafood.

Beyond the buffets, Nevada does have a good representation of ethnic eateries. Basque restaurants will fill you up with both food and heritage. You'll find these restaurants clustered in small pockets throughout the state. Gardnerville, Reno, Carson City, Winnemucca, and Elko all have Basque restaurants. Throughout the state, and even in most small towns, you'll also find a good representation of Mexican, Asian, and Italian restaurants. In rural Nevada you'll find plenty of steak and potatoes; after all, this is farming and ranching country. In fact, Winnemucca is famous for its spuds, which you'll find on restaurant menus in town.

Bargain meals may not qualify as a type of cuisine, but in Nevada they're staples. Prime rib is de riguer at Nevada's casinos—you'll find all sizes, shapes, and prices. Another state icon is the bargain shrimp cocktail. It's a tradition that began at the Golden Gate Hotel in the 1960s and has become a requirement for any self-respecting casino snack bar. Breakfast is an important meal in Nevada—so important that you can order it any time of day just about anywhere you go. Casinos are famous for luring patrons into their coffee shops with graveyard (late-night) specials, which usually come with a slab of ham, a big pile of hash browns, and toast, and they cost about $1.99.

For haute cuisine, you can't go wrong at most of the gourmet rooms in Nevada's casinos. At Las Vegas's Bellagio alone there are more fancy eateries with big-name chefs associated with them than there are in some major metropolitan cities. At places like the Mirage, MGM Grand, and Mandalay Bay you'll find Wolfgang Puck and other trendy restaurants transplanted from Los Angeles, San Francisco, and New York. Themed restaurants are also big in

Las Vegas—look for several Planet Hollywoods as well as a Harley-Davidson Cafe, an All-Star Cafe, a Rainforest Cafe, Dive!, and many others.

OUTDOOR ACTIVITIES

Nevada offers so many outdoor activities that visitors can have a tough time squeezing in all the possibilities. Just about any town you visit in Nevada will have at least one golf course, so golfers shouldn't leave home without their clubs and knickers. The Las Vegas area has more than 20 courses while the Reno-Tahoe area has close to 30 courses. Skiing is popular at both ends of the state. In Reno skiers can choose from more than a dozen alpine resorts surrounding the lake that fit all skill levels and budgets. In Las Vegas skiers and snowboarders head to Mount Charleston. For the extreme skier who appreciates virgin slopes, Elko offers heli-skiing where skiers drop out of a helicopter onto fresh powder. A more tame option is the Elko Snobowl, a small community ski hill.

Cross-country skiers will find plenty of trails in Nevada. Up north, several downhill resorts offer cross-country trails, too. In rural towns like Austin and Ely skiers can pull off on any flat, snowy area and schuss to their heart's delight. And just about anywhere you find snow, you'll also find tobogganing, sledding, and snowmobiling.

In summer, hiking is a popular pastime in Nevada. There is no shortage of spectacular trails and views. Lake Tahoe offers the Tahoe Rim Trail, and Reno has the heart-pounding trek up to Mount Rose. The mountains of eastern Nevada are meccas for hikers, as is Mount Charleston in southern Nevada. At Red Rock National Conservation Area near Las Vegas, you'll find hiking as well as rock climbing.

Nevada is fast becoming a destination for mountain bikers. The Flume Trail near Lake Tahoe is a challenging, narrow trail with lofty views of the lake. Word is starting to spread about Austin, which recently designated and established mountain-bike trails and opened a bike shop.

Calmer pursuits such as fishing, sailing, horseback riding, and bird-watching are plentiful in the Silver State. Nevada allows visitors the opportunity to try parasailing and roller coaster riding or to sip daiquiris while relaxing poolside. In Nevada there's every extreme and everything in between.

PLANNING YOUR TRIP

Before you set out on your trip, you'll need to do some planning. Use this chapter in conjunction with the tools in the appendix to answer some basic questions. First of all, when are you going? You may already have specific dates in mind; if not, various factors will probably influence your timing. Either way, you'll want to know about local events, the weather, and other seasonal considerations. This chapter discusses all of that, while the Calendar of Events in the appendix provides a month-by-month view of major area events.

How much should you expect to spend on your trip? This chapter addresses various regional factors you'll want to consider in estimating your travel expenses. How will you get around? Check out the section on local transportation. If you decide to travel by car, the Planning Map and Mileage Chart in the appendix can help you figure out exact routes and driving times, while the Special Interest Tours provide several focused itineraries. The chapter concludes with some reading recommendations, both fiction and nonfiction, to give you various perspectives on the state. If you want specific information about individual cities or counties, use the Resource Guide in the appendix.

HOW MUCH WILL IT COST?

Nevada offers vacations that can suit everyone, from high rollers to low rollers. For high rollers the possibilities are astounding, especially in Las Vegas. To be considered a high roller, you have to spend lots of money at the blackjack or baccarat table, or the $100 slot machines. Then the hotel will usually comp your meals and entertainment as well as provide you with the best suites in the hotel. For the low roller, the lifestyle isn't quite as glamorous, but you can find excellent rooms at good prices, depending on when and how you travel. One of the best options is to find a hotel package (usually in the travel section of newspapers) that includes your meals and entertainment. Once you're in town, you can clip coupons from free tourist magazines for cheap buffets and discounts on attractions.

Las Vegas caters to all budgets. For visitors who want to splurge, several hotels such as Bellagio, Mirage, Caesars Palace, and the Desert Inn cater to big spenders looking for luxury accommodations that range from $150 to $1,000 per night. In the middle of the road are hotels like Treasure Island, New York-New York, and the Monte Carlo where you can expect to pay about $60 to $100 per night. For families and budget travelers, Circus Circus and Excalibur are excellent options—the rooms are great and there are activities for the kids—and the rooms run from $30 to $50.

Keep in mind that rates fluctuate wildly in Las Vegas. Weekdays are always less expensive than weekends and holidays, and two-night stays are often required on weekends. Big conventions like the computer trade show Comdex will send hotel rates sky-high and restrict availability. Another way to beat high rates is to stay at a property that is off the Strip. Travelers will find good hotel bargains downtown in "Glitter Gulch," where the properties are older and smaller but have been refurbished. These hotels still have the Las Vegas polish and are by no means second-rate, and the rooms range from $30 to $80 per night.

Also in southern Nevada, bargain hunters travel in droves to the Colorado River town of Laughlin, which has always been famous for its very inexpensive rooms ($15 to $30 per night), especially in the summer when temperatures routinely hit the century mark. Laughlin is a small-scale Las Vegas and offers excellent hotel-casinos as well as production shows and buffets galore.

Up north, room rates in Reno are comparable to those in Las Vegas. In the downtown casino core, rooms range from about $60 to $80 per night. At Stateline, on the south shore at Lake Tahoe, you get a view of the lake and access to a wide range of outdoor activities, which makes the price of an average hotel room about $40 to $60 more expensive than in Reno. Carson City and Gardnerville are the bargain pockets in northern Nevada, where you'll pay anywhere from $30 to $60 for a night's stay.

Happily, dining is still a bargain just about anywhere you travel in Nevada. Buffets are king in the Silver State, and for a family of four you can usually escape for about $40 for dinner. On Friday nights, when the seafood spreads are rolled out, the price jumps to about $80 for a family of four. Laughlin buffets are usually the least expensive, but it's wise to peruse the selections before you pay—just to make sure the quality is up to par.

Aside from Laughlin, other bordertowns like Wendover, Primm, and Jackpot also offer high-quality accommodations as well as many of the perks you'll find in the big cities—without the higher prices. Other rural Nevada towns also are a bargain just about any time you travel, with the exception of holidays and special events such as train season in Ely and cowboy poetry time in Elko. But hotels and even most bed-and-breakfasts in rural Nevada rarely charge more than $70 a night.

If you don't mind the heat, southern Nevada is one of the few places in the United States where it actually becomes less expensive to travel in the summer. In Las Vegas and Laughlin, room rates drop as the heat goes up. In the winter, skiers flock to Lake Tahoe, so it's less expensive to travel there in the spring and fall.

If you come to Nevada primarily to gamble, another way to save money and earn freebies is by joining a slot club. Joining a slot club allows the casino to give you free meals, rooms, and show tickets based on how much you spend while you play.

WHEN TO GO

Nevada has distinct seasons, and each has its own influences on the southern, northern, central, and eastern sections of the state—even if you don't detect much of a temperature change.

Spring is the best time to visit southern Nevada. The desert wildflowers put on a colorful show, and temperatures are mild. The summers in southern Nevada are just plain hot. In June 1994, Laughlin recorded a record high of 125 degrees. Las Vegas gets hot, too, but if you stay indoors, you'll find that the city's hotel-casinos have some of the world's most efficient air-conditioning systems—you won't even notice that it's 101 degrees outside while you're pumping nickels into a slot machine in cool comfort.

Summer is a good time to be in northern Nevada because the temperatures rarely climb over 95. In the winter, the weather can get cold and snowy in both the northern and eastern areas of the state, but if you're a skier, either cross-country or downhill, you won't mind a bit. The roads often require snow tires or chains, especially in the higher climes, so make sure you're prepared before you set out.

Fall is one of the best times to visit Reno, Lake Tahoe, and the other mountainous towns in the northern tier, where the changing leaves put on shows that would rival those in New England. In fall the heat of summer has faded, and there are fewer tourists, especially around Tahoe. Some of the area's biggest events are held in the fall—the Great Reno Balloon Race, the Camel Races in Virginia City, and the National Air Races in Reno. Consequently, rooms can fill up quickly and rates are usually higher on those weekends.

In the winter in rural Nevada, the pace definitely slows down, and some museums, parks, and attractions close up shop until spring. The major exception is Elko, which, despite its icy winters, attracts huge crowds to town during the Cowboy Poetry Festival in January. Elko is often one of the coldest spots in the state in the winter, and in the summer it also can be the most temperate.

SPECIAL EVENTS

Camels, cantaloupes, cowboys, cars, ribs, snow, and even Shakespeare are just a few of the reasons that Nevadans celebrate with big events. During every season, visitors will find a major celebration in some corner of the state.

Cowboys and cowgirls take over Las Vegas in January during the National Finals Rodeo, where everything from casino showrooms to dance halls features Western entertainment. Spring is powwow season in Nevada. You'll find Native Americans celebrating the earth with dance competitions and performances in Carson City, Las Vegas, and other areas of the state. Summer is packed with events ranging from state fairs, car races, music festivals, and Basque festivals. Rodeo season heats up in the summer—the Reno Rodeo, which has been going for close to 80 years, is held in June. In August, classic-car fans converge on Reno for Hot August Nights, a weekend of sock hops, '50s music, and car parades. Summer and fall are the seasons for food festivals. Ribs are honored in Sparks near Reno, Fallon celebrates its famous Hearts of Gold cantaloupes, Genoa cooks up candy, and chili cooks compete at festivals throughout the state.

Fall is Reno's biggest event season. The Great Reno Balloon Race and the Virginia City International Camel Races are usually held on the same weekend. The Reno National Championship Air Races, where biplanes and old war birds race around pylons and put on shows, usually follows later in the month. In southern Nevada balloons take flight during RiverFlight in Laughlin and the Las Vegas Balloon Classic in October.

Nevadans don't take their state's admission day, October 31, lightly. Nevada Day is a state holiday, and in Carson City, a major U.S. highway is closed to make room for the state's longest parade. Christmas is another great season to spend in Nevada. Even small communities get decked out for the holidays. Sparks holds a chilly but festive parade. At Lake Mead near

Las Vegas, the Parade of Lights features a string of boats that are draped in lights.

ORIENTATION AND TRANSPORTATION

For air travelers, Nevada has two gateways: Las Vegas and Reno. Las Vegas is served by McCarran International Airport. Visitors to Reno arrive via the Reno/Tahoe International Airport.

Visitors are often surprised to learn that these two bright spots on the map are so far apart—more than 400 miles of mountains and sagebrush separate the two. By air the trip between Reno and Las Vegas is just over an hour; by car it's nearly eight hours. But once you're in the state, navigating by car is a breeze (although there are some long, lonely stretches of highway between certain towns). U.S. 95 cuts a north-south path between Reno and Las Vegas. I-80 goes east and west through Wendover, Elko, Winnemucca, and Reno. U.S. 50, named the Loneliest Road in America by Life Magazine, does indeed have its desolate stretches as it connects such communities as Ely, Eureka, and Austin to Carson City.

Nevada's remote towns and lonely highways make for great road trips. Between towns, undulating ribbons of highways seem to stretch on forever into the distance. You can travel for many miles before you ever meet another car; that can have both benefits and pitfalls. Make sure you have plenty of water, food, and gasoline before you leave town—and in very remote areas drivers should pay attention to those "Last Services for 150 Miles" signs.

While traversing Nevada's wide expanses of sagebrush, playas, and mountains you'll find another benefit to these isolated highways—high speed limits. At one time there were some roads in Nevada that didn't have any speed limit at all. Today you'll find that you can top out at 75 mph on most highways. A cautionary note: Make sure you slow down and abide by speed limits as you roll into town. Drivers also should note that Nevada has free-range country, meaning that cattle aren't always fenced off from the roadways. Therefore, drivers need to watch out for cows on the highway, especially at night.

RECOMMENDED READING

Nevada's preeminent author is Robert Laxalt. He has written a number of fictional works based on his Basque roots and his family's experiences in Nevada. Laxalt's father was a Basque sheepherder, and Laxalt's tales are compelling and weave a rich fabric of the state's—and his own—heritage. His *The Basque Hotel* (University of Nevada Press) was nominated for a Pulitzer Prize, but any of his books will give readers a glimpse into Laxalt's vision of Nevada and his affection for the state. Among his other works are *Child of the Holy Ghost, Sweet Promised Land,* and *Dust Devils.*

The Complete Nevada Traveler (Gold Hill Publishing) by Gold Hill author David W. Toll offers a warm look at Nevada's towns and their people, quirks, and histories. The *WPA Guide to 1930s Nevada* offers an intriguing perspective on what it was like to travel in Nevada during the pre-WWII years. Reno author and trivia buff Richard Moreno is the author of three excellent Nevada books: *The Backyard Traveler, The Backyard Traveler Returns,* and the *Nevada Trivia Book. The Backyard Traveler* series is a compilation of Moreno's newspaper columns about Nevada's outback that includes lots of history and interesting details about the places that are off the beaten path.

Explorers can learn about Nevada's turbulent past by checking out *Nevada Ghost Towns and Mining Camps* (Nevada Publications), a coffee-table-sized hardback by Stan Paher that is loaded with photographs, maps, and histories of the state's old mining camps. Paher has seen every inch of Nevada's numerous lost cities and has carefully documented each town's buildings, residents, and stories.

Wildlife watchers on the lookout for Nevada's animals should bring along the *Nevada Wildlife Viewing Guide* (Falcon Press). It pinpoints designated Wildlife Viewing Areas.

Gamblers will find hundreds of books about how to play the games and beat the odds. One of the best sources for these books is Huntington Press, a Las Vegas-based publishing company staffed by gambling and casino experts. Huntington Press also produces recreation guides to Las Vegas as well as titles that cover the history and people behind the gaming industry. Huntington Press's *Las Vegas Advisor* is a monthly eight-page newsletter available by subscription that is packed with up-to-the-minute advice for bargain hunters about shows, top-10 bargains, dining, and gambling.

Slot machine fanatics can learn everything they ever wanted to know about the one-armed bandits in *Slot Machines: The First 100 Years* (Liberty Belle Books) by Reno resident Marshall Fey, whose grandfather invented the slot machine.

History buffs should read *A Short History of Reno* (University of Nevada Press) by Barbara Land and her late husband, Myrick. The book gives visitors insight into the Biggest Little City, its colorful forefathers, its days as a divorce capital, and some of its landmarks, such as the Mapes and Riverside hotels.

Nevada Magazine, based in Carson City, is the state's bimonthly. It is filled with stories about history, recreation, people, restaurants, events, and casino happenings throughout the state.

1
LAS VEGAS

While Las Vegas, which is Spanish for "the meadows," used to be a hot, dusty outpost in the middle of nowhere, today it has more neon per square inch than Hollywood and Times Square combined. Las Vegas has continued to define itself by incorporating the best of all areas of the globe. It has replicated the great pyramids and the Venetian canals. It has built exploding volcanoes and lakes that spout water choreographed to opera music. But, while gambling has always been the mainstay, Las Vegas has become a city of more than just casinos. Each resort tries to outdo its predecessor. Bugsy Siegel, who opened the first glamour joint, the Flamingo, in the 1940s, wouldn't believe his eyes today. Each new resort may rely on its blackjack tables and slot machines to pay the bills, but today's casinos are offering more of everything—entertainment, food, shopping, and far-out attractions, from Star Trek to white tigers and pirate ships to Picasso.

A PERFECT DAY IN LAS VEGAS
You should begin your day with a breakfast buffet at either the Rio's massive buffet or Main Street Station, which is smaller but a bit more elegant. Next it's time to visit the priceless works of van Gogh and others at the Bellagio, where you can stop to smell the flowers in the conservatory before entering the gallery. Put on your shopping shoes and aim for the Forum Shops at Caesars, where you can admire the works of Gucci, Versace, and other designers while

DOWNTOWN LAS VEGAS

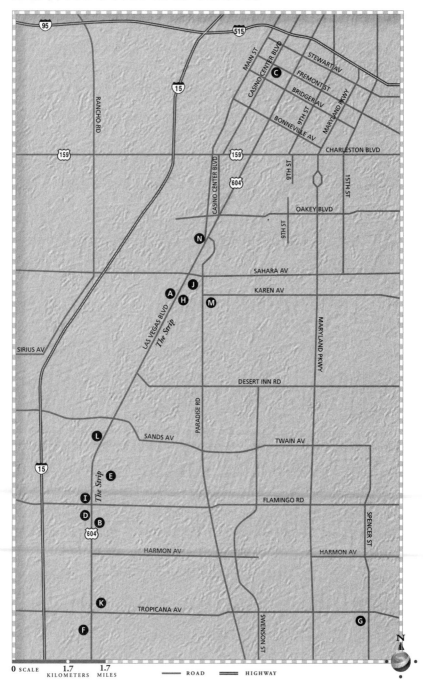

you chow down on the giant salads and wraps at the Cheesecake Factory. If there's time, take a ride aboard the 3-D simulated chariots at the Race For Atlantis. You'll find more virtual thrills at the Star Trek Experience at the Las Vegas Hilton. Or, try the real ups and downs on the Manhattan Express roller coaster at New York–New York, a casino that's worth taking the time to stroll through to see its Greenwich Village and other replicated Big Apple neighborhoods. The Las Vegas Strip, which is a designated Scenic Byway, is the place to be after the sun goes down. After absorbing the explosive sights of the Strip, you should cruise up to downtown Las Vegas for dinner at the Top of the Tower at the Stratosphere. Afterward you can take in the city's best view of the Las Vegas Valley. Be sure to catch the brief performance of the light-and-sound show at the Fremont Street Experience before you end the evening with a performance of *Mystère* at Treasure Island.

SIGHTSEEING HIGHLIGHTS: THE STRIP

★★★★ GALLERY OF FINE ART AND CONSERVATORY
Bellagio, 3600 Las Vegas Blvd. S., 888/987-7111

Would Vincent van Gogh cut off the other ear if he knew that his name was appearing on a marquee at a Las Vegas casino? Probably not if he knew it was at Bellagio. Bellagio is a $1.6 billion masterpiece that honors the master and other artists who share space inside the hotel's Gallery of Fine Art. Who would've thought that one day visitors could jump up from a blackjack table and stroll over to gaze upon the

SIGHTS

- Ⓐ Circus Acts and Carnival Midway, Circus Circus
- Ⓑ Eiffel Tower, Paris
- Ⓒ Fremont Street Experience
- Ⓓ Gallery of Fine Art and Conservatory, Bellagio
- Ⓔ Imperial Palace Auto Museum
- Ⓕ King Tut Museum, Luxor
- Ⓖ Liberace Museum
- Ⓗ Madame Tussaud's, Venetian
- Ⓘ Omnimax Theatre, Caesars Palace
- Ⓙ Sahara Speedworld, Sahara
- Ⓚ Showcase Mall
- Ⓛ Siegfried and Roy's Secret Garden, The Mirage
- Ⓜ Star Trek Experience, Las Vegas Hilton
- Ⓝ Stratosphere Tower

masterful works of such artists as Cézanne, Picasso, de Kooning, Renoir, and Warhol? Bellagio CEO Steve Wynn decided to introduce Las Vegas visitors to the world of fine art. The gorgeous gallery contains a collection of more than $300 million worth of art. Visitors can peruse it with the benefit of an audio guide. The conservatory, a 12,500-square-foot botanical garden, sets the mood for gazing upon masterpieces. The garden has a massive glass ceiling that lets in light for the live flowers and trees, which are watered, pruned, and pampered by a staff of 115 folks in the hotel's garden department. Every few months the garden is completely changed to reflect the season.

Details: Gallery of Fine Art open daily 9–11. $12 (audio wand included); reservations required. Conservatory free. (1–2 hours)

★★★★ STRATOSPHERE TOWER
2000 Las Vegas Blvd. S., 702/380-7777 or 800/998-6937
The 1,149-foot Space Needle–shaped Stratosphere Tower is the best perch from which to get some perspective on Las Vegas. The tower has a 360-degree view and is a peaceful escape from the din of slot machines and the hectic casino pace. The elevator is half the fun—the escorted ride zips up 1,000 feet, making your ears pop along the way. Atop the glass-enclosed pod are signs that offer a little history and other information about what you're gawking at. There's also an outdoor observation deck where the winds wreak havoc with hairdos and acrophobes cling to the railings as the screams from passengers on the two tower-top thrill rides are carried through the air. The phenomenal view provides a perfect setting for the Top-of-the-Tower Restaurant and the wedding chapel.

Details: Tower open 24 hours. $6 for elevator, $3 for NV residents. Ride hours Sun–Thu 10–1 a.m., Fri–Sat 10–2 a.m. $5 High Roller Coaster. $6 Big Shot. (1–2 hours)

★★★ IMPERIAL PALACE AUTO MUSEUM
3635 Las Vegas Blvd. S., 800/634-6441
This museum will rev up your interest in automotive history with its rotating collection of more than 800 antique autos. The emphasis at this museum is on cars with famous—and infamous—owners. You'll find an intriguing display on Nazi Germany and the 1939 Mercedes Benz that was owned by Hitler as well as the 1939 Alfa Romeo that was driven by Benito Mussolini. Visitors will find a doozie of a display in the Dusenberg Room. The $50 million collection of Dusenbergs

includes cars that were owned by the rich and famous, such as James Cagney and chewing gum millionaire Philip Wrigley. Another major section of the museum is dedicated to presidential cars such as the 1962 Lincoln Continental Bubble Top owned by JFK. The specific cars on display are periodically rotated. The museum also has displays dedicated to military vehicles, motorcycles, and fire engines.

Details: Open daily 9:30–11:30. $6.95 adult, $3 children 12 and under. Coupons for free admission available at the hotel. (1 hour)

★★★ LION HABITAT AT MGM GRAND
MGM Grand Hotel, 702/891-7777 or 800/929-1111

MGM Grand's icon is the lion, so it's only natural that the hotel has opened a habitat at which visitors can see the magnificent cats. Inside the 5,345-square-foot habitat, a see-through tunnel allows gawkers to walk right into the midst of the pride and watch the lions romp amid African foliage and waterfalls. The trilevel habitat has 18 cats, including a couple of descendants from MGM Studios' marquee lion, Metro.

Details: Open daily 11–11. Free. (30 minutes–1 hour)

★★★ OMNIMAX THEATRE
Caesars Palace, 3570 Las Vegas Blvd. S., 702/731-7110

This little casino secret is a good spot for leaving behind the crowds and clanking slot machines. Escape to another world of elephants, oceans, or Mount Everest—whichever movie may be showing at the time. The Omnimax was one of the first attractions that gave kids something do at the upscale Roman casino. It opened in 1979 and has been a popular spot ever since.

Details: Shows Sun–Thu 2–10, Fri–Sat 11–10. Call for show times. Shows are 45 minutes. $7 adults, $6 Nevada residents, $5 hotel guests, military, seniors, and physically challenged. (1 hour)

★★★ SAHARA SPEEDWORLD
Sahara, 2535 Las Vegas Blvd. S., 702/737-2111

Race-car fans will find their hearts accelerate on this ride. It's the next best thing to actually getting into a real Indy car on the racetrack. Racers climb into a three-quarter-scale Indy car, which rumbles as you wait for the checkered flag. You feel every bump, shake, and g-force that you would in a real car. The best part of the ride is that racers get to zoom up the Strip, past the hotel-casinos, and the Fremont Street Experience. Riders who get into wrecks have to pull into the pits. At the end of the race you receive a printout of your stats. If you'd rather be a passenger than a driver, you can attend one of three 3-D motion simulator theaters that will give you a chance to ride with professional NASCAR racers.

Details: Sun–Thu 10 a.m.–11 p.m., Fri–Sat 10 a.m.–12 a.m. $3 for 3-D motion show, $8 for eight-minute race. (1 hour)

★★★ SIEGFRIED AND ROY'S SECRET GARDEN
Mirage Resort, 3400 Las Vegas Blvd. S., 702/791-7111 or 800/627-6667

Several of the majestic animals of the Mirage reside in the Secret Garden, a tropical hideaway that almost makes you feel as though you're on a wildlife-watching safari. The tour begins at the 2.5-million-gallon saltwater tanks where the hotel's pod of Atlantic bottlenose dolphins resides. A guide tells visitors about the animals and takes them to the underwater viewing area. Inside the garden area, visitors receive radios on which Mirage owner Steve Wynn provides narration about the garden's residents, including the white tigers that appear during Siegfried and Roy's magic extravaganza at the hotel. White lions, a snow leopard, black panthers, and other huge felines yawn and nap while you pause to admire their huge teeth and paws at a fairly close distance. An Asian elephant occupies another area of the garden and often performs for passersby.

Details: Mon–Fri 11–5, Sat–Sun 10–5 (open fewer hours during winter). $10 adults, free ages 10 and under. (1–2 hours)

★★ CIRCUS AND CARNIVAL MIDWAY
Circus Circus, 2880 Las Vegas Blvd. S., 702/794-0410 or 800/634-3450

A visit to Circus Circus is a requirement if you've got kids in tow. The action is on the second level, overlooking the slot machines. Circus performers—everything from trapeze and juggling acts to clowns and animal stars—take the stage in the center of the midway every hour on the hour. One of the most popular acts is Housecats, during which former Moscow Circus performer Gregory Popovich shows off the talents of his trained domestic cats. For acts that don't take place from the trapeze, you'll want to arrive at the midway seating area about 20 minutes before each show to ensure a good view. Aside from the shows, the midway area is crammed with kids and grownups playing the numerous carnival games. The best time to visit this area is weekdays, preferably before

noon—on the weekends, the midway can be extremely crowded.
Details: Daily 11 a.m.–12 a.m. Free. (1–3 hours)

★★ MADAME TUSSAUD'S
CELEBRITY ENCOUNTER
Venetian, 3355 Las Vegas Blvd. S., 888/2-VENICE

If you've ever wanted to rub elbows with Brad Pitt, the Rat Pack, or Wayne Newton, Madame Tussaud's might give you your best chance. This London import features intricate celebrity wax figures dressed in the stars' original clothing. Visitors are allowed to mingle with the celebs in a party atmosphere and put their arms around their favorite figures for photos. The end of the tour features a short multimedia production about Las Vegas entertainment.

Details: Daily 10–10. $12.50 adults, $10.75 seniors and Nevada residents, $10 children. (1 hour)

★★ SHOWCASE MALL
3785 Las Vegas Blvd. S.
702/736-7611

You can't miss the giant see-through Coke bottle on the Strip next to the MGM Grand. Fans of the popular pop will enjoy a tour of the World of Coca-Cola Museum, which offers a nostalgic look at how the beverage came to be. There's a Time Walk that reveals Coke's beginnings more than 100 years ago. The popular soda fountain dispenses exotic Coca-Cola drinks, such as Simba Piña, a pineapple-flavored drink. Entrance to the huge gift shop is free, and visitors will find all sorts of Coke-themed merchandise, including stuffed polar bears from the TV commercials, Coke machines, and everything wearable. Also enclosed in the Showcase Mall are M&Ms World and Ethel M Chocolates, both of which are dedicated to chocoholics. At M&Ms World you can pick and choose a grab bag of exotically colored M&Ms, such as gray and bright pink. You can also purchase M&M-themed merchandise, including T-shirts, stuffed animals, and even beaded evening gowns and handbags. Adjacent to the mall you'll find a movie theater and GameWorks, which is packed with state-of-the-art video games and a climbing wall.

Details: Open Sun–Thu 10 a.m.–12 a.m., Fri–Sat 10 a.m.–1 a.m. Closed Christmas and New Year's, 702/736-7611. M&Ms World and Ethel M are free. World of Coca-Cola Museum admission $3.50, age 3 and under free; 800/720-COKE. GameWorks Las Vegas 702/597-3122. (1–2 hours)

GREATER LAS VEGAS

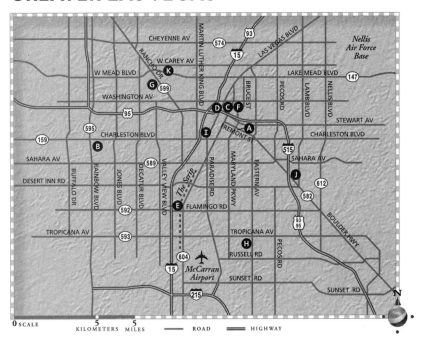

SIGHTS

A Fremont Street Experience
B Las Vegas Art Museum
C Las Vegas Natural History Museum
D Lied Discovery Children's Museum

SIGHTS (continued)

E Masquerade Village, Rio Suite Hotel
F Old Mormon Fort
G Southern Nevada Zoological-Botanical Park

FOOD

H Bootlegger's
I El Sombrero

LODGING

J Boulder Station
K Texas Station

★ **EIFFEL TOWER**
Paris Las Vegas, 3655 Las Vegas Blvd. S., 702/967-4401

The Paris hotel's most striking feature is the 540-foot replica of the Eiffel Tower, which rises amid the pyramids and other outlandish architecture on the Strip. For a bird's-eye view of Las Vegas's lights and landmarks, climb aboard the Eiffel Tower's elevator, which whisks visitors to an observation deck at the 50-story level. A few modern innovations were used in the tower's construction, but

---

architects used the Parisian plans as a guide.
Details: Daily 10–2. $8. (1 hour)

★ KING TUT MUSEUM
Luxor, 3900 Las Vegas Blvd. S., 702/262-4000

History buffs who've always wondered what King Tut's tomb looked like when Howard Carter discovered it in 1922 should stroll through King Tut's Tomb and Museum in the Egyptian-themed Luxor. Each artifact, down to the statues, baskets, and pottery, has been painstakingly reproduced and arranged just as Carter found them in Tutankhamun's burial chamber. The exhibit is narrated through Carter's eyes and includes a film about the discovery of the tomb.
Details: Open daily 9 a.m.–11 p.m. $5. (1 hour)

SIGHTSEEING HIGHLIGHTS: DOWNTOWN

★★★★ FREMONT STREET EXPERIENCE
702/678-5600 or 702/678-5777

This strange-looking white-metal canopy covering a four-block stretch of Glitter Gulch provides a surprisingly good little pocket of entertainment. Stretched between Sassy Sally's, the Golden Gate, the Golden Nugget, and other downtown casinos, the canopy covers a pedestrian mall, which—every hour on the hour—explodes into an animated light and sound show. Powered by 2.1 million lights, more than 200 speakers, and enough computer power to make Bill Gates envious, the Fremont Street Experience features various facets of Las Vegas entertainment, attractions, and holidays. The Fremont Street attractions, which include cart vendors, roaming performers, and outdoor stages, are expanding and will soon include outdoor cafés and more shopping. At an outdoor museum, visitors can stroll amid historic neon signs that were salvaged from the neon graveyard. The signs, such as the gaucho on horseback from the Hacienda and the lamp from the Aladdin, are scattered along Fremont Street in various locations.
Details: Fremont Street Experience light and sound shows appear hourly 11–11. Free. (1 hour)

★★★ SOUTHERN NEVADA ZOOLOGICAL-BOTANICAL
PARK 1775 N. Rancho Dr., 702/648-5955

This little zoo is a relaxing place to take the kids to. They'll learn about desert and exotic animals. The zoo, which became Nevada's first when it opened in 1980, offers a wide range of critters, including the country's only family of Barbary apes. Because of the southern Nevada climate, zoo founder and director Pat Dingle tends to acquire animals that don't mind the heat, such as apes and emus, wallabies, and golden eagles. A number of the zoo's residents were rescued and rehabilitated at the zoo. Cougie the mountain lion was one such animal. He was abandoned as a cub and raised at the zoo, where he still resides. Desert denizens living at the zoo include a badger, coyotes, iguanas, and Gila monsters. Dingle also offers tours and eco-excursions to various locations surrounding Las Vegas where you can learn about the geology, flora, fauna, and history of southern Nevada.

Details: *One-half block south of Texas Station. Open year-round daily 9–5. $5.95 adults, $3.95 seniors and children under 12. (1–2 hours)*

★ OLD LAS VEGAS MORMON FORT STATE HISTORIC PARK
908 Las Vegas Blvd. N., 702/486-3511

Traces of early Las Vegas are difficult to find in this city of bright lights and gambling fortunes, but the Mormon Fort provides a glimpse into what the city was like before the pyramids and castles were here. The fort was built in 1855 by Latter Day Saints missionaries as a refuge for weary travelers headed for the California gold rush. It was abandoned by the Mormons in 1858 and later became a Union Pacific Railroad stop. The area houses artifacts unearthed on the old fort's grounds. You'll also find a garden planted with the same crops that pioneers grew there.

Details: *Open daily year-round except Christmas–New Year's, 8:30–3:30. Donation. (30 minutes)*

SIGHTSEEING HIGHLIGHTS: OFF-STRIP AND SURROUNDING AREAS

★★★★ LIED DISCOVERY CHILDREN'S MUSEUM
833 Las Vegas Blvd. N., 702/382-KIDS

Kids clambering for a chance to escape the casino arcades will enjoy an excursion to the Lied Discovery Children's Museum. The first floor of the museum is dedicated to the "World of Arts and Humanities." Kids can draw using computers or learn about sound waves at the Music Pavilion. The second floor has science exhibits, including an eight-story Science Tower with a weather station. Another section of the museum introduces children to what it's like to be a grownup—they can earn a paycheck, go to the bank, and shop at the grocery store. One of the most popular exhibits at the museum is KKID Radio where kids can host their own radio shows.

Details: *Open Tue–Sat 10–5, Sun 12–5; summer Wed–Sat 10–5, Sun 12–5. $5 adults, $4 seniors, military, and ages 12–17, $3 children 3–11. (1–2 hours)*

★★★★ MASQUERADE VILLAGE
Rio Suite Hotel, 3700 W. Flamingo Rd., 702/252-7777 or 800/888-1808

The main attraction at this promenade is the Masquerade Show in the Sky, a Mardi Gras–style parade suspended from the ceiling of the casino. The exotic and colorful floats include such characters as a flying swan. The parade includes live singers and musicians as well as dancers and acrobats who perform on the floats, the floor of the casino, and a nearby stage. The shows alternate between themes, including Mardi Gras, Disco Swing Street Parade, and others. You can watch from the mezzanine and catch the beads that performers toss to audience members, or pay $9.95 to don a costume and ride the floats. The mezzanine also has restaurants and shops.

Details: *Daily every 2 hours between 1 and 11. Free. (1 hour)*

★★★ LAS VEGAS NATURAL HISTORY MUSEUM ·
900 Las Vegas Blvd. N., 702/384-DINO

Grownups with dinosaur-loving kids should make a stop at the Las Vegas Natural History Museum. It has a Dino Den featuring a giant animatronic Tyrannosaurus Rex, raptors, and other prehistoric creatures that move their heads and tails and roar. This ever-expanding museum is a great place to learn about animals both ancient and modern. You'll find exhibits on animals from Nevada, Africa, and several places in between. One of the most popular areas of the museum is the marine-life room, which has a tank with live sharks. Visitors can watch the shark feedings at 10 a.m. on Tuesday and Thursday, and 2 p.m. on Saturday.

Details: *Open year-round 9–4. $5 adults, $4 seniors, military, and students, $2.50 ages 4–12, free children under 4. (1 hour)*

★★★ LIBERACE MUSEUM
1775 E. Tropicana Ave., 702/798-5595

Most visitors are surprised when they step inside this rather inauspicious building in a red-tiled-roof mini-mall on East Tropicana. The world of Liberace—"Mr. Showmanship" and longtime Las Vegas resident—comes to life inside the museum that aptly reflects his sparkling tastes and penchant for expensive cars, pianos, clothing, and jewelry. Inside the main museum you can see 18 of the 39 pianos that Liberace owned, including the Baldwin concert grand that is covered with mirrored tiles and was one of Liberace's favorites. The Car Gallery includes Lee's Mercedes Excalibur that is covered with Austrian rhinestones as well as the "Volks Royce," a pink Volkswagen that Liberace had customized to look like a Rolls Royce. Naturally, the costumes on display are out of this world—especially the King Neptune number that is covered in shells and pearls and weighs 200 pounds. You can also gaze upon the flamboyant performer's eye-popping candelabras and jewelry, including a piano-shaped ring that has 260 diamonds in it. The walls of the museum are filled with photographs of the late fun-loving performer with celebrities, fans, and family. The legacy of Liberace lives on through scholarships that the Liberace Foundation awards to promising young musicians as well as in the Liberace Play-Alike competitions, held during Liberace's birthday celebration in May.

Details: Open Mon–Sat 10–5, Sun 1–5. $6.95 adults, $4.50 seniors, $3.50 students, $2 children 12 and under. (1–2 hours)

★★★ STAR TREK EXPERIENCE
Las Vegas Hilton, 3000 Paradise Rd., 888/GO-BOLDLY
www.startrekexp.com

Visitors can boldly explore the world of Starfleet at the Las Vegas Hilton's Star Trek Experience. This attraction offers a museum devoted to all things Trekkie, a simulated ride aboard a shuttlecraft, a bar with out-of-this-world beverages, and a gift shop. After you and your fellow "passengers" purchase tickets, you enter an area that resembles the bridge of the starship *Enterprise*, which is occupied by the Star Trek museum. Here you can follow the Federation timeline and see uniforms, tricorders, phasers, and other props from the original series, the three spin-off series, and the numerous movies. Then you're greeted by folks wearing Starfleet uniforms who masterfully carry out a script in which you are caught in a time-shift continuum and brought on board the "real" *Enterprise*. They load you into the shuttlecraft (a motion simulator) for the hair-raising ride back to the twenty-first century. One of the best parts of the ride is zooming over the Las Vegas Strip (although, because the Strip changes so quickly, the scene is now a bit outdated). The ride spits you out at Quark's Bar where you can order a Beam Me Up Jim Beam and other spacey concoctions. While you sip your drink and soak up the techno-atmosphere, Klingons, Ferengi, and other beings from far-away planets stroll about the bar and make conversation with twenty-first century visitors. The next stop is the gift shop where you can buy Federation-insignia key chains and stuffed tribbles.

Details: Open daily 11–11. Ride $15.95. (2 hours)

★ LAS VEGAS ART MUSEUM
9600 W. Sahara Ave., 702/360-8000

This museum helps defray Las Vegas's reputation for having more glitz than culture. Founded in 1950, the Las Vegas Art Museum is Nevada's oldest and, since it moved to the sprawling 30,000-square-foot Sahara West Library and Fine Arts Museum building in 1997, largest. The massive museum has huge ceilings, minimalist decor, and an emphasis on contemporary art. The museum holds art classes and special exhibits ranging from the work of Salvador Dali to local artists. It's worth the trip to inject some culture into a Las Vegas visit.

Details: Open Tue–Sat 10–5, Sun 1–5. Free for members, $3 non-members. (1 hour)

THRILL RIDES AND AMUSEMENT PARKS

An assortment of amusement parks has sprung up in Las Vegas in recent years. One of the best is Grand Slam Canyon, 702/734-0410 or 800/634-3450, under the shiny-pink dome next to Circus Circus. The dome has the Canyon Blaster, a decent roller coaster thrill with a double loop, double corkscrew—worth a few good screams, anyway. The Rim Runner flume ride offers a refreshing remedy to the summer heat. The dome also has the Fun House Express (a clown-themed motion-simulator ride), a rock climbing wall, arcade, several rides for little tikes, and clown shows throughout the day. Admission to the dome is free; an all-rides pass is $15.95 for adults, $11.95 for children under four-feet tall.

Las Vegas has some of the West's best outdoor roller coasters, too, including the Manhattan Express, 702/740-6969 or 800/693-6763, a rollicking ride that zips around New York-New York at top speeds of 67 miles per hour. Passengers enter through subway-style turnstiles to board the ride, which costs $5 per run. For a truly hair-raising experience, the Stratosphere Tower, 702/380-7777 or 800/998-6937, offers two rides atop the observation pod. The High Roller ($5) is a roller coaster that is wrapped around the top of the tower, and the Big Shot ($6) catapults its victims to the top of the needle—both are worth the new gray hairs just for the view. The ride to the top of the elevator is $6 ($3 for Nevada residents).

If you're looking to cool off while you get your thrills, Wet 'n Wild, 2601 Las Vegas Blvd. S., 702/737-3819 or 800/565-0786, which is open April through October, is a popular water park that offers a few slides and chutes that are not for the faint of heart. Der Stuka has a 75-foot drop that gives you the sensation of a free fall. A more calming option is a float down the Lazy River. Admission is $22.95 adults and $18.95 children 3–12.

Thrillseekers will find several motion-simulator rides. One of the best is the Race for Atlantis, 702/893-4800, at the Forum Shops at Caesars. A statue depicting Neptune guides visitors into the dungeonlike entrance, covered in a dense fog lit with blue lights. Passengers don wraparound headsets and race aboard futuristic chariots in the 3-D, computer-animated movie. Tickets are $9.50.

SHOPPING

Las Vegas doesn't just have shopping malls—it has shopping *experiences*. The best by far is the Forum Shops at Caesars, 702/893-4800, adjacent to Caesars Palace, where you can shop amid the cobblestone streets, fountains, and frescoes. The scene is reminiscent of a quaint yet upscale Italian village, and the ceiling overhead slowly changes from night to day. The mall is packed with shopping heavyweights, including Gianni Versace, Gucci, Estée Lauder, and others. Dining is an experience here, too, and can be done alfresco at such highbrow eateries as Spago, Palm, or Bertolino's. If you need to put a little fire into your shopping, stroll down to the Festival Fountains where, every hour on the hour, a statue of Neptune rises from the floor to try to referee a battle between his two heirs to the throne—one the goddess of ice and the other the god of fire. Naturally the two engage in battle, resulting in the sinking of Atlantis in a fiery—and watery—explosion. This newest section of the Forum Shops also has some of the mall's most unusual stores, such as the giant NikeTown (a multimedia exhibit as well as a shoe store), and FAO Schwartz, where a two-story Trojan horse dominates the breezeway.

Another place to shop on the Strip is the Fashion Show Mall, 702/369-8382, next door to Treasure Island, which doesn't have any statues but does have Saks Fifth Avenue, Nieman Marcus, and Macy's, among others. This mall is another good place to find unusual restaurants, including Dive! (a cartoonlike eatery designed and owned by Steven Spielberg).

Bargain hunters congregate at Belz Outlet Mall, 7400 Las Vegas Blvd. S., on the south end of the Strip, 702/896-5599. This sprawling indoor mall has Levi's, Spiegel, Espirit, Reebok, Casual Corner, and Burlington brands among its more than 140 stores. Kids can climb aboard the carousel and go for a ride for $1. If you're looking for designer bargains, you can check out the Off Fifth Saks Fifth Avenue and Calvin Klein outlets adjacent to Belz's parking lot.

Las Vegas has traditional malls, too, such as The Boulevard, at Maryland Parkway and Desert Inn Road, 702/732-8949, www.blvdmall.com, which is Nevada's largest with 144 stores and 1.2 million square feet of shopping space. The Meadows, at U.S. 95 North at Valley View Blvd., 702/878-4849, has 50-cent carousel rides. In Henderson, the area's newest mall is the Galleria Mall at Sunset, 702/434-0202, situated across the street from the Sunset Station.

Casinos have always offered upscale shops for clothing and jewelry, but Bellagio, 888/987-6667, transcends the standard with its array of stores that have been transplanted from Rodeo Drive in Hollywood and Fifth Avenue in New York. You'll find Chanel, Gucci, Hermes, Tiffany and Co., Moschino, Prada, and several others.

FITNESS AND RECREATION

Visitors will find a jackpot of outdoor recreation in Las Vegas. Duffers will find more than a dozen public courses where they can get into the swing. The only course on the Las Vegas Strip is the Desert Inn Golf Club, 3145 Las Vegas Blvd. S., 702/733-4290, established in 1952 and home to such prestigious tournaments as Tournament of Champions and the Las Vegas Invitational. The privilege of playing amid the palm trees and undulating greens is not cheap— guests of the hotel pay $150 while non-guests pay $215. Call the Las Vegas Convention and Visitors Authority, 702/892-0711, for a guide to the area's golf courses.

The Las Vegas Motor Speedway, 7000 Las Vegas Blvd. N., 702/644-4443, across from Nellis Air Force Base, offers a full racing schedule, including Winston Cup series races and others. If you've ever dreamed of getting behind the wheel of a race car, you can sign up for instruction at the Speedway's Richard Petty Driving Experience, 800/BE-PETTY. You can ride shotgun for three laps in a two-seater stock car driven by an instructor ($90) or go for the three-hour Rookie Experience, which allows you to put the pedal to the metal for eight laps ($330). Advanced classes also are available.

DOWNTOWN LAS VEGAS

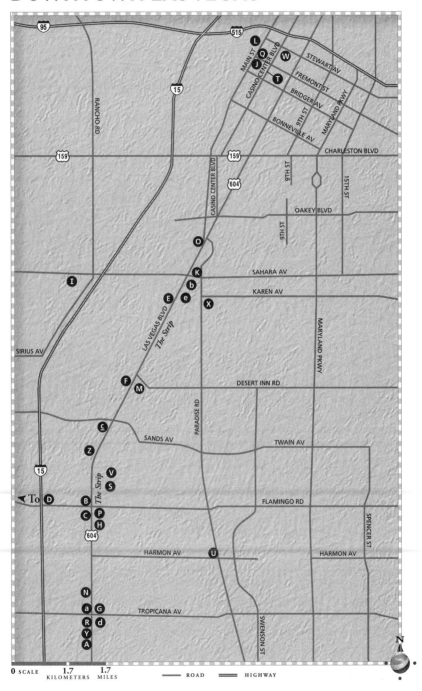

95
515
L
Q W
J
STEWART AV
MAIN ST
CASINO CENTER BLVD
T
FREMONT ST
15
BRIDGER AV
5TH ST
6TH ST
MARYLAND PKWY
BONNEVILLE AV
CHARLESTON BLVD
RANCHO RD
159
159
9TH ST
15TH ST
604
OAKEY BLVD
9TH ST
O
SAHARA AV
K
b
KAREN AV
E e
I
X
MARYLAND PKWY
LAS VEGAS BLVD
The Strip
SIRIUS AV
F
DESERT INN RD
M
PARADISE RD
C
SANDS AV
TWAIN AV
Z
15
V
The Strip
S
To D
B
FLAMINGO RD
C P
SPENCER ST
H
604
HARMON AV
U
HARMON AV
N
a G
TROPICANA AV
R d
SWENSON ST
Y
A
N

0 SCALE   1.7   1.7
        KILOMETERS MILES   ROAD   HIGHWAY

The All-American SportPark, located just south of the Strip, 702/798-7777, is a huge sports complex where you can golf, rock climb, rollerblade, try your batting skills in the batting cages, and race five-eighth-scale NASCAR cars.

Thrillseekers can go bungee jumping next to Circus Circus at A. J. Hackett Bungy, 810 Circus Circus Dr., 702/385-4321. It'll cost you $49 for your first jump, $79 with a T-shirt and videotape of your fall, and $29 for the second and third jumps. The fourth jump is free.

Surrounded by all this decadence and excitement, it's not surprising that Las Vegas offers some of the most opulent spas in the world. The Venetian, 800/494-3556, imported the highly regarded Canyon Ranch SpaClub from Tucson, Arizona, which *Condé Nast Traveler* readers have consistently voted as the world's best. Surrounded by gardens, the spa has exercise rooms, lap pools, and a Canyon Ranch restaurant as well as spa and skin treatments designed to melt away the fatigue. The Spa at the Desert Inn, 800/634-6909, and the Spa at Caesars, 800/634-6001, will help work out those sore muscles you earned from too many pulls on the slot-machine handles.

FOOD

- Ⓐ Aureole (Mandalay)
- Ⓑ Bacchanal (Caesars)
- Ⓒ Bellagio
- Ⓐ Border Grill (Mandalay)
- Ⓑ Caesars Magical Empire (Caesars)
- Ⓓ Carnival World Buffet (Rio)
- Ⓔ Circus Circus
- Ⓕ Chin's at the Fashion Show Mall
- Ⓖ Coyote Cafe (MGM)
- Ⓗ Eiffel Tower (Paris)
- Ⓖ Emeril Lagasse's New Orleans Fish House (MGM)
- Ⓑ Empress Court (Caesars)
- Ⓘ Feast Buffet (Palace Station)
- Ⓙ Golden Gate Hotel
- Ⓚ Holy Cow!
- Ⓒ Le Cirque (Bellagio)
- Ⓗ Le Village Buffet (Paris)

FOOD *(continued)*

- Ⓛ Main Street Station Microbrewery
- Ⓗ Mon Ami Gabi (Paris)
- Ⓜ Monte Carlo (Desert Inn)
- Ⓝ Monte Carlo Pub and Brewery (Monte Carlo)
- Ⓒ Olives (Bellagio)
- Ⓑ Palace Court (Caesars)
- Ⓒ Picasso (Bellagio)
- Ⓞ Top of the World (Stratosphere)
- Ⓐ Trattoria del Lupo (Mandalay)
- Ⓓ Voodoo Cafe (Rio)
- Ⓖ Wolfgang Puck Cafe (MGM)

LODGING

- Ⓟ Bally's
- Ⓒ Bellagio
- Ⓠ Binion's Horseshoe
- Ⓑ Caesars Palace

LODGING *(continued)*

- Ⓔ Circus Circus
- Ⓜ Desert Inn
- Ⓡ Excalibur
- Ⓢ Flamingo Hilton
- Ⓙ Golden Gate Hotel
- Ⓣ Golden Nugget
- Ⓤ Hard Rock Hotel
- Ⓥ Harrah's
- Ⓦ Lady Luck
- Ⓧ Las Vegas Hilton
- Ⓕ Luxor
- Ⓛ Main Street Station
- Ⓐ Mandalay Bay
- Ⓖ MGM Grand
- Ⓩ Mirage
- Ⓝ Monte Carlo
- ⓐ New York–New York
- Ⓘ Palace Station
- Ⓗ Paris
- Ⓓ Rio Suite Hotel
- ⓑ Sahara
- Ⓢ Treasure Island
- ⓓ Tropicana
- ⓔ The Venetian

Note: Items with the same letter are located in the same area.

FOOD

Dining offerings don't get much more diverse than in Las Vegas. The options run from snack bars serving 99-cent shrimp cocktails to four-star gourmet rooms, with a dash of everything in between.

The buffet, which originated as the "chuck wagon" in the late 1940s at the El Rancho in Las Vegas, has been perfected and elevated to an art form. Virtually every hotel-casino has a buffet, but the cream of the crop are those that offer numerous serving stations (many with international cuisines) and "action" stations where the dishes, such as omelettes, steaks, and spinach salads, are prepared while you watch. **Carnival World Buffet at the Rio**, 3700 W. Flamingo Rd., 702/252-7777, is one of Las Vegas's finest—and a pioneer in the modern buffet. This massive spread is considered a "super" buffet because of the numerous individual serving stations offering Chinese, Mexican, Italian, and American cuisines. The Rio also has a separate daily seafood buffet. Both are worth the extra trip to the workout room. The **Feast Buffet** at the Palace Station, 2411 W. Sahara Ave., 702/367-2411, introduced the "action" buffet and continues to lure patrons with its fresh entrées prepared while you wait. Generally speaking, the higher the price of the buffet, the better the quality of food, although you can always ask to peruse the offerings before you pay. And hotels such as Bellagio often have top-notch buffets. If you're looking for bargain buffets it's wise to scout them out first. **Circus Circus,** 2880 Las Vegas Blvd. S., 702/734-0410, is the most popular inexpensive buffet (breakfast is $2.99, lunch $3.99, dinner $4.99)—on average, it serves more than 10,000 people per day.

Of course, casinos offer more than just buffets for hungry patrons. You'll find many lavish gourmet rooms. The **Monte Carlo** at the Desert Inn, 3145 Las Vegas Blvd., 702/733-4524 (jackets required), is a classic, elegant room offering indulgent French continental cuisine, most of it prepared or served tableside. The à la carte entrées range from $25 to $40.

Equally indulgent is the **Bacchanal** at Caesars Palace, 3570 Las Vegas Blvd. S., 702/731-7110, where right before dessert male diners are treated to neck massages by goddesses dressed in togas. The price is $70 per person for a feast of seven courses. Visitors of all genders and ages can enjoy the experience at **Caesars Magical Empire**, 702/731-7333 or 800/445-4544, where the $75 admission includes a three-course meal hosted by a wizard (half-price for kids ages 5–10). Non-meal tours are available. The **Palace Court** at Caesars, 702/731-7547 (reservations and jackets required), is the hotel's traditional gourmet room, serving French cuisine seasoned by herbs grown next to the pool. Caesars' **Empress Court**, 702/731-7110, is probably the city's fanciest Asian restaurant, serving Cantonese and Szechuan dishes.

You can't beat the view at the Stratosphere's highly rated gourmet room, the **Top of the World**, 2000 Las Vegas Blvd. S., 702/380-7777, which specializes in such dishes as prime filet mignon and the towering chocolate stratosphere dessert. The 106th-floor restaurant makes one revolution about every hour and a half.

All the restaurants at the Bellagio, 3600 Las Vegas Blvd. S., offer dining with an artistic flair, both with the cuisine and the decor. **Picasso**, 702/693-7223 or 888/987-7111, features dining amid original Picasso artwork. You'll also find **Olives**, 702/693-7223, a casual Mediterranean-style café imported from Boston, and the legendary New York City restaurant **Le Cirque,** 702/693-8150, which serves French cuisine overlooking the lake and dancing fountains.

Other hotels that offer superb dining include the Rio, where the **Voodoo Cafe**, 3700 W. Flamingo Rd., 702/252-7777, offers an exotic, superstitious theme and huge windows with views of the Strip, and the MGM, 3799 Las Vegas Blvd., which specializes in restaurants with celebrity chefs such as Mark Miller's **Coyote Cafe**, 702/891-7349 (southwestern food), the **Wolfgang Puck Cafe**, 702/891-3019, and **Emeril Lagasse's New Orleans Fish House**, 702/891-7374.

Naturally, the cuisine at Paris Las Vegas, 3655 Las Vegas Blvd. S., 702/967-4401, has a French flair, and all the restaurants are top-shelf. The hotel's signature room is its **Eiffel Tower** restaurant, which serves up a good view of the Strip. But you'll find excellent dining at the other cafés, including **Le Village Buffet** (don't miss the crème brûlée) and **Mon Ami Gabi,** a steak house that offers a rarity among casino restaurants—outdoor seating.

Mandalay Bay, 3950 Las Vegas Blvd. S., 877/632-7000, the $950 million resort that opened in March 1999, includes such restaurants as Chef Charlie Palmer's **Aureole**, Wolfgang Puck's **Trattoria del Lupo**, and Mary Sue Milliken and Susan Feniger's **Border Grill.**

At the other end of the spectrum, you can find several good restaurants and meal deals without paying a gourmet price. One of the best bargains in town is the 99-cent shrimp cocktail at the **Golden Gate Hotel**, 1 E. Fremont St., 800/426-1906, downtown under the Fremont Street Experience. The tradition of the inexpensive shrimp cocktail began at this tiny joint in 1955, when the first one sold for 49 cents. Today, at 99 cents it's still a good deal—you won't find any lettuce or other fillers in your glass of ice-cold shrimp. The atmosphere is great, too. The brass and dark-wood accents and photographs of San Francisco are reminiscent of the City by the Bay, and a musician tickles the ivories on the piano in the center of the snack bar.

A rash of theme restaurants has appeared in Las Vegas, including Planet Hollywood, Harley-Davidson Cafe, All-Star Cafe, Motown Cafe, and the Hard

Rock Cafe, among others. The food usually is a bit overpriced for what you get, although the atmosphere can sometimes make up for it. Another popular trend is the appearance of brewpubs, and there are some good ones. Choices include the **Main Street Station Microbrewery**, 200 N. Main St., 800/713-8933, located downtown at Main Street Station, the **Monte Carlo Pub and Brewery**, 1770 Las Vegas Blvd. S., 702/730-7777, inside the Monte Carlo, and **Holy Cow!**, 2423 Las Vegas Blvd. S. 702/732-2697, a bovine-themed brewpub that became one of Las Vegas's first breweries when it opened in 1993.

Las Vegas also has a number of excellent restaurants that are not affiliated with casinos. For Italian cuisine, **Bootlegger's**, 5025 Eastern Ave., 702/736-4939, owned by Nevada's lieutenant governor, Lorraine Hunt, can't be beat. **Chin's**, at the Fashion Show Mall, 3200 Las Vegas Blvd., 702/733-8899, is another popular local haunt where you'll find creative Asian appetizers and entrées that are attractively presented. Near downtown at **El Sombrero**, 807 S. Main St., 702/382-9234, you'll find another Las Vegas original. Owned by the same family since it opened in 1951, this unassuming little restaurant serves authentic Mexican cuisine at very reasonable prices.

LODGING

The Las Vegas Strip is the only place on earth where you'll find an Egyptian pyramid, medieval castle, exploding volcanoes, the Eiffel Tower, and the Statue of Liberty all on one glitzy street. If you're going to splurge and stay at the best, the **Bellagio**, 3600 Las Vegas Blvd. S., 888/987-6667, with its dancing fountains, art gallery, exquisite restaurants, and elegant atmosphere is the place to do it. Since it opened in October 1998, the $1.6 billion Bellagio ushered in a new frontier of upscale, themed resorts—and this one doesn't allow children under 18 unless they are guests at the hotel. The lobby, with its huge, glass-flower sculptures hanging overhead and opera music playing in the background, sets the tone for guests at the Bellagio.

Mandalay Bay, 3950 Las Vegas Blvd. S., 877/632-7400, a Circus Circus resort that opened on the south end of the Strip in March 1999, offers some fresh amenities, including a wave pool with surfing on six-foot waves, a House of Blues, and several restaurants. The 35th through 39th floors of the hotel are occupied by a Four Seasons Resort. **The Venetian**, 3355 Las Vegas Blvd. S., 800/494-3556, which opened in April 1999, has Italian canals with serenading gondoliers in addition to its three thousand 700-square-foot suites geared toward conventioneers. **Paris**, 3650 Las Vegas Blvd. S., 702/946-7000, opened in fall 1999, has a 50-story "Eiffel Tower" occupied by a French restaurant and an observation deck.

If you're looking for something a little more classic you can check into

WEDDING BELLS

On the Strip and throughout town, you can't miss the little wedding chapels that lure couples to tie the knot where Liz Taylor, Jon Bon Jovi, and other celebrities have exchanged vows under the bright lights. Most hotel-casinos also have beautifully appointed wedding chapels, and several have wedding planners on staff.

- At the **Little White Chapel**, 1301 Las Vegas Blvd. S., 702/382-5943 or 800/545-8111, several notable couples have tied the knot, including Bruce Willis and Demi Moore, Ricki Lake, and Joan Collins. This chapel also has a drive-up window for couples on the go.

- At the **Graceland Wedding Chapel**, 619 Las Vegas Blvd., 702/474-6655 or 800/824-5732, you can have your wedding officiated by an Elvis impersonator.

- The **Candlelight Wedding Chapel**, 2855 Las Vegas Blvd. S., 702/735-4179 or 800/962-1818, www.candlelightchapel.com, is one of the most popular chapels due to its location on the heart of the Strip. Michael Caine, Whoopi Goldberg, and Bette Midler have gotten hitched here.

- Plan a wedding with a Victorian, gangster, Camelot, or Elvis theme at the **Viva Las Vegas Wedding Chapel**, 27 S. Ninth St., 702/384-0771 or 800/574-4450, www.vivalasvegasweddings .com.

Caesars Palace, 3570 Las Vegas Blvd. S., 702/731-7110 or 800/634–6661, which set a new standard for opulence when it opened in 1966. One of the best attractions at this Roman-themed property, aside from the shopping and superb restaurants, is the pool, or the Garden of the Gods, which is set against Roman columns and has private cabanas. Slightly more understated is the **Desert Inn**, 3145 Las Vegas Blvd. S., 702/733-4444 or 800/634-6906, a posh hotel that feels more like a desert resort than a hotel-casino. Once a former hideaway for reclusive billionaire Howard Hughes, the hotel has one of Las Vegas's most esteemed golf courses as well as a spa, tennis courts, and top-of-the-line restaurants. Other high-end glitz palaces include the tropical paradise **Mirage**, 3400 Las Vegas Blvd. S., 702/791-7111 or 800/627-6667, and the massive emerald-colored **MGM Grand**, 3799 Las Vegas Blvd. S., 702/891-1111 or 800/929-1111, the world's largest hotel with 5,005 rooms. Each of the major hotel-casinos along the Strip has a unique theme and amenities. **Luxor**, 1900 Las Vegas Blvd. S., 702/262-4800 or 800/288-1000, gets high marks for its pyramid-shaped hotel, and **New York-New York**, 3790 Las Vegas Blvd. S., 702/740-NYNY or 800/NY-FOR-ME, is a bit cramped but has hotel towers lifted from the Big Apple, such as the Chrysler Building. **Harrah's**, 3475 Las Vegas Blvd. S., 702/369-5000 or 800/634-6765, has an excellent reputation for offering its patrons personalized and friendly service, and visitors are rarely disappointed. **Monte Carlo**, 1770 Las Vegas Blvd. S., 702/730-7777 or 800/311-8999, with its French Riviera feel, is elegant but affordable, and the huge property gives visitors a little more elbow room. If you're traveling with kids, a popular spot is **Treasure Island**, 3300 Las Vegas Blvd. S., 702/894-7111 or 800/944-7444, where the pirate-ship theme is carried out in every facet of the hotel, from the buccaneer swords on the doors at the entrance to the pirate battle that takes place out front. Not all of the old hotels from the 1970s and earlier have been "imploded." The **Tropicana**, 1801 Las Vegas Blvd. S., 702/739-2222 or 800/634-4000, **Bally's**, 3645 Las Vegas Blvd. S., 702/739-4111 or 800/634-3434, the recently renovated **Sahara**, 2535 Las Vegas Blvd. S., 702/737-2111 or 800/634-6666, and the **Flamingo Hilton**, 3555 Las Vegas Blvd. S., 702/733-3111 or 800/732-2111, famous for its founder Bugsy Siegel, are all excellent hotels. And, if you're traveling with kids and don't mind crowds, you'll find good deals and kid-style excitement at the **Excalibur**, 3850 Las Vegas Blvd. S., 702/597-7777 or 800/937-7777, as well as the venerable **Circus Circus**, 2880 Las Vegas Blvd. S., 702/794-0410 or 800/634-3450.

The downtown hotels offer some of the city's best lodging deals. One of the most elegant hotels is the **Golden Nugget**, 129 E. Fremont St., 702/385-7111 or 800/634-3454, a little sister of the Mirage and Bellagio. **Main Street Station**, 300 N. Main St., 702/387-1896 or 800/634-6255, which is furnished with antiques and resembles an old train station, is another good option. You can also opt for one of the older, smaller places like the **Lady Luck**, 1308 E. Fremont St., 702/385-1093, **Binion's Horseshoe**, 128 E. Fremont St., 702/382-1600 or 800/622-6468, and one of my favorites, the **Golden Gate Hotel**, 1 E. Fremont St., 702/385-1906 or 800/426-1906, which opened in the 1950s and has a lot of character.

Don't forget about the hotels located off the Strip, many of which have devised ways to entice visitors with exceptionally good restaurants, attractions, or inexpensive rooms. The **Rio Suite Hotel**, 3700 Flamingo Rd., 702/252-7777 or 800/PLAY-RIO, is one of the best, offering suites that range from $60 to $300. The **Hard Rock Hotel**, 4455 Paradise Rd., 702/693-5000 or 800/473-7625, is an attractive place with a sandy-bottom pool, music memorabilia, a youthful clientele, and rooms ranging from $95 to $175. All of the Station properties, including **Boulder Station**, 4111 Boulder Hwy., 702/432-7777 or 800/683-7777, **Palace Station**, 2411 W. Sahara Ave, 702/367-2411 or 800/634-3101, and **Texas Station**, 2101 Texas Star Lane, 702/631-1000 or 800/654-8888, are popular with locals and offer rooms in the $60 to $70 range as well as some of Las Vegas's best buffets. The **Las Vegas Hilton**, 3000 Paradise Rd., 702/732-5111 or 800/732-7117, which is marketed as a convention hotel, has attractive rooms in the $100 range.

NIGHTLIFE

The quantity and quality of the nightlife in Las Vegas makes one wonder if anything goes on during the day. The city is famous for its production shows, and you should try to see at least one while you're in town. For a classic Las Vegas production show with beautiful, topless showgirls, plenty of feathers and rhinestones, and dancing, one of the best is the long-running *Jubilee!* at Bally's, 702/739-4567 or 800/237-SHOW. The dance and music spectacular by the legendary late producer Donn Arden features costumes designed by Bob Mackie and includes tributes to the *Titanic* and the Ziegfeld Follies. *The Best of Folies Bergere . . . Sexier Than Ever* at the Tropicana, 702/739-2411, is another spectacle featuring feathers and massive 20-pound hats on the heads of showgirls. *EFX* at the MGM Grand, 800/929-1111 or 702/891-7777, is a special-effects show that has been updated several times. The latest version stars Tony Award–winning Tommy Tune. *Enter the Night* at the Stardust, 702/732-6111 or 800/824-6033, is a surreal show featuring music and dance. Less traditional but much more popular and accessible to showgoers of all ages is Cirque du Soleil's *Mystère* at Treasure Island, 702/894-7111. *"O"* at Bellagio, 888/987-6667, is another Cirque du Soleil production featuring a stage that has been transformed into a lake. Siegfried and Roy put on quite a magic show at the Mirage, 800/374-9000 or 702/792-7777, making white tigers and other jungle animals appear and disappear, but the ticket price of $89.35 might be prohibitive for most visitors. A more down-to-earth option is Lance Burton, a folksy, talented magician who uses humor to spice up his illusions at the Monte Carlo, 702/730-7000. Kids can sink their teeth into the *King Arthur's Tournament* at the Excalibur, 702/507-7600.

Most of the big hotels feature headliners in their showrooms. Wayne Newton, the Midnight Idol and Las Vegas perennial, still performs occasionally, but you'll be able to catch nearly every other big name in show business these days, from Drew Carey and Carrot Top to LeAnn Rimes and Neil Diamond. Most hotel-casinos have lounges, and many host decent live bands just about every night. And the nightclub scene is making a comeback. At the MGM, Studio 54, 702/891-1111, has been resurrected from its New York City ashes. Club Rio at the Rio Suite Hotel, 800/634-6787 or 702/597-5970, and Club Ra, 702/262-4000, at the Luxor, also are happening joints these days.

2
GREATER
LAS VEGAS—EAST

This quadrant of southern Nevada showcases some of the state's most diverse and exotic outdoor attractions, proving to visitors that there's more to the Las Vegas environs than casinos and bright lights.

Although it's only 24 miles south of Las Vegas, Boulder City seems worlds apart from its glitzier sister city. A small, historic burg established in the early 1930s to house the workers at Hoover Dam, Boulder City has maintained its small-town charm—this is Nevada's only town where gambling is illegal. The grassy, tree-lined streets, classic restaurants, and antiquated buildings lure visitors to escape the bright lights of Las Vegas and stroll amid the shops or pause in the park to watch wild bighorn sheep graze on the grass.

Boulder City is also a gateway to Lake Mead and Hoover Dam, an architectural wonder that rivals even some of the flashiest Las Vegas casinos. When Hoover Dam was built to harness the power of the Colorado River, Lake Mead was formed, creating a scenic recreation area for anglers, water-skiers, boaters, sunbathers, and sightseers.

On the geologic time line, Lake Mead is an infant compared to the grand-fatherly formations of Valley of Fire State Park, which became Nevada's first state park in 1935. An ancient and sacred stomping ground for Native Americans, Valley of Fire now hosts hikers, picnickers, and other recreationalists. Native Americans also left their marks at Overton where the museum there has carefully preserved remnants of the Pueblo culture's housing and other artifacts. Just up I-15 is Mesquite, a formerly quiet Mormon farming

GREATER LAS VEGAS—EAST

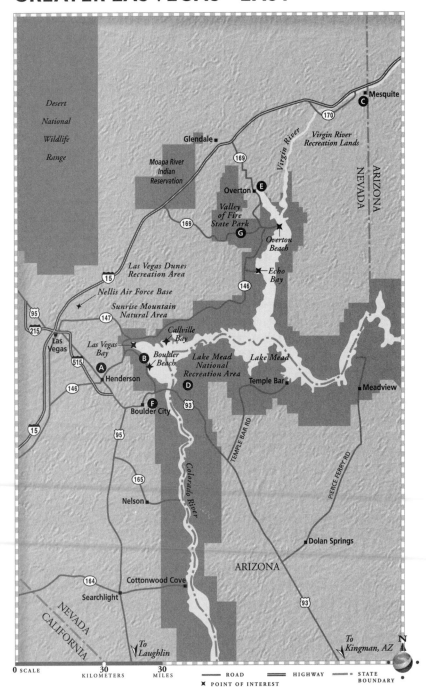

Desert
National
Wildlife
Range

Glendale

Virgin River

Virgin River
Recreation Lands

Mesquite **C**

170

169

Moapa River
Indian
Reservation

Overton **E**

169

Valley
of Fire
State Park

G

Overton
Beach

Echo
Bay

146

Las Vegas Dunes
Recreation Area

15

Nellis Air Force Base

Sunrise Mountain
Natural Area

95

147

215

Las
Vegas

Callville
Bay

Las Vegas
Bay

B

Boulder
Beach

Lake Mead
National
Recreation Area

Lake Mead

515

A

Henderson

D

Temple Bar

Meadview

146

F

Boulder City

93

15

95

TEMPLE BAR RD

165

PIERCE FERRY RD

Colorado River

Nelson

Dolan Springs

ARIZONA

164

Cottonwood Cove

93

Searchlight

NEVADA

CALIFORNIA

To
Laughlin

To
Kingman, AZ

N

ARIZONA
NEVADA

0 SCALE   **30**
KILOMETERS   **30**
MILES   ROAD   HIGHWAY   STATE
BOUNDARY

✕ POINT OF INTEREST

community that is becoming an oasis of spas, golf courses, and Las Vegas-caliber casinos.

A PERFECT DAY EAST OF LAS VEGAS

The best way to begin a tour of this area is with a big breakfast at the nostalgic Coffee Cup in Boulder City. It will charge your batteries for a day of exploring some of southern Nevada's most striking scenery, both natural and man-made. The first stop from Boulder City should be Hoover Dam where you can take a guided tour and marvel at this monolithic wonder. From there, hop in the car and head for scenic Lakeshore Road, which meanders alongside the western shore of Lake Mead. Lakeshore Road will guide you to Valley of Fire State Park. Here you can picnic atop the ancient red sandstone formations. If there's time, the Lost City Museum in Overton is worth a visit. As you make your way back to I-15 and head south back to Henderson, you can end your tour with a buffet dinner at the Reserve. If you'd rather leave the driving to someone else, you might miss out on some of the small attractions, but a ride on the *Desert Princess* is a great way to see Lake Mead, and it might be worth the sacrifice if you'd rather relax and soak up some rays while you scan the horizons for bighorn sheep and other wildlife.

SIGHTS

- Ⓐ Clark County Heritage Museum
- Ⓑ Desert Princess
- Ⓒ Desert Valley Museum
- Ⓓ Hoover Dam
- Ⓔ Lost City Museum of Archaeology
- Ⓕ Old Town Boulder City and the Boulder Dam Hotel

FOOD

- Ⓐ Barley's Casino and Brewing Company
- Ⓐ Capri Italian Ristorante
- Ⓐ Carver's Steaks and Chops
- Ⓕ Coffee Cup Cafe
- Ⓐ Congo Jack's (Reserve)

FOOD *(continued)*

- Ⓐ Costa del Sol (Sunset Station)
- Ⓕ Evan's Old Town Grille
- Ⓐ Feast Around the World (Sunset Station)
- Ⓐ Grand Safari Buffet (Reserve)
- Ⓕ Happy Days Diner
- Ⓔ Inside Scoop
- Ⓐ Pasta Mombasa Italian Eatery (Reserve)
- Ⓒ Redd Room Steak House
- Ⓐ Rosalita's Mexican Cantina (Sunset Station)
- Ⓐ Sonoma Cellar (Sunset Station)
- Ⓔ Sugar's Home Plate

FOOD *(continued)*

- Ⓐ Sunset Brewing Company (Sunset Station)
- Ⓕ Tiffany's
- Ⓕ Vanna's Gourmet Beverage and Cafe
- Ⓐ Wildfire (Reserve)

LODGING

- Ⓒ CasaBlanca
- Ⓒ Rancho Mesquite
- Ⓐ The Reserve
- Ⓒ Si Redd's Oasis
- Ⓐ Sunset Station
- Ⓒ Virgin River

CAMPING

- Ⓑ Lake Mead National Recreation Area
- Ⓖ Valley of Fire State Park

Note: Items with the same letter are located in the same area.

SIGHTSEEING HIGHLIGHTS

★★★★ HOOVER DAM
702/294-3523, www.hooverdam.com

There's no doubt about it: Hoover Dam is one of the greatest man-made structures on the planet. Constructed by the Bureau of Reclamation in 1935 at a cost of $175 million, the dam was completed ahead of schedule. The construction of Boulder Dam, as it was originally called, provided jobs for several thousand men during the Depression, but the project was not without its sacrifices. The working conditions were horrific at times. The southern Nevada heat was oppressive, and the workers had to scramble on rocky, steep canyon walls and work with dangerous equipment—94 men gave their lives to this project. (Contrary to the popular myth, none of them is buried in the concrete.) Ultimately, seven million tons of concrete were used to form the dam, which is 660 feet thick at the base, 1,244 feet long, and 726 feet high. A beautiful new visitors center and covered parking garage, both designed to blend in and complement the dam and the red rock that surrounds it, opened in 1995. While Hoover Dam's sole purpose was to harness the power of the Colorado and provide electricity, the Bureau of Reclamation put careful consideration into the architecture and design of all the structures. Touches such as the terrazzo floors and sculptures at both the visitors center and dam are worth taking the time to explore. You can learn the history and engineering of the dam by taking the 35-minute guided tours. For a more in-depth exploration, you can take a hard-hat tour. The visitors center also has exhibits and a movie about the dam.

Details: *30 miles south of Las Vegas. Visitors center open 8–6 year-round except Thanksgiving and Christmas. Guided tours, 8:35–5:15, leave every 10 minutes. $8 adults, $7 seniors, $2 ages 6–16. One-hour hard-hat tours $25. (2–3 hours)*

★★★ CLARK COUNTY HERITAGE MUSEUM
1830 S. Boulder Hwy., Henderson, 702/455-7955

This fascinating little museum has extensive displays that cover everything from Native American life to railroads. Heritage Street is lined with a collection of historic homes that have been moved from other Nevada locales. Each house has been refurbished and furnished to reflect the era in which it was built. There's also a replicated 1900s newspaper print shop as well as a 1932 depot from Boulder City along with rolling stock.

Details: *Open daily 9–4:30. $1.50 adults, $1 ages 3–15. (1–2 hours)*

★★★ DESERT PRINCESS
Lakeshore Road, Lake Mead Cruises Landing and Ferry Terminal, 702/293-6180, www.pcap.com/lakemead.htm

While this festive-looking paddlewheeler may look out of place this far from the Mississippi River, passengers don't seem to mind as they enjoy the relaxing cruise chugging across Lake Mead in the middle of the desert. The *Desert Princess*, Lake Mead's only paddlewheeler, is a leisurely way to see the lake as well as learn about the dam and the geology of the surrounding area. Passengers can choose from four cruises: the breakfast buffet, midday excursion, the early dinner, and dinner dance.

Details: *About 22 miles south of Las Vegas on Lakeshore Road. Open year-round. Departure times vary, and reservations are recommended. Breakfast cruise $21 adults, $10 children (under 12); midday cruise $16 adults, $6 children; early dinner cruise $29 adults, $15 children; dinner-dance cruise $43 adults (children not recommended). (2–3 hours)*

★★★ OLD TOWN BOULDER CITY AND THE BOULDER DAM HOTEL
1305 Arizona St., 702/293-7731

The grand Boulder Dam Hotel is the centerpiece of Boulder City's historic district, which makes for a fine stroll back in time. Established as a company town in the 1930s, Boulder City still reflects a small-town charm that can renew the spirits of visitors fresh from the neon overload in Las Vegas. The Boulder Dam Hotel was a haven for the rich and famous in the 1930s and 1940s—Fred MacMurray, Bette Davis, and other celebrities often absconded to the hotel for some R and R. After the 1950s the hotel fell into decline and became a flophouse. In 1993, a group of local citizens banded together to save the stately Dutch Colonial hotel and opened shops, galleries, and the Boulder City/Hoover Dam Museum.

Details: *Open daily. Museum is free. (1–2 hours)*

★★ LOST CITY MUSEUM OF ARCHAEOLOGY
Overton, 702/397-2193

The "Enemies of Our Ancestors," or the Anasazis, inhabited this arid stretch of desert near the Muddy River. The legacy of the Pueblo Grande de Nevada, or the Lost City, is preserved at this museum. It's crammed with pottery, baskets, and other artifacts from the Puebloans who occupied this area from 10,000 years ago to about

ELEPHANT ROCK (Valley of Fire State Park)

© Mel Lewis/Nevada Commission on Tourism

A.D. 500 to 1150. The southern Nevada Paiutes moved into the area around A.D. 1000. The museum chronicles the excavation of the Lost City in 1924 with a series of intriguing black-and-white photographs further illustrated with artifacts. The re-creation of the dig site shows how the strata were studied and artifacts carefully extracted. The pioneer exhibit shows how the most recent settlers lived and established a farming community in the Moapa Valley. At the front of the pueblo-style museum is a pit house and a pueblo created from actual foundations.

Details: *63 miles northeast of Las Vegas. Open daily 8:30–4:30. $2 adults, age 18 and under free. (1 hour)*

★ DESERT VALLEY MUSEUM
35 W. Mesquite Blvd., Mesquite, 702/346-5705
This slightly homespun museum is situated in a rock building that was built in 1941 and served as a library, and later a hospital. Exhibits include an impressive collection of basketball trophies from 1915 and 1916 as well as clothing, toys, old telephones, and other items donated by local residents.

Details: *Open Mon–Sat 8–5. Donation. (30 minutes)*

FITNESS AND RECREATION

The recreational opportunities are endless in this area of southern Nevada. First and foremost is Lake Mead National Recreation Area, 702/203-8906, created when the Colorado River backed up behind Hoover Dam. The 110-mile-long lake provides 822 miles of shoreline, so sunbathers and swimmers will find plenty of territory in which to cool off during the blazing southern Nevada summers. Boulder Beach is one of the most popular and accessible spots for swimmers. Boaters will find five marinas and numerous coves. Of course, there's plenty of fishing—bass, trout, and crappie lurk in the lake. Forever Resorts, based at Callville Bay Marina on Northshore Road, 800/255-5561, offers houseboat and jetboat rentals on the lake.

The Colorado River is no slouch when it comes to recreation. One of the most popular ways to explore the river is aboard a raft. Black Canyon River Raft Tours based in Boulder City, 702/293-3776 or 800/696-RAFT, www.pcap.com/blackcny.htm, offers three-and-a-half-hour rides down this calm section of the river. Guides point out the sights, and occasionally visitors will see elusive bighorn sheep in the canyon. The ride ends at Willow Beach where you have lunch, and after which you are delivered via a bus back to Boulder City. Tour takers gather at the Expedition Depot at 1297 Nevada Highway in Boulder City. The season runs February through November, and rides cost $69.95 per person.

A visit to the Lake Mead area must include a stop at Valley of Fire State Park, at the northern tip of Lake Mead 75 miles northeast of Boulder City on NV 169, 702/397-2088. The ancient burning-red sandstone formations are spectacular, making the park an excellent place to sightsee, take photographs, hike, or have a picnic. The best place to begin is the visitors center, which has maps and information as well as interpretive exhibits that explain the park's geologic history. The park is covered with intriguing formations and hiking trails, and, since Native Americans occupied the area, you'll also find petroglyphs. Entrance to the park is $5 per vehicle.

This corner of Nevada also is ripe with numerous hiking opportunities. The 6.2-mile U.S. Government Construction Railroad Hiking Trailhead, located just north of Boulder City off Pacifica Way on U.S. 93, follows a portion of the old Hoover Dam Railroad system that was dismantled in 1962. The historic trail winds through tunnels, into Lake Mead National Recreation Area, and to superb views of Hoover Dam. In Boulder City, the River Mountain Hiking Trail, 702/293-2034, is an interpretive trail that shows hikers the flora and fauna as well as the geology.

Of course, there's golf in this section of southern Nevada. Boulder City has its 18-hole Municipal Course, 1 Clubhouse Dr., 702/293-9236. Henderson has four public courses, the most glamorous of which is the new Lake Las Vegas Course, 75 MonteLago Blvd., 702/558-0022, designed by Jack Nicklaus.

Mesquite is the place to go to unwind. Aside from its three golf courses, you'll find two luxurious spas—the CasaBlanca Spa at the CasaBlanca Resort, 800/459-PLAY, and the Green Valley Spa at Si Redd's Oasis, 800/21-OASIS. You'll find such delectable treatments as a crushed pearl body rub and a full-body canyonland mud pack. In case you feel you need a workout to earn a spa treatment, the CasaBlanca also has tennis courts and offers mountain-bike rentals. Marksmen can show their skills at Si Redd's Oasis Ranch and Gun Club, 800-21-OASIS, which has ponds, fields, and cliffs from which to take aim at the clay pigeons.

FOOD

Since Henderson's roots are primarily as an industrial town, it has not yet become a hotbed for haute cuisine. But visitors will find several good restaurants and buffets at both the major hotel-casinos—Sunset Station and the Reserve. Sunset Station is owned by Station Casinos, owner of three other Las Vegas properties that have a strong reputation and local following for superb dining. Sunset Station, 1301 W. Sunset Rd., has a massive buffet—the **Feast Around the World** offers several nationalities of cuisine—and no one leaves without letting out the belt a notch. The casino's other restaurants include **Capri Italian Ristorante**, **Costa del Sol** (seafood), the **Sonoma Cellar** (a steak house), **Rosalita's Mexican Cantina**, and the **Sunset Brewing Company** (featuring an on-site brewery).

The Reserve, 777 W. Lake Mead Dr., has the **Grand Safari Buffet**, **Congo Jack's** (it has a crashed airplane in the dining room and specializes in Chinese and California-style cuisine), **Pasta Mombasa Italian Eatery**, and **Wildfire** (steaks and seafood).

If you venture beyond the major casinos you'll find **Barley's Casino and Brewing Company**, 4500 E. Sunset Rd., 702/458-2739, which has a sports book and dancing fountains in addition to handcrafted microbrews and wood-fired ovens. Beyond the casinos and for more upscale dining, **Carvers Steaks and Chops**, 2061 W. Sunset Rd., 702/433-5801, has a cigar bar as well as an elegant atmosphere.

Boulder City has a couple of restaurants that reflect its nostalgic atmosphere. At the **Coffee Cup Cafe**, 558 Nevada Highway, 702/294-0517, you might expect to see James Dean swaggering in looking for a cup of joe and eggs sunnyside up. Similarly, you might watch for Fonzie or Potsy at the **Happy Days Diner**, 512 Nevada Highway, 702/294-COKE, a genuine '50s diner plastered with memorabilia—the shakes here will knock your bobby

FACTORY TOURS AT HENDERSON

Henderson is Nevada's industrial pocket, and visitors who like to see everything from how clowns to chocolates are made can check out the Henderson factories: Ethel M Chocolate Factory and Cactus Garden, 2 Cactus Garden Dr., 702/458-8864 or 888/627-0990, www.ethelm.com, Cranberry World West, 1301 American Pacific Dr., 702/566-7160 or 800/289-0917, www.lasvegas-nv.com/cranworldwest, and Ron Lee's World of Clowns, 330 Carousel Pkwy., 702/434-1700.

The famed chocolatier Ethel M (created by the Mars family and named for Ethel Mars) opened its factory in the 1970s because of Nevada's liberal export laws, which made it easier to ship the confections filled with liqueur. Before filling up on sweets, visitors can meander through the garden and inspect the cacti. You'll see cacti ranging from the common beavertail to more exotic South American species. If you have kids in tow, it might be worth the stop to meet Carinna the Cran-Cran Girl and see how Ocean Spray bottles its cranberry beverages at Cranberry World West. Popular clown sculptor Ron Lee's factory is especially intriguing for collectors.

socks off. The downtown area is beginning to blossom with restaurants, including **Vanna's Gourmet Beverage and Cafe**, 1300 Arizona St., 702/294-4255, which serves excellent sandwiches and gourmet coffee drinks in a former soda fountain. **Evan's Old Town Grille**, 1129 Arizona St., 702/294-0100, is a neighborhood cafe that serves lunch and dinner. One of the more elegant—and historic—eateries in town is **Tiffany's**, located inside the Boulder Dam Hotel, 1305 Arizona, 702/293-7731, which is open for lunch and dinner.

In Overton, the main eatery in town is **Sugar's Home Plate**, 309 S. Moapa Valley Blvd., 702/397-8084, a sports-themed restaurant that serves burgers and other coffee-shop regulars. For sweets, check out the 32 flavors of ice cream at the **Inside Scoop**, 395 S. Moapa Valley Blvd., 702/397-2055.

In Mesquite, you'll find a variety of cuisines as well as some dining bargains at the four major hotel-casinos. Si Redd's Oasis and the Virgin River have buffets. One of the best gourmet rooms in town is the **Redd Room Steak House** at Si Redd's Oasis, 897 W. Mesquite Blvd., 702/346-5232.

LODGING

Henderson's hotel-casinos are a great way to escape the crowds on the Las Vegas Strip. **Sunset Station**, 1301 W. Sunset Rd., Henderson, 702/547-7777, 888/SUNSET9, www.sunsetstation.com, is a spacious hotel-casino with lots of amenities and good rooms (it's also right across the street from the Galleria Mall—a nice perk for shoppers). **The Reserve,** 777 W. Lake Mead Dr., 800/899-7770, is fast becoming a popular local spot. It's packed with excellent eateries, and the African decor is inviting.

Mesquite, with its spas and golf courses, is becoming a popular getaway for Las Vegas residents seeking solitude from the hectic Sin City scene. Little wonder—the pace here is peaceful. One of the most restful resorts in town is **CasaBlanca**, 600 Mesquite Blvd., 775/346-7529 or 800/896-4567, where guests are greeted by an attractive waterfall at the entrance to the resort. The other major hotel-casinos include **Si Redd's Oasis**, 897 W. Mesquite Blvd., 702/346-5232, **Virgin River**, 100 N. Pioneer Blvd., 702/346-7777, and **Rancho Mesquite**, 301 Mesa Blvd., 702/346-4600.

NIGHTLIFE

For a taste of the exotic, the Gaudi Bar is the centerpiece of Sunset Station and is a colorful salute to renowned Spanish architect Antoni Gaudi. There are no right angles at this bar—everything is curved—and cut glass covers the ceiling and fixtures. All of the hotel-casinos in Henderson and Mesquite offer lounge and headliner entertainment as well as dancing in some of the bars. The Virgin River in Mesquite also has a two-screen movie theater.

CAMPING

The best bets for camping are **Valley of Fire State Park** and **Lake Mead National Recreation Area**. Valley of Fire, 702/397-2088, has two campgrounds, totaling 51 units, which offer shaded tables, water, and rest rooms. Rates are $12 per night per vehicle. The National Park Service, 702/293-8907, operates eight campgrounds, scattered along the shoreline of Lake Mead, that offer fire pits, tables, water, and rest rooms. Rates are $8 per night, and RVs are allowed although there are no utility hookups. You'll find hookups at a number of commercial RV campgrounds, which are usually clustered near the marinas.

3
GREATER
LAS VEGAS—WEST

This side of Las Vegas proves once and for all that the area offers more than massive casinos, bright lights, and fast-shuffling blackjack dealers. Diversity abounds here. Mountains, prehistoric sandstone, and grapevines beckon travelers who may be ready for a change of pace. One of the most dramatic signs of this diversity is Mount Charleston, 30 miles northwest of Las Vegas, where visitors enjoy the escape from 100-degree desert temperatures to the cool breezes in this mountain oasis. In fact, it's feasible that you could spend the morning skiing in Lee Canyon and the afternoon swimming or golfing in the valley.

The desert environment is at its best at Red Rock Canyon National Conservation Area. The fiery Jurassic sandstone has been sculpted over millions of years into monolithic statues that have become havens for hikers and climbers. A historic ranch situated on the conservation area land adds a human element. You're also likely to encounter wild burros and other wildlife there. The attractions become more modern as you head for the Nevada-California border, where you'll find the curious little mining town of Goodsprings as well as the larger gambling towns of Jean and Primm. The two towns demonstrate the bordertown phenomenon, capitalizing on visitors who are anxious to try Lady Luck on their way to Las Vegas from California. Both towns have developed their own personalities and attractions, and often lure visitors with their more intimate atmospheres, unusual attractions like a giant roller coaster, and dining and room bargains.

GREATER LAS VEGAS—WEST

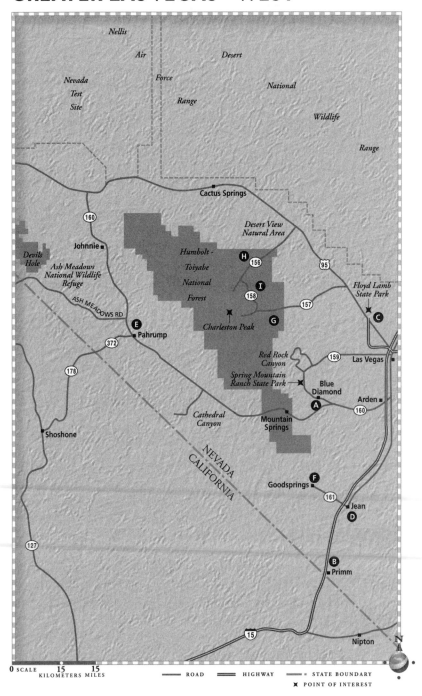

Nellis

Air

Force

Desert

National

Nevada
Test
Site

Range

Wildlife

Range

Cactus Springs

160

Desert View
Natural Area

Johnnie

Devils
Hole

Ash Meadows
National Wildlife
Refuge

Humbolt -

Toiyabe

National

Forest

H 156

95

Floyd Lamb
State Park

ASH MEADOWS RD

I 158

157

C

E

372

Pahrump

Charleston Peak

G

Red Rock
Canyon

159

Las Vegas

178

Spring Mountain
Ranch State Park

Blue
Diamond

Arden

A

160

Cathedral
Canyon

Mountain
Springs

Shoshone

NEVADA

CALIFORNIA

F

Goodsprings

161

Jean

D

127

B

Primm

15

Nipton

N

0 SCALE   15   15
KILOMETERS MILES

━━━ ROAD   ▭▭▭ HIGHWAY   ▬ ▬ STATE BOUNDARY
✕ POINT OF INTEREST

Pahrump, on the other hand, was an established town before it had gambling, and these days it's becoming a popular spot for retirees and big-city refugees looking for a slower pace. The centerpiece here is the Pahrump Valley Vineyards, which introduced a little piece of the Mediterranean to this desert town.

A PERFECT DAY WEST OF LAS VEGAS

The best way to begin the day exploring the western edge of southern Nevada is to take a hike at Red Rock Canyon National Conservation Area. That way, you can capitalize on the cool and save the heat of the day for a drive up to Mount Charleston. I'd recommend coming prepared with a picnic lunch to enjoy among the red rocks or on the sprawling grassy lawns of Spring Mountain Ranch State Park. From there you can loop down to Primm where you can send the kids to Desperado, the huge roller coaster at Buffalo Bill's, while you shop at the Las Vegas Factory Stores at the Primm Valley Resort. You can freshen up with a late-afternoon beer or soda at the Goodsprings Saloon. The folks there eagerly welcome visitors and enjoy sharing

SIGHTS

- Ⓐ Bonnie Springs/ Old Nevada
- Ⓑ Desperado Roller Coaster
- Ⓑ Fashion Outlet of Las Vegas
- Ⓒ Gilcrease Wildlife Sanctuary
- Ⓓ Jean
- Ⓔ Pahrump Valley Vineyards
- Ⓕ Pioneer Saloon
- Ⓑ Whiskey Pete's

FOOD

- Ⓑ Baja Bar and Grille (Buffalo Bill's)
- Ⓓ Gold Strike
- Ⓑ GPs (Primm Valley Resort)

FOOD *(continued)*

- Ⓖ Mount Charleston Hotel
- Ⓖ Mount Charleston Lodge
- Ⓓ Nevada Landing
- Ⓔ Pahrump Valley Vineyards
- Ⓑ Rebecca's Restaurant and Oyster Bar (Buffalo Bill's)
- Ⓑ Whiskey Pete's Silver Spur (Buffalo Bill's)

LODGING

- Ⓑ Buffalo Bill's
- Ⓓ Gold Strike Hotel
- Ⓖ Mount Charleston Hotel
- Ⓖ Mount Charleston Lodge
- Ⓓ Nevada Landing

LODGING *(continued)*

- Ⓔ Pahrump Station–Days Inn
- Ⓑ Primm Valley Resort
- Ⓔ Saddle West
- Ⓑ Whiskey Pete's

CAMPING

- Ⓗ Dolomite at Lee Canyon
- Ⓖ Fletcher View Campground
- Ⓘ Hilltop Campground
- Ⓖ Kyle Canyon Campground
- Ⓖ Kyle Canyon RV Park
- Ⓗ McWilliams at Lee Canyon
- Ⓘ Mahogany Grove
- Ⓑ Primadonna RV Village

Note: Items with the same letter are located in the same area.

tales about the historic saloon and town. The best place to end the day is with the scent of pine in your nose and a romantic dinner at the Mt. Charleston Hotel. You might easily forget that you're just minutes away from a sagebrush-covered desert.

SIGHTSEEING HIGHLIGHTS

★★★★ DESPERADO ROLLER COASTER
Buffalo Bill's Casino Resort, Primm
702/382-1212 or 800/FUN STOP
www.primadonna.com
Acrophobics will shudder at the sight of Desperado, the world's tallest and fastest roller coaster, which looms above the horizon as you approach its home base at Buffalo Bill's. After mustering up enough nerve to mount up inside the casino, riders clickety-clack to a height of 209 feet before dropping 225 feet at speeds surpassing 80 miles per hour. The screams can be heard inside and outside the casino. For a dramatic change of pace, the casino has a tame log ride that meanders past animatronic characters. For more thrills, visitors will find a motion simulator and a movie theater.

Details: East of I-15 in Primm. Desperado runs Sun–Thur 10–10, Fri–Sat 10 a.m.–12 a.m. $6 per person. (1–1 1/2 hours)

★★★★ PAHRUMP VALLEY VINEYARDS
3810 Winery Rd., 775/727-6900 or 800/368-WINE
After a few fits and starts, including wild horses with an appetite for wine grapes, the Pahrump Valley Vineyards has managed to produce a pleasing label of wines as well as a winery and gift shop that are worth a tour. Nevada's only winery is perched right in the desert overlooking the scenic valley. Most of the grapes are trucked in from California, but owner Jack Sanders has installed mustang-resistant fencing around his latest crop of grapes. The free, self-guided tour shows the production and bottling procedures, and there's tasting in the gift shop where you'll also find wine-themed T-shirts and aprons as well as a host of cooking wines, books, and utensils. Of course, you can buy Pahrump Valley wines and even have your own personalized label made for special occasions.

Details: Lunch and dinner daily. Winery tours daily 10–4:30. Free. (1 hour)

★★★ FASHION OUTLET OF LAS VEGAS
Primm, 702/874-1400, www.fashionoutletlasvegas.com
Primm is becoming a shopper's retreat due to the 1998 opening of this flashy outlet mall. Big billboards rather than traditional signs announce the names of the stores inside—a tactic designers used to give the mall a Times Square atmosphere. An upscale warehouse effect is achieved through the mall's exposed ceilings, painted-concrete floors, murals, statues, and minimalist chrome benches. Shoppers can check out the more than 90 stores, which include some big-name designers and names you wouldn't expect to find in an outlet mall. Look for J. Peterman, Versace, Kenneth Cole, Banana Republic, Williams Sonoma Marketplace, Pottery Barn, and Donna Karan.

Details: *Located adjacent to the Primm Valley Resort. Open Mon–Sat 10–9, Sun 10–8. Daily shuttle from New York–New York on the Las Vegas Strip departs from the north casino lobby at 9:15, 12 p.m., and 2, and returns at 1, 3, and 6. Cost for round-trip shuttle ticket is $10. Reservations recommended. (2–3 hours)*

★★★ PIONEER SALOON
NV 161, Goodsprings, 702/874-9362
If you have a few minutes to spare enroute to Jean and Primm on I-15, a quick tour of Goodsprings is worth the stop. The hot spot to slake your thirst in this ramshackle town is the Pioneer Saloon. It has withstood the harsh elements and hard-drinking miners since 1913. The folks are friendly to a fault and are eager to relay the history of the saloon, which is evident in the pressed-tin walls, wood floors, and creaky old back bar. Resting nonchalantly atop the wood-burning stove is a melted, macabre piece of metal that the barflies claim is a piece of Carole Lombard's airplane, which crashed nearby in 1942, killing the actress and all the plane's passengers. There's also a pool table, historic photos, and snacks. Paul Newman has been known to come in and shoot some stick, and locals say he's drawn to the peace and quiet of the place.

Details: *Take I-15 south 20 miles to Jean, right on NV 161 for eight miles to Goodsprings. Free. (1 hour)*

★★ BONNIE SPRINGS/OLD NEVADA
NV 160, Blue Diamond, 702/875-4191
Kids love the petting zoo at Bonnie Springs, a funky replicated Old West town. Folks dressed in Western trappings greet visitors and put on melodramas throughout the day. Llamas, chickens, prairie dogs, ferrets,

goats, foxes, burros, and other feathered and furry creatures reside at the zoo and petting area. Next to the pond filled with ducks and geese is the restaurant and saloon, the walls and ceilings of which are peppered with dollar bills signed by visitors.

Details: *About 16 miles west of Las Vegas on NV 160. Take I-15 south to exit 33, right toward Arden and Blue Diamond. Open daily 10–6. $6.50 adults, $4 children 5–11. (1–2 hours)*

★★ GILCREASE WILDLIFE SANCTUARY
8103 Racel St., 702/645-4224

This sanctuary 10 miles north of Las Vegas is a peaceful retreat for both birds and humans. Animal lovers can come here to see turkey vultures, hawks, ravens, and other birds that are on the mend. This sanctuary is home to the Wild Wing Project, an all-volunteer, nonprofit organization that rehabilitates injured, ill, and orphaned birds, and, when possible, returns them to the wild. The sanctuary is situated in a scenic greenbelt and is adjacent to the Gilcrease family farm, where visitors can buy and pick fruits and vegetables during harvest season.

Details: *About 10 miles north of Las Vegas via U.S. 95, just south of Floyd Lamb State Park. Open Wed–Sun 11–3. $3 adults, $1 children, free for children under 5. (1 hour)*

★★ WHISKEY PETE'S
Primm, 702/382-1212 or 800/FUN STOP
www.primadonna.com

Believe it or not, there really was a Whiskey Pete who ran a small gas station on the site where Whiskey Pete's Casino now stands. Pete McIntyre was a cantankerous character who told his cronies that when he died, he wanted to be buried standing straight up so that he could watch highway travelers. Unfortunately, the ground was too hard, so Pete was laid to rest at a slant. But he still rests under the billboard for the casino that bears his name. There are a few other quirky discoveries to make at this castle-shaped casino, such as the Bonnie and Clyde Death Car, riddled with bullets from the fateful day, May 23, 1934, when the couple's famous crime spree was ended by federal agents. Visitors will find easy access to the Primm Valley Resort and Buffalo Bill's via the sleek monorail that crosses I-15.

Details: *West of I-15 in Primm. Free attractions. (1 hour)*

★ JEAN
I-15 S. Exit 12, 702/874-1360 (visitors center)
There are two big casinos here—Nevada Landing and Gold Strike—both of which are owned by Circus Circus Enterprises. Both have good-sized casinos and are tailor-made for bargain hunters or visitors who have the misfortune of planning a Las Vegas vacation during a big convention, when rooms can be astronomically expensive or hard to come by. The Jean Welcome Center near the Gold Strike is a good place to stock up on brochures and information.

Details: *Gold Strike, 702/477-5000 or 800/634-1359, www.goldstrike-jean.com; Nevada Landing, 702/387-5000 or 800/628-6682, www.nevadalanding.com. (30 minutes–1 hour)*

FITNESS AND RECREATION
The red-and-purple landscape of Red Rock Canyon National Conservation Area, 15 miles west of Las Vegas, 702/363-1921, beckons visitors to discover its wildlife, flowers, waterfalls, history, and geology. A 13-mile loop slices through the park, which offers several scenic picnic areas and numerous hiking trails that lead to scenic overlooks and into canyons. To enter the park, which is overseen by the Bureau of Land Management, visitors pay $5 at the gate. Rangers offer a full year-round schedule of guided hikes that explore topics such as the geology of the Keystone Thrust (where older sandstone was thrust atop younger sandstone) or reptile-watching expeditions.

For a more hands-on experience at Red Rock, rock climber Randal Grandstaff and his company, Sky's the Limit, 702/363-4533 or 800/733-7597, www.skysthelimit.com, lead low-impact rock-climbing adventures for climbers of all skill levels. The Discover Climbing class ($169) allows beginners the chance to learn to scramble up the red rocks. Sky's the Limit also offers daily hikes for $69 per person.

Escape the City Streets, 702/596-BYKE, offers mountain-bike tours and rentals in Red Rock. Guided rides range from a 29-mile asphalt excursion into Red Rock Canyon from Las Vegas to an off-road trek on a trail created by wild horses.

For a more intimate learning experience, Rocky Trails, 702/869-9991 or 888/86-ROCKY, www.rockytrails.com, has guides that provide intriguing facts about Red Rock Canyon and the natural attractions surrounding Las Vegas. On Rocky Trails' six-hour excursion, you learn about the Jurassic sandstone of the park as well as the Native Americans and pioneers who occupied the area. The tour, $139, includes lunch.

Another pleasant hideaway on the Red Rock Canyon National Conservation

Area is Spring Mountain Ranch State Park, 15 miles west of Las Vegas via NV 159, 702/875-4141, a picturesque, historic park sprawled at the foothills of the Wilson Range. Visitors pay $5 at the entrance to the park, where you can explore an original 1869 stone cabin as well as the spacious lawn suitable for picnicking.

Few people would expect to find alpine hiking and skiing 42 miles northwest of Las Vegas, but Mount Charleston has become a cool retreat for southern Nevada residents and visitors alike. The scenic Spring Mountains and Charleston Peak, elevation 11,912 feet, is part of the Humboldt-Toiyabe National Forest and is a welcome surprise to hikers and skiers. The recreation area has two major canyons, Kyle (on NV 157) and Lee (on NV 156). In Kyle Canyon, you'll bump into the Mt. Charleston Hotel, 702/872-5500, which has a bar, big open fireplace, restaurant, golf course, and horse-drawn wagon rides. The Kyle Canyon road ends at the Mt. Charleston Lodge, 702/872-5408 or 800/955-1314, mtcharleston@ahm-w.com, which has individual cabins and several hiking trails in the neighborhood. The main attraction on the Lee Canyon road is the Las Vegas Ski and Snowboard Resort, 702/646-0008, a good hill that's been a local favorite since it opened in the 1960s. It's not unusual to see showgirls and lounge singers staying in shape by skiing on the slopes here. You'll find a ski school, three double chairs, 1,000 vertical feet of skiing, and runs named for gambling words such as Blackjack and Slot Alley. This area is also popular for snow play, and you'll find good terrain for snowmobiling, tubing, and sledding near the resort.

At Floyd Lamb State Park, 10 miles north of Las Vegas off U.S. 95, 702/486-5413, visitors will be greeted by peacocks patrolling the former ranch house buildings and ponds. The park, originally known as Tule Springs, is a lush, desert oasis that was once a watering hole for Native Americans. In the 1950s, the working ranch also operated as a dude ranch, where divorcées could wile away their troubles while they lounged, swam, took horseback rides, partied, and waited out the six-week residency requirement for a Nevada divorce. Today the park has excellent picnicking around the ponds (which are occupied by geese and ducks), fishing, a shooting range, and historic buildings to explore.

Wildlife watchers should make a side trip to Ash Meadows National Wildlife Refuge, 25 miles north of Pahrump, 775/372-5435, which features a series of springs and wetlands that are home to 20 species of plants and animals that are unique to the area (spring and fall are the best times to visit). The most famous denizen is the Devil's Hole pupfish, an ancient species that is only found here.

One of the main attractions at Primm, a bordertown 43 miles south of Las Vegas, is golfing. Primm Valley Golf Club, 702/679-5510 or 800/386-7867, has two 18-hole courses, the Lakes Course, which has greens arranged amid lakes and streams, and the Desert 18, which, not surprisingly, has a desert layout. Calvada Valley Golf and Country Club in Pahrump, 63 miles west of Las Vegas, also has two 18-hole courses: a championship course, 702/727-4653, and an executive course, 702/727-6388.

FOOD

Bargain hunters will enjoy dining in Primm where the restaurants in the three hotel-casinos are all inexpensive—from the buffets to the steak houses. All the resorts have buffets and 24-hour coffee shops. Primm Valley Resort, 31900 Las Vegas Blvd. S., 702/382-1212 or 800/386-7867, has **GPs**, a casual restaurant that offers steak and seafood.

Buffalo Bill's, 31700 Las Vegas Blvd. S., 702/382-1111 or 800/386-7867, stirs up the mix with **Rebecca's Restaurant and Oyster Bar** as well as the Mexican-themed **Baja Bar and Grille**.

Locals often make the drive to **Whiskey Pete's Silver Spur**, 100 W. Primm Blvd., 702/382-4388 or 800/386-7867, where they serve massive cuts of beef at good prices.

Thirteen miles north of Primm is Jean. There you'll also find inexpensive meals at both the **Nevada Landing**, 2 Goodsprings Rd., 702/387-5000 or 800/628-6682, and **Gold Strike**, 400 E. Ogden, 702/384-8444 or 800/634-6703, hotel-casinos. Both are owned by the massive Circus Circus Enterprises, which is famous for its super-cheap dining specials and buffet prices. Don't expect superior quality, but it's worth it if you're feeding a large family.

The ambiance goes decidedly uphill—both figuratively and literally—as you head up to Mount Charleston. The **Mt. Charleston Hotel**, 2 Kyle Canyon Road, 702/872-5500 or 800/794-3456, is an elegant resort with a romantic, elegant restaurant overlooking the golf course (the hotel is a popular wedding spot). Just up the hill at the **Mt. Charleston Lodge**, 1200 Old Park Rd., 702/872-5408 or 800/955-1314, the restaurant is a bit more rustic, although you will find a bar and live music.

In Pahrump, the eatery of choice is the **Pahrump Valley Vineyards**, 3810 Winery Road, 702/727-6900 or 800/368-WINE, which serves California cuisine with its Pahrump Valley Chardonnay, Sauvignon Blanc, Burgundy, and other wines.

LODGING

Again, Primm and Jean offer good rooms at bargain rates. The two towns can often be a good alternative to staying in Las Vegas during big conventions and holidays, when hotel rates go soaring. The quality of rooms and amenities are slightly better at the resorts in Primm, which include **Primm Valley Resort**, 31900 Las Vegas Blvd. S., 702/382-1212 or 800/386-7867, **Buffalo Bill's**,

31700 Las Vegas Blvd. S., 702/382-1111 or 800/386-7867, and **Whiskey Pete's**, 100 W. Primm Blvd., 702/382-4388 or 800/386-7867. In Jean, the rooms are fairly basic, but the room rates at the **Gold Strike Hotel**, 400 E. Ogden, 702/384-8444 or 800/634-6703, and **Nevada Landing**, 2 Goodsprings Rd., 702/387-5000 or 800/628-6682, are in the $22 to $30 range.

Up the hill you'll find 63 rooms at the **Mt. Charleston Hotel**, 2 Kyle Canyon Road, 702/872-5500 or 800/794-3456, which range from $50 to $140 per night. The **Mt. Charleston Lodge**, 1200 Old Park Rd., 702/872-5408 or 800/955-1314, has 13 cabin-style rooms that rent for $125 to $220 per night. In Pahrump, the biggest hotel-casino in town is the **Saddle West** hotel-casino, 122 NV 160, 775/727-1111 or 800/433-3987, which has 110 rooms and rates that range from $30 to $90. The **Pahrump Station–Days Inn**, NV160 Loop Road, 775/727-5100 or 800/329-7466, is the next largest with 45 rooms and rates from $39 to $85.

CAMPING

The best way to commune with nature between trips to the casino is to camp at Mount Charleston, which, with its pine forests and a peak elevation of more than 11,000 feet, seems worlds away from Las Vegas. If you plan to camp up here, be sure to check with the Las Vegas Ranger District Office of the Humboldt-Toiyable National Forest, 2881 S. Valley View, Suite 16, 702/873-8800—most of the campgrounds are open from about May through September, depending on the weather. The fee for staying at the Mount Charleston campgrounds is $10. **Kyle Canyon Campground** is the first area you encounter on Kyle Canyon Road, and it has pine-surrounded sites that can accommodate tents or RVs up to 40 feet. Since this campground is the most accessible, it often fills up quickly, so it's wise to call 800/280-CAMP for reservations. Next up is **Fletcher View Campground**, where tenters or RVers up to 32 feet can put down stakes for the night (no reservations accepted here). **Kyle Canyon RV Park** across the highway can hold RVers. **Hilltop Campground** on NV 158, which links the two canyon roads, was recently renovated and has coin-operated showers. **Mahogany Grove** nearby is a group-camping area. At Lee Canyon you have your choice of two campgrounds: **McWilliams** and **Dolomite**. The Lee Canyon campgrounds are slightly higher in elevation. McWilliams has 40 sites, and Dolomite, closest to the ski area, has 31.

RVers who don't want to get too far from the casino action can hook up at the **Primadonna RV Village**, 702/382-1212 or 800/386-7867, adjacent to the Primadonna hotel-casino in Primm.

4
LAUGHLIN

It might be hard to imagine when you look at the bright lights, glittering casinos, and boats skipping along the Colorado River, but Laughlin didn't even show up on the Nevada state map until 1977. Casino visionary and developer Don Laughlin saw potential in this hot stretch of desert on the river between Nevada and Arizona. In 1964, Laughlin visited a tiny fishing spot called Mike's Camp. It consisted of a bar and little else. He bought the land and the bar, and in 1966 opened Don Laughlin's Riverside, a small casino with a few slot machines, two gaming tables, and a cheap chicken buffet dinner. Bullhead City folks and other Arizonans drawn to the gambling began to bolster the success of the Riverside, and soon other casinos began to pop up along the banks of the river. When Laughlin received its own post office, the postal inspector suggested "Laughlin," and the name stuck.

Today Laughlin is a bustling little boomtown with an airport and a bridge spanning the river from Bullhead City, Arizona. The Riverside now has 1,405 rooms, and the town has a total of 11,035. Laughlin has an intimacy that Las Vegas has far outgrown, and low rollers are the town's main clientele. Numerous nickel machines, cheap hotel rooms, and even cheaper buffets keep a steady stream of RVers, seniors, and bargain hunters rolling into town.

Visitors seems to enjoy the smaller casinos, but the town still manages to offer some of the glamour, nightlife, and attractions that you would find in Las Vegas. And there is one attraction that Laughlin has that Las Vegas doesn't—the Colorado River. In summer, when the sidewalk is sizzling, a younger set of visitors arrives to hop on Jet Skis, water skis, and beaches.

LAUGHLIN

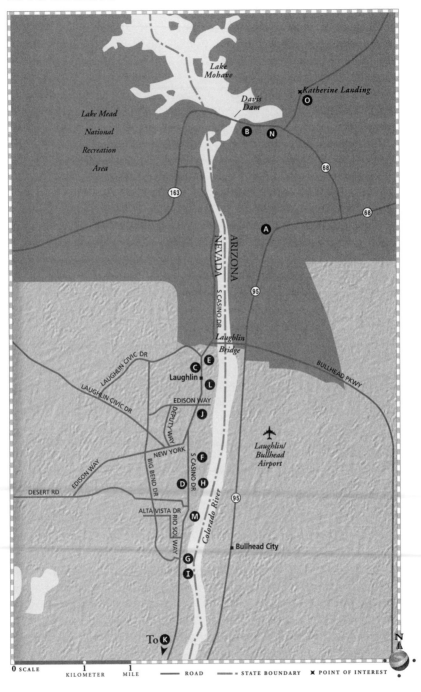

Lake Mohave

Lake Mead National Recreation Area

Davis Dam

Katherine Landing ✕
O

B **N**

68

163

NEVADA ARIZONA

A

68

95

S CASINO DR

Laughlin Bridge

LAUGHLIN CIVIC DR

C **E**

Laughlin ▪

LAUGHLIN CIVIC DR

L

EDISON WAY

DEPUTY WAY

J

BULLHEAD PKWY

NEW YORK

F

Laughlin/ Bullhead Airport

EDISON WAY

BIG BEND DR

S CASINO DR

D **H**

DESERT RD

ALTA VISTA DR

RIO SOL WAY

M

95

Colorado River

Bullhead City ▪

G

I

To **K** ▼

N

A PERFECT DAY IN LAUGHLIN

Morning in Laughlin should begin with a buffet breakfast—both the Pioneer Club and Harrah's offer good options. If you want to see the river, the *Little Belle*, docked at the Colorado Belle, offers an enjoyable cruise aboard a nostalgic replica sidewheeler. After seeing wildlife and desert scenery you'll be ready to quench your thirst with a tall cool one at the Colorado Belle's Boiler Room brew pub. A stop at the Ramada Express to see *On the Wings of Eagles*, a multimedia show about WWII, followed by a trip to the Horizon Outlet Mall will fill up your afternoon. Late afternoon is a good time to drive out to Grapevine Canyon; the sun will be setting on the petroglyphs, carved into the red- and bluff-colored rocks. The evening is a good time to do some casino hopping, ending at Harrah's Laughlin, where you can finish with a steak dinner at William Fisk's steak house. You can work off the filet mignon with a night of two-stepping at the Western Ballroom at the Riverside, and you can also sample the $1 Riverside-label light beer.

SIGHTS

- **A** Colorado River Museum
- **B** Davis Dam self-guided tour
- **C** Horizon Outlet Center Mall
- **D** Ramada Express Train Ride and Shop
- **D** Ramada Express WWII Exhibit and Show
- **E** Riverside Automobile Museum

FOOD

- **F** Boiler Room Brewery (Colorado Belle)
- **G** D'Angelo's Italian Bistro (River Palms)
- **H** Granny's Gourmet Room (Pioneer)

FOOD *(continued)*

- **I** La Hacienda (Harrah's Laughlin)
- **G** Madeline's Gourmet Room (River Palms)
- **G** No Ka Oi (River Palms)
- **D** Passaggio Italian Gardens (Ramada Express)
- **E** Prime Rib Room (Riverside)
- **D** Ramada Express
- **D** Roundhouse (Ramada Express)
- **I** William Fisk's (Harrah's Laughlin)
- **J** Winner's Circle (Edgewater)

LODGING

- **K** Avi Resort and Casino
- **F** Colorado Belle
- **J** Edgewater
- **L** Flamingo Hilton Laughlin
- **M** Golden Nugget
- **I** Harrah's Laughlin
- **H** Pioneer
- **D** Ramada Express
- **G** River Palms
- **E** Riverside

CAMPING

- **K** Avi Resort
- **N** Christmas Tree Pass
- **O** Katherine Landing
- **E** Riverside RV Park

Note: Items with the same letter are located in the same area.

TRAVELER'S NOTE

The weather gets scorching in Laughlin during the summer. The temperatures in June, July, and August can reach 115 degrees or hotter. The casinos are well-equipped inside, but if you step outside, make sure you carry a hat, sunscreen, and water—even for short trips. Of course, when the temperature heats up, the room rates go down so, if you can take the heat, you can cash in on some good bargains. The climate is more temperate during the spring, fall, and winter, but the town becomes a bit more crowded and the bargains less plentiful (although it's still a good deal).

Visitors also should note another bordertown phenomenon—time zones. Laughlin is on Pacific time, and Arizona is on Mountain time. Arizona doesn't observe daylight saving time, so in summer the two states are on the same time. But, in winter, Arizona is an hour ahead.

SIGHTSEEING HIGHLIGHTS

★★★★ RAMADA EXPRESS WWII EXHIBIT AND SHOW
2121 S. Casino Dr., 702/298-4200 or 800/243-6846
www.ramadaexpress.com

This exhibit and multimedia show will bring out the patriot in everyone. The pavilion between the hotel towers and casino houses an auditorium where visitors can watch *On the Wings of Eagles*, a 15-minute multimedia show presented on four giant screens and complemented with lights and lasers. You'll see photographs and hear sound bites from such notables as Franklin D. Roosevelt, Winston Churchill, and Adolf Hitler. There are photos that show people of all genders and races who contributed to the war effort. You'll catch glimpses and hear the sounds of entertainers of the day, such as Glen Miller and Bing Crosby. The show spans the era from the day Pearl Harbor was attacked to the time John F. Kennedy was president and Martin Luther King Jr. made his "I Have a Dream" speech. The show also reveals highlights from subsequent decades, including the lunar landing and the fall of the Berlin Wall. Fireworks and images of the flag mark the finale. The walls of the auditorium are filled with war-era memorabilia, from an extensive radio exhibit to uniforms, posters, military displays, and a cockpit from a Flying Fortress.

Details: *Shown daily, every hour on the hour, 9–4. Free. (30 minutes–1 hour)*

★★★ HORIZON OUTLET CENTER MALL
S. Casino Dr., 702/298-3003

Shoppers rejoiced when the Horizon Outlet Mall opened in the heart of Laughlin in 1997. Although small by metropolitan standards, shoppers will find more than 50 outlet stores, including Bugle Boy, Linen Barn, Polo/Ralph Lauren, Geoffery Beene, Reebok, and Wild Things. The growing mall also has a food court, movie theater, and covered parking (a must during summer).

Details: *Southern end of Casino Dr. next to the Ramada Express. Mon–Sat 9–8, Sun 10–6. Free covered parking. (1–3 hours)*

★★ RAMADA EXPRESS TRAIN RIDE AND SHOP
2121 S. Casino Dr., 702/298-4200 or 800/243-6846
www.ramadaexpress.com

The locomotive theme is prevalent here. For a cheap (free) thrill you might want to climb aboard the small-scale replica of the Virginia and Truckee Railroad (made famous in Virginia City) and take the short loop ride around the hotel. You can board at the small train station at the front of the hotel and pass the locomotive-shaped swimming pool. Inside the hotel at the train shop, railroad buffs will find everything from books and videotapes to conductor's caps and train whistles.

Details: *Free. (30 minutes–1 hour)*

★★ RIVERSIDE AUTOMOBILE MUSEUM
1650 S. Casino Dr., 702/298-2535 or 800/227-3849
www.riversidecasino.com

Riverside owner Don Laughlin has a love for old cars, and he showcases them at this surprisingly diverse automobile collection. You'll find more than 70 classic cars, including a few one-of-a-kinds as well as some that once were owned by celebrities, such as John Wayne's Travel-All. You'll also see the Indian motorcycle owned by Steve McQueen.

Details: *Located on the third floor of the south tower. Free. (30 minutes–1 hour)*

★ COLORADO RIVER MUSEUM
355 Hwy. 95, 520/754-3399

This museum houses a wide range of exhibits, from 240-million-year-old fossils to a 1960s model of the Riverside Resort. Housed inside a building that was constructed for Davis Dam workers in 1947, the museum contains artifacts from the Mojave Indian tribes that live in the area, including a replica of a village and descriptions of petroglyphs found nearby. There's an extensive section devoted to the Katherine gold mine, the area's big mine near Lake Mohave. Artifacts include a replica of the mine shaft. Visitors can take a look at the old Bullhead City Post Office, the town's first, which also served as a general store.

Details: *U.S. 95, one-half mile north of the Laughlin Bridge at Davis Camp. Open April, May, June, Sept, Oct Tues–Sat 9:30–2:30 (Arizona time); Nov–Mar Mon–Sun 9:30–2:30 (Arizona time). By appointment during summer (closed July and Aug). (1 hour)*

★ DAVIS DAM
520/298-2214

Davis Dam is dwarfed by its larger cousin upstream, Hoover Dam, but the free, self-guided tour is intriguing, especially for engineering buffs. Built in 1953, the dam's architecture, government-green furnishings, and equipment reflect the era. You can scope out the photographs and interpretive exhibits, and see the turbines and the control room with its big knobs and lights that make it resemble the set of a 1950s sci-fi movie.

Details: *On the north end of Laughlin. Open weekdays 9–4. Free. (30 minutes)*

FITNESS AND RECREATION

The Colorado River is right out the back door, so water-related recreation is a must in Laughlin. A few of the hotels along the riverwalk offer Jet Ski rentals although you can bring your own and launch from Fishermen's Park just north of the Riverside Hotel. The hotels also offer a number of sightseeing cruises. The *Fiesta Queen*, 702/298-1047 or 800/228-9825, docked at the Edgewater offers cruises aboard a sidewheeler. The USS *Riverside* at the Riverside, 702/298-2535 or 800/227-3849, and the *Celebration* at the Flamingo Hilton, 702/298-5111, also are sightseeing boats. At Harrah's Laughlin, the Del Rio Beach Club, 702/298-6828 or 800/74-BEACH, has yacht cruises as well as Wave Runner and jet boat rentals. Blue River Safaris, 702/298-0910, based at the Colorado Belle, offers eight-hour tours to Lake Havasu for $60. London Jet Boat Tours, 888/505-3545, is based at the Pioneer boat dock and offers similar tours to Lake Havasu.

If you'd like to stretch out away from the casinos, Big Bend of the Colorado State Recreation Area, 702/298-1859, Nevada's newest state park, has 2,343 acres next to the river for boating, fishing, picnicking, and wildlife watching. The park entrance fee is $3 and an additional $5 to use the boat ramp.

RELAX AT THE RIVER

On one side are the serene sights and sounds of the Colorado River—on the other are the neon lights and bells of the slot machines. The riverwalk divides the two worlds and makes a pleasurable stroll (although you might not enjoy it quite as much midday in the summer). The riverwalk begins at Fishermen's Park on the north end of Laughlin and meanders by the eight big resorts that are perched on the Colorado. Along the way you can duck into the casinos, wander out onto the docks, or pause at the numerous park benches and admire the petunias. For a quicker tour, climb aboard one of the water taxis that shoot between the Arizona side and a few of the clubs on the Nevada side (fare is $2 one way or $3 round-trip).

There's more water recreation nine miles north of Laughlin at Katherine Landing on Lake Mohave, which occupies the southern tip of Lake Mead National Recreation Area. Katherine Landing, 530/298-1859, which sits on the Arizona side of the lake, has a national park visitors center where visitors can learn about the area as well as join the ranger-led nature hikes. Katherine Landing also has a boat launch, boat rentals, marina, restaurant, docks, swimming, water-skiing, and fishing.

Native Americans occupied this area, and visitors can explore the petroglyphs and small caves at Grapevine Canyon, seven miles west of Davis Dam. Park rangers based at Katherine Landing offer guided tours, 530/754-3272. You'll find even more hiking trails and picnicking above Grapevine Canyon on the dirt road to Christmas Tree Pass. It leads into the Newberry Mountains and offers spectacular canyons and desert scenery. The road is bumpy and there are no facilities up here, so be sure you have a good spare tire and plenty of water—it's a long, hot walk back to town.

Golfers can tee off at the two surprisingly verdant courses in Laughlin. The Emerald River Country Club, 1155 W. Casino Dr., 702/298-0061, has holes next to the river and is divided by a roadway. The Mojave Resort Golf Club, 16 miles south of Laughlin near the Avi Casino, 9905 Aha Macav Pkwy., 702/535-4653, is proving to be a popular new course with its numerous (80) sand bunkers and wide fairways.

FOOD

Buffet lovers will find many ways to fill their plates in Laughlin. Prime rib, fried chicken, salads, ice cream—you'll find a little bit of everything at every Laughlin hotel-casino, and you'll find it at reasonable prices. One of the most elegant—and popular—is the Sunday brunch at **Granny's Gourmet Room** at the Pioneer, 2200 S. Casino Dr., 702/298-2442 or 800/634-3469. Be sure to call ahead because it fills up a couple of weeks in advance. At $21.95, this brunch is a bit more expensive than the average Laughlin buffet, but the gourmet fare is worth it.

The decor and buffet food are above average at the **No Ka Oi** at the River Palms, 2700 S. Casino Dr., 702/298-2242 or 800/835-7904, and at the **Roundhouse** at the Ramada Express, 2121 S. Casino Dr., 702/298-4200 or 800/243-6846.

You'll also find a variety of cuisines beyond the buffets, such as **D'Angelo's Italian Bistro** at the River Palms, 2700 S. Casino Dr., 702/298-2242 or 800/835-7904, **Passaggio Italian Gardens** at the Ramada Express, 2121 S. Casino Dr., 702/298-4200 or 800/243-6846, and **La Hacienda** at Harrah's Laughlin, 2900 Casino Dr., 702/298-4600 or 800/447-8700. Nothing is more refreshing on a scorching summer day in Laughlin than a freshly brewed glass of beer—you'll find one at the **Boiler Room Brewery** at the Colorado Belle, 2100 S. Casino Dr., 702/298-4000 or 800/477-4837. The Boiler Room also serves mesquite-grilled pizzas, herb-seasoned salmon, and burgers. Most of the hotel-casinos have good gourmet rooms, too. For steaks you can bring your appetite to **William Fisk's** at Harrah's Laughlin, 2900 S. Casino Dr., 702/298-4600 or 800/447-8700, or **Madeleine's Gourmet Room** at River Palms, 2700 S. Casino Dr., 702/298-2242 or 800/835-7904. Meat lovers also will enjoy the prime rib carved tableside at the **Prime Rib Room** at the Riverside, 1650 S. Casino Dr., 702/298-2535 or 800/227-3849.

If you're on the go, the **Ramada Express**, 2121 S. Casino Dr., 702/298-4200 or 800/243-6846, will pack a picnic lunch for you with sandwiches, chips, and snacks in a cooler that you get to keep. For a quick yet filling bite, the **Winner's Circle** at the Edgewater, 2020 S. Casino Dr., 702/298-2453 or 800/677-4837, has good snack-bar deals, including a half-pound hot dog and huge shrimp cocktail, for $1.99 each.

LODGING

Lodging in Laughlin has always been known as a bargain, and it becomes ridiculously cheap during summer. Most hotels range from about $15 during the hot season to $90 during the winter, when snowbirds from the cold climes come to Laughlin to thaw out.

Each of the nine major hotel-casinos in Laughlin has its own personality and amenities, and all of them sit right next to the Colorado River except for the Ramada Express (across from the rest on Casino Drive). The **Colorado Belle**, 2100 S. Casino Dr., 702/298-4000 or 800/477-4837, which recently underwent a renovation, is the most striking with its riverboat theme. The Colorado Belle and the southwestern-themed **Edgewater**, 2020 S. Casino Dr., 702/298-2453 or 800/677-4837, are both Circus Circus properties, so both offer decent although not luxurious rooms at reasonable prices. The **Flamingo Hilton Laughlin**, 1900 S. Casino Dr., 702/298-5111 or 800/352-6464, is a comfortable resort where you can enjoy concerts at the hotel's outdoor amphitheater in the fall. The tropical theme at the **Golden Nugget**, 2300 S. Casino Dr., 702/298-7111 or 800/237-1739, is reminiscent of its mother property, the Mirage in Las Vegas. **Harrah's Laughlin**, 2900 S. Casino Dr., 702/298-4600 or 800/447-8700, on the southern end of Casino Row has a Mexican-resort theme and offers the same high quality and friendly staff as its other Nevada properties. All of the rooms have a river view, and the grounds are covered with blooming bougainvilla. Harrah's also has its own private beach reserved for hotel guests. The **Pioneer**, 2200 S. Casino Dr., 702/298-2442 or 800/634-3469, with its giant neon mascot

COLORADO BELLE

River Ric, is a popular spot for gamblers, who flock to the numerous nickel slots. **River Palms**, 2700 S. Casino Dr., 702/298-2242 or 800/835-7904, has an open, industrial feel with huge exposed ceiling beams. You take an escalator down to the main casino or stay up on the mezzanine that overlooks the action. The **Ramada Express**, 2121 S. Casino Dr., 702/298-4200 or 800/243-6846, is a compact little hotel-casino that has pleasant decor, good restaurants, and intriguing attractions, such as a small-scale train, a locomotive-shaped swimming pool, and a WWII museum and multimedia presentation. Town founder Don Laughlin opened the **Riverside**, 1650 S. Casino Dr., 702/298-2535 or 800/227-3849, the first hotel-casino, in 1966. His resort has blossomed and now in addition to the casino you'll find a movie theater, automobile collection, and some of the town's best lounges. The Fort Mohave Indian Tribe owns the **Avi Resort and Casino**, 10000 Aha Macav Parkway, 702/535-5555 or 800/284-2946, 16 miles south of Laughlin. The resort is geared toward golfers, who can choose from the area's three championship courses.

CAMPING

In winter, thousands of snowbirds traveling in RVs descend upon Laughlin. **Riverside RV Park**, 702/298 2535 or 800/227-3849, which has a whopping 900 spaces across the street from the hotel, becomes its own little community, albeit one that's a little cramped. But you'll find all the amenities, including full hookups, showers, and a laundromat for $16 per night (and a pedestrian walkway connects the park and the hotel). **Katherine Landing**, 530/298-1859, has a campground for both tents and RVs, a popular option for anglers. **Avi Resort**, 702/535-5555 or 800/284-2946, also has an RV park. The hundreds of acres surrounding **Christmas Tree Pass** offer plenty of opportunities for primitive camping. Because of the winding, bumpy road, large RVs are not recommended.

NIGHTLIFE

Despite the fact that Laughlin is less than a tenth the size of Las Vegas, the entertainment in the lounges and showrooms of the hotel-casinos is on par with its sister city. The Riverside, 702/298-2535 or 800/227-3849, probably has the most diverse offerings for entertainment on the river. Big-name performers such as Willie Nelson and Anne Murray appear at Don's Celebrity Theater, where, on Sundays, Catholic church services are also held. In the hotel's Western Ballroom, you can dance to country music videos, DJ music, or live music. Rock 'n' rollers can head over to the Losers Lounge, which is

SIDE TRIP: SEARCHLIGHT

A visit to Laughlin should include a stop at the historic little mining town of Searchlight, 40 miles north of Laughlin. Founded after gold was discovered in 1898 and named for the brand of matches used by miners, Searchlight has become a gateway to Lake Mohave, 14 miles east, and the southern end of Lake Mead National Recreation Area. The town also has a few attractions of its own as well as some intriguing claims to fame. It has one of the world's last 10-cent cups of coffee at the Searchlight Nugget's coffee shop, 702/297-1201. Notable Hollywood costume designer Edith Head grew up in Searchlight, and silent-film star Clara Bow and husband Rex Bell resided near Searchlight at their Walking Box Ranch. You can learn about the famous residents and other history at the Searchlight Historic Museum and Mining Park, 200 Michael Wendoll Way (Cottonwood Cove Highway), 702/297-1201. Art critics should tour the Searchlight Gallery, 702/297-1540, where artist and Searchlight resident Don Schaeffer shows his paintings of Western landscapes.

decorated with the trappings of famous disasters, such as the *Titanic*, and disasterous people, like George Custer. At the Flamingo Hilton Laughlin, 702/298-5028 or 800/435-8469, the hotel usually offers a production show, such as *Dancin' to the Hitz,* as well as concerts during the spring and fall in the outdoor amphitheater. Such performers as Wynonna Judd and Lynyrd Skynyrd also appear here. At Harrah's Laughlin, 702/298-4600 or 800/447-8700, you'll find a production show in its Fiesta Showroom, and performers such as Chuck Berry at its Rio Vista Outdoor Amphitheater. The River Palms Resort, 702/298-2242 or 800-835-7904, also offers a production show in its Crystal Sands Showroom. The Colorado Belle's Boiler Room, 702-298-4000, the Golden Nugget's Tarzan Lounge, 702/298-7111 or 800/237-1739, and the Edgewater's Kokopelli's Lounge, 702/298-2453, are also popular places to dance and listen to live music.

SPECIAL EVENTS

One of the most colorful—and noisy—events in Laughlin is the Laughlin River Run, 909/340-0094, www.laughlinriverrun.com, during which thousands of Harley-

Davidson owners descend upon the Colorado River town. The event is usually held in the spring and includes rides to nearby attractions and show 'n' shines.

You can also get your motor revved during the Laughlin Desert Challenge, 800/227-5245, www.score-international.com, which is held in January and is part of the SCORE International Off-Road Racing six-race circuit. One of the most popular competitions during the event is the Laughlin Leap during which trucks vie for the longest jump.

5
THE GOLDEN TRIANGLE

While this particular stretch of U.S. 95 offers only small towns that are on the way to larger attractions, visitors who keep their eyes open will find some unusual and inviting places to explore. Inevitably, if you're traveling between Las Vegas and Reno, you will bump into these little places, each with its own flavor and brand of hospitality. Along the way are Beatty, Rhyolite, Goldfield, Tonopah, and Hawthorne. The common thread that ties them together, aside from their location on U.S. 95, is history. This is Nevada's mining belt—tons of gold and silver ore were culled from this area in the late 1800s and early 1900s, creating cosmopolitan cities that were, at the time, larger than Las Vegas and Reno combined. But the wealth didn't last forever, and many of the boomtowns quickly went bust. In some cases, the towns disappeared forever; others are mere remnants of what they once were. But some, such as Tonopah and Hawthorne, managed to hold on and develop other industries and attractions. The histories of these towns are what draw many visitors to the museums and ruins where one can almost imagine grizzled old miners wandering along the dirt streets with their burros.

A PERFECT DAY IN THE GOLDEN TRIANGLE

Because of the distances involved in traveling this remote, unpopulated area of Nevada, you may find it difficult to see everything the area has to offer in one day. But if you begin in Beatty, you can drive to Rhyolite for a quick tour of the desert sculptures and the remains of the ghost town. The next stop is Goldfield,

THE GOLDEN TRIANGLE

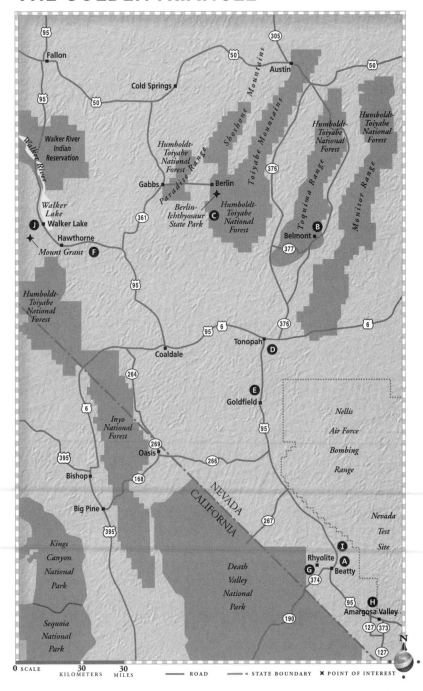

where the historic buildings scattered through town make it a good candidate for a quick driving tour (although you should stop for refreshments at the Santa Fe Saloon). In Tonopah, you can grab a quick bite at Burger Master and walk it off at the Tonopah Mining Park. For campers, the best place to end your tour is Berlin-Ichthyosaur State Park where you can tour the ghost town and see the fossilized bones of dinosaurs still partially buried in the ground. If you'd rather stay at a bed-and-breakfast and explore one of Nevada's most intriguing ghost towns, the final stop for the day should be the Belmont Monitor Inn in the ramshackle ghost town of Belmont. Fishermen and golfers can opt to spend the final hours of the day in Hawthorne. You can have a romantic dinner at the Cliff House overlooking Walker Lake or enjoy nine holes of golf in twilight at the Walker Lake Country Club.

SIGHTSEEING HIGHLIGHTS

★★★★ CENTRAL NEVADA MUSEUM
Logan Field Rd., Tonopah 775/482-9676

SIGHTS

- Ⓐ Beatty Trading Post
- Ⓑ Belmont
- Ⓒ Berlin-Ichthyosaur State Park
- Ⓓ Central Nevada Museum
- Ⓔ Goldfield
- Ⓕ Mineral County Museum
- Ⓖ Rhyolite and the Gold Well Open Air Museum
- Ⓓ Tonopah Mining Park

FOOD

- Ⓐ Alexander's Steak House
- Ⓑ Belmont Monitor Inn
- Ⓓ Burger Master
- Ⓖ Cliff House Lakeside Resort

FOOD (continued)

- Ⓔ El Capitan
- Ⓓ El Marques
- Ⓔ Joe's Tavern
- Ⓔ Maggie's
- Ⓓ Rex Chinese
- Ⓐ Rita's Restaurant
- Ⓓ Station House Casino

LODGING

- Ⓑ Belmont Monitor Inn
- Ⓕ Best Western Desert Lodge
- Ⓓ Best Western Hi-Desert Inn
- Ⓐ Burro Inn
- Ⓕ Cliff House Motel
- Ⓓ Clown Motel
- Ⓔ El Capitan
- Ⓐ Exchange Club
- Ⓗ Longstreet Inn and Casino

LODGING (continued)

- Ⓐ Phoenix Inn
- Ⓓ Silver Queen
- Ⓐ Stagecoach Casino and Hotel
- Ⓓ Station House

CAMPING

- Ⓘ Bailey's Hot Springs
- Ⓒ Berlin-Ichthyosaur State Park
- Ⓐ Burro Inn
- Ⓐ Stagecoach Motel
- Ⓙ Sportsmen's Beach Recreation Site
- Ⓙ Tamarack Beach
- Ⓙ 20-Mile Beach

Note: Items with the same letter are located in the same area.

The emphasis at this museum is hands-on, making it an entertaining as well as educational place for kids. You'll find a section devoted to the area's desert wildlife, including a taxidermied golden eagle in flight. You'll also see an old telephone switchboard that was used from 1906 to 1961. There is an extensive display devoted to the history of the Tonopah Army Air Field, including the wreckage and photographs of a B-25 that crashed near Tonopah (all eight crew members survived). The exhibits show how the pioneers dressed and cooked—even how they curled their hair. You can sit in the beauty chair and attach the archaic-looking electric curlers to your head. The playhouse area has an old typewriter at which kids can peck away, as well as a kitchen with an old stove and cookware. There's a selection of clothing and hats for dress up. Outside there are more exhibits of mining equipment, out-houses, and old automobiles. The museum also has an extensive research area complete with newspapers, books, photographs, and videos.

Details: *Open Apr–Sept daily 9–5; Oct–Mar Mon–Sat 11–5. Donation. (1 hour)*

★★★★ RHYOLITE
775/553-2424

Visitors can hardly believe their eyes when they drive up to this former Nevada boomtown. Situated near the decaying structures of the Rhyolite ghost town is the **Gold Well Open Air Museum**, a series of surreal sculptures perched in the parched desert. The museum was started by Belgian artist Albert Szukalski in 1984. For his life-sized *Last Supper*, ghostly figures made of plaster and fiberglass, he used Beatty and Rhyolite residents as models to give him the proper shapes. The *Ghost Rider* appears ready to take a spin on a bicycle. Other artists have joined Szukalski and made their own contributions to the desert art museum. Painter Fred Bervoets created the sculpture of Shorty Harris, a legendary prospector who roamed Rhyolite in search of riches. Hugo Heyrman created the pink-cinderblock *Lady Desert: The Venus of Nevada*, and David Spicer made the stone sculpture *Chained to the Earth*. *Icara*, by Andre Peeters, represents the female counterpart to Icarus who, according to Greek mythology, tried to fly to the sun.

Juxtaposed against the surreal artwork are the even more surreal ruins of Rhyolite. After gold was discovered in 1904, the town quickly became one of Nevada's most cosmopolitan cities. Between

1905 and 1912, between 3,500 and 10,000 people lived in Rhyolite. At the time, the town had more than 50 saloons, three water systems, three newspapers, an opera house, two hospitals, and a red-light district. But as quickly as they were born, the promises of major gold strikes dissipated, and today all that remains is a ghostly skeleton. This colorful little ghost town has been preserved and has some fascinating structures scattered amid the sagebrush. Signs reveal what each structure was. You can't miss the three-story Cook Bank building, one of Rhyolite's most striking landmarks. A caretaker watches over the ruins and offers tours of the Rhyolite Bottle House, built in 1906 out of thousands of bottles. You can help with preservation efforts by buying a T-shirt or making a donation.

Details: *Five miles west of Beatty; 775/553-2424. Open year-round. Donation. (1–2 hours)*

★★★ BERLIN-ICHTHYOSAUR STATE PARK
775/964-2440

This state park combines two attractions. At one end of the park are the remains of ancient fish-lizards known as ichthyosaurs, which swam in the sea that once covered Nevada. Archaeologists first excavated the fossilized bones in the 1950s, and the remains have been preserved in the ground and covered by a shelter. At the other end of the park are the remains of Berlin, a mining camp that has been preserved in a state of "arrested decay." Visitors can peer into the old mill and a miner's shack that is still furnished with the accoutrements of its final occupant. The surrounding juniper-covered hillsides are excellent for hiking and exploring, and the relative remoteness of the park means that the place is rarely overcrowded.

Details: *128 miles north of Tonopah. Park open year-round. Berlin Townsite Tour (by request) Memorial Day–Labor Day. Fossil Shelter Tour Memorial Day–Labor Day daily 10, 2, and 4; Mar 18–Memorial Day and Labor Day–Nov 13 Sat–Sun 10, 2, or by request; Nov 14–Mar 15 by request only. $3 entry fee to park. (2 hours minimum)*

★★★ GOLDFIELD
775/485-3560

One glance at the towering remains of this once-thriving city tells yet another tale of boom and *borrasca*. The most notable landmark is the deserted four-story Goldfield Hotel. Built in 1908, the stone hotel had 150 rooms and numerous amenities, including telephones in every room and a huge, grand dining room. It closed in 1946 never to be reopened, but the solidly built hotel still stands sentinel over the town. You can pull off the highway and drive by a number of other buildings that reveal Goldfield was once a large city, peaking at a population of 10,000 people in 1907. The Southern Nevada Consolidated Telephone Company, now home to a mining office, and the boarded-up Goldfield High School speak of a more prolific time. The Esmeralda County Courthouse still serves residents, and visitors are allowed to tour inside. Be sure to pay a visit to the Santa Fe Saloon, built in 1905, where the old Brunswick back bar is well worn, and you can order a drink and strike up a conversation with the mannequin that is dressed like Wyatt Earp. The Mozart Club, with a skeleton mural painted on the outside of the building, is worth a stop for a drink. You can shop and learn about the town at Glory Hole Antiques, although you'll also find tourist information at the Goldfield Chamber of Commerce on the highway in the center of town.

Details: 26 miles south of Tonopah on U.S. 95. (30 minutes– 1 hour)

★★★ MINERAL COUNTY MUSEUM
400 10th St., Hawthorne, 775/945-5142
This wide-open museum, housed in a former grocery store, includes a cornucopia of local historical displays, including Hawthorne's first fire truck, military displays, and pioneer clothing. Visitors should pause to admire the Gold Key Drugstore diorama with its apothecary and waiting room as well as the mural depicting Hawthorne's history painted by a local artist for the bicentennial. The collection of turn-of-the-century photographs taken by E. F. Box shows exceptional photography skills and reveal how early Hawthorne citizens enjoyed leisure time picnicking and relaxing at Walker Lake and other sites.

Details: Open Tue–Sat 11–5. Donation. (1 hour)

★★ BELMONT
NV 376
At its peak in the 1860s, two thousand people lived in Belmont, a silver camp that became the county seat of Nye County. Alas, the silver played out, and residents skedaddled in search of riches elsewhere. The buildings were left to looters and the destructive desert environment, but fortunately the town was declared a National Historic District, which saved the ghostly Belmont Courthouse. Visitors can occa-

sionally luck out and find a resident willing to give a quick tour inside the building, but most often you'll have to enjoy the sights from the outside. In summer, you can whet your whistle at Dirty Dick's Saloon, a rustic watering hole owned by part-time resident Dick Ashton.

Details: *46 miles north of Tonopah on NV 376. (2 hours)*

★★ LOST RIVER TRADING COMPANY
U.S. 95 and McDonald St., Beatty
775/553-2233

Shopping options can be sparse in rural Nevada, but the Lost River Trading Company provides a suitable opportunity. Stocked with antiques, artwork by local artisans, and jewelry, the Beatty Trading Post is worth browsing.

Details: *Open daily 9–5. Free (30 minutes)*

★★ TONOPAH MINING PARK
Mizpah Ave., Tonopah, 775/482-9274 or 775/482-9676
www.tonopahminingpark.com

Perched atop the original mining claim that gave birth to Tonopah, the Tonopah Mining Park makes for an intriguing stroll through the town's mining history. The most striking feature of the park is the steel head-frame of the Mizpah Mine, which plucked valuable silver ore from the earth between 1902 and 1948. The mine belonged to town founders Jim and Belle Butler. Jim first discovered the rich ore when his burro wandered off and he picked up a rock to chuck at the ornery critter. The weight of the rock caught his attention, and the subsequent assay proved that the ground was rich with silver. The Tonopah Mining Park is a walking tour of the Butlers' once prolific mining area. The tour begins with an informative video about Tonopah history. Visitors can then see the deep stopes and the buildings filled with giant mining equipment.

Details: *Call for hours and tour times. $3 adults, $5 couples, $7 families. (1 hour)*

FITNESS AND RECREATION

Although it's a minor remnant of an ancient sea that once covered Nevada, Walker Lake, 10 miles north of Hawthorne, is a big lake that appears to have been plopped down in the middle of the desert. Nearly 30 miles long, the lake stretches out in the shadow of Mount Grant. It's also next to U.S. 95, where the water is a welcome sight to road-weary travelers. The lake offers water-skiing, swimming, bird-watching, boating, and camping, but of course the main attraction is the fishing. Anglers are drawn to Walker for its cutthroat trout—an annual fishing derby keeps fishermen dreaming of the lunkers that may lurk in the depths. And speaking of lunkers, Walker Lake is rumored to harbor a friendly sea serpent, which townsfolk have popularized as Cecil. An incarnation of Cecil appears in hometown parades, and the high school sports teams are called the Serpents. The lake is also home to other types of wildlife—a migration of loons makes biannual stopovers at Walker. The town holds an annual Walker Lake Loon Festival, during which the Nevada Division of Wildlife schedules loon-watching tours on the lake.

You can scarcely arrive in any small town in Nevada without running into a golf course, and Hawthorne is no exception. Hawthorne's Walker Lake Country Club, 775/945-1111, is situated on the Army Ammunitions Plant and is one of Nevada's most picturesque rural courses. The nine-hole course was established in 1952 by military personnel, and has gorgeous greens and tall cottonwoods—a worthwhile stop if you need a quick golf fix.

Beatty is the Nevada gateway to Death Valley National Park, 775/553-2200, a small corner of which crosses into Nevada from California. Among the park's numerous attractions is the Furnace Creek Resort, which offers golf, horseback riding, and other forms of recreation amid the gothic desert landscape. With place names such as Dante's View and the Devil's Golf Course, and an elevation below sea level, you can easily conclude that this place gets downright inhabitable during the summer. If you do go in summer, bring plenty of water—both for you and your automobile.

FOOD

One of the most romantic places to dine in this area is the **Cliff House Lakeside Resort**, 1 Cliff House Rd., Hawthorne, 775/945-5253. The bar and dining room overlook Walker Lake—the scene is even more dramatic during full moons. The menu matches the ambiance—steaks, Alaskan king crab, Australian rock lobster, and other forms of surf and turf. You'll find a more casual atmosphere at **Maggie's**, 785 E. Main St., 775/945-3908, which serves superb fried chicken and chicken-fried steak. All the items on the extensive menu are made fresh, including the breads, cakes, and pies. Maggie's also has another unusual feature for rural restaurants—patio dining. You'll also find good pies and other coffee-shop fare as well as a dinner buffet at the **El Capitan**, 540 F St., 775/945-3321, the town's big casino. Across the street at **Joe's Tavern**, 526 E St., 775/945-2302, you won't find much more food than beer nuts, but the venerable old saloon is worth a visit. A longtime locals' hangout, the saloon is stocked with antiques and has occasional weekend entertainment, a dance hall, and a few slot machines.

In Tonopah the 24-hour coffee shop at the **Station House Casino**, 1100 Erie-Main St., 775/482-9777, has good American grub, and **Burger Master**, 607 Erie-Main St., 775/482-6402, has great cheeseburgers, fries, and shakes. Even in this small mining town you'll find good international cuisine at **Rex Chinese**, 137 Main St., 775/482-5377, and **El Marques**, 348 Main St., 775/482-3885. In Belmont (pop. 7), 46 miles north of Tonopah, the **Belmont Monitor Inn**, Hwy. 377, 775/487-2417, set in a historic surrey house built in 1866, has a steak house and a bar.

In Beatty, the Stagecoach Hotel, 800/4-BIGWIN, has **Alexander's Steak House** and **Rita's Restaurant**.

LODGING

To truly immerse yourself in the spirit of Nevada's gold-mining ghost towns, the best place to pack it in for the night is the **Belmont Monitor Inn**, Hwy. 377, 775/487-2417. The rustic bed-and-breakfast inn is the work of local Chris Bramwell. He transformed a dilapidated surrey house into a cozy lodging house. The rooms are furnished with antiques, and the bathrooms have clawfoot tubs and pedestal sinks. Originally Chris was using the house to provide shelter for hunters visiting the area, but he decided to turn it into a full-fledged bed-and-breakfast. The result is an inviting, homey lodge.

In Hawthorne the main hotel-casino is the **El Capitan**, 540 F St., 775/945-3321, which has large although sparsely decorated hotel rooms. If you'd rather be close to the water, the **Cliff House Motel**, 3113 Cliff House Road at Walker Lake, 775/945-2444, sits near the shore and overlooks the activities on the lake. The **Best Western Desert Lodge**, 1402 E. Fifth St., 775/945-2660, is the most expensive in town ($55 per night); most of the hotel rooms in Hawthorne range from $30 to $40 per night.

In Tonopah the main hotel-casino is the **Station House**, 1100 Erie-Main St., 775/482-9777, on the south end of town. (The historic Mizpah Hotel has been closed for renovations, and a reopening date is undetermined.) Downtown you'll find Tonopah's largest motel, the 85-room **Silver Queen**, 255 Main St., 775/482-6291. The most unusual feature of this motel is its detached lobby, a round building of classic '60s architecture that resembles a jester's hat. You'll find a handful of little motels, including the **Best Western Hi-Desert Inn**, 323 Main St., 775/482-3511 or 800/528-1234, and the **Clown Motel**, 521 N. Main St., 775/482-5920, that offer good rooms at very reasonable rates.

Beatty is a good oasis and stopping point if you plan to spend the day exploring Rhyolite or Death Valley National Park. **Stagecoach Casino and Hotel** on U.S. 95, 775/553-2419 or 800/4-BIGWIN, has been renovated and has two restaurants, weekend entertainment, and a swimming pool and Jacuzzi. The 54-room **Phoenix Inn**, U.S. 95 and First St., 775/553-2250 or 888/845-7401, has a casino and offers a free continental breakfast. The **Burro Inn**, Hwy. 95 S. and Third St., 775/553-2225 or 800/843-2078, and the **Exchange Club**, 119 Main St., 775/553-2333, each have motel rooms and a casino. Another gateway to Death Valley is Amaragosa Valley, 29 miles south of Beatty, which has the **Longstreet Inn and Casino**, Hwy. 127, Death Valley Junction, 775/372-1777.

CAMPING

In Hawthorne at Walker Lake, camping is allowed at **20-Mile Beach**, **Tamarack Beach**, and **Sportsmen's Beach Recreation Site**. You'll find well-developed sites with showers and restrooms at **Berlin-Ichthyosaur State Park**, 74 miles east of Hawthorne near the tiny town of Gabbs. The Beatty area is a haven for RVers. Both the **Burro Inn**, 775/553-2225 or 800/843-2078, and the **Stagecoach Motel**, 775/553-2419 or 800/4-BIGWIN, have RV parks with hookups. **Bailey's Hot Springs**, 775/553-2395, six miles north of Beatty, is a hot springs resort with a campground.

SPECIAL EVENTS

What happens when you combine ornery critters, determined racers, and Bisquick? You get the Beatty 49er Burro and Flapjack Races, usually held in the fall. You don't have to be fast to enter—you just have to have a good pancake recipe and a burro that isn't too stubborn and has a strong love for flapjacks. Burros were the partners of prospectors in the early 1900s, and in that tradition, contestants assume their roles. The human becomes the prospector and loads his or her beast of burden with pancake supplies as well as a pick and shovel. The human and burro race around the track and, at the end of the course, the prospector has to build a fire, prepare a pancake, and serve it to the burro—a breed that is particularly fond of flapjacks. The result is a bizarre spectacle, but one worthy of watching.

6
FALLON AREA

It doesn't take long to realize that this little green pocket of Nevada is the state's breadbasket. While the bucolic scenery of rolling fields of corn, old tractors, and pastures dotted with cattle are reminiscent of old-fashioned farm towns, you can look up in Fallon and see navy jets roaring overhead—a juxtaposition that creates an intriguing mix of old and new. As you pass through town you see an old-fashioned root beer stand and a downtown movie theater, remnants of a simpler time, and a sculpture of a fighter jet along with signs pointing the way to the Top Gun Raceway. In Yerington and Wellington and the other tiny farm communities south of Fallon, the pace is even slower. In the Smith and Mason valleys, a few old farmhouses have become bed-and-breakfasts, the cows outnumber the trucks, and folks gather to discuss the weather at the country store.

A PERFECT DAY AROUND FALLON

Bird-watchers should rise at the crack of dawn and head to the Stillwater National Wildlife Refuge to scope out the birds and other critters as they set about their day. Find a tall cattail blind and watch the sunrise while you're serenaded by the calls of red-winged blackbirds, geese, and other early risers. Once the sun is up, you can get on the road and head to Yerington where you can grab a cappuccino at Greenfield Espresso and stroll the old-fashioned downtown area. Nearby, stop in at the Lyon County Museum, and on your way out of town gas up at the Hillygus station, a locals' favorite and one of the few full-service-only stations in Nevada.

FALLON

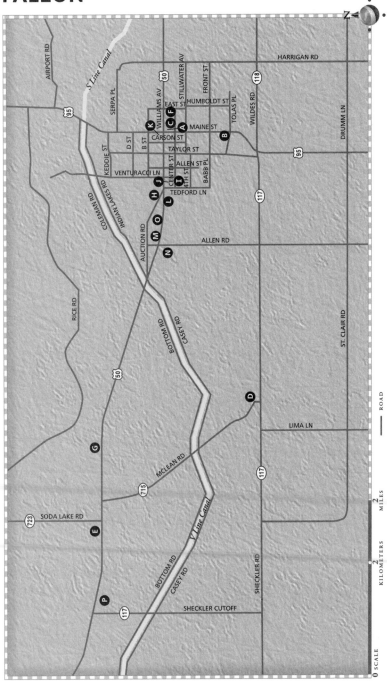

Head back to Fallon for an afternoon root beer float at Bob's followed by a tour of downtown Fallon. Then you can catch a movie at the historic Fallon Theatres.

SIGHTSEEING HIGHLIGHTS

★★★★ LYON COUNTY MUSEUM
215 S. Main St., Yerington, 775/463-2245

This well-stocked museum is located inside a former Baptist church that was built nearby in 1911 and moved to its current site in 1930. Inside you'll find a re-created sheriff's office and barber shop as well as collections of dolls, hats, and lanterns from the V&T Railroad. There's a case filled with relics such as opium bottles and carved jade from the Chinese people who lived in this area. The Native American section has baskets as well as photographs of local Paiute prophet Wovoka. Some of the more unusual exhibits include a picture of flowers made from human hair. Outside is a collection of old schoolhouses, including the one-room East Walker schoolhouse, which was moved from its location nearby. Another old schoolhouse contains natural history exhibits.

Details: *Open Thu–Sun 1–4. Donation. (1 hour)*

★★★ CHURCHILL COUNTY MUSEUM AND ARCHIVES
1050 S. Maine St., Fallon, 775/423-3677

This museum reveals how this fertile valley's Native Americans and pioneers lived. At the Tule Hut exhibit you can see the intricately

---

SIGHTS
- **A** Churchill County Courthouse
- **B** Churchill County Museum and Archives
- **C** Fallon Theater
- **D** Lattin Farms
- **E** Workman Farms

FOOD
- **F** Apple Tree Grille and Tavern

FOOD (continued)
- **G** Bob's Root Beer
- **H** Cafe Nations
- **I** El Comedor
- **J** Fallon Depot Casino, Depot Diner
- **J** Heidi's
- **G** Java World
- **G** La Cocina
- **I** La Fiesta
- **J** Stockman's

LODGING
- **K** 1906 House
- **L** Best Western Fallon Inn
- **M** Comfort Inn
- **N** Oxbow Motor Inn
- **O** Stockman's Holiday Inn Express

CAMPING
- **P** Fallon RV Park

Note: Items with the same letter are located in the same area.

---

woven blankets, baskets, and cradleboards used by the area's early inhabitants—the Paiute Indians. Visitors can see how the pioneers cooked, cleaned, and sewed. Check out the Springfield Steam Road Roller (used to build Lahontan Dam in 1915) as well as the buildings outside the museum such as the restored Woodliff Novelty Store, one of the oldest buildings in Fallon.

Details: Apr–Dec Mon–Sat 10–5, Sun 12–5; Jan–Mar call for hours. Donation. Two-hour tours of the Hidden Cave Archaeological Site depart from the museum on the second and fourth Sat of the month at 9. (1 hour)

★★★ FALLON THEATER
71 S. Maine St., Fallon, 775/423-6210 or 775/423-4454

This little gem of history in downtown Fallon is the longest continuously operating movie theater in Nevada—and it's well worth a visit. The once-lavish theater opened in 1920 and was rebuilt in the 1930s to accommodate "talkies," at the time becoming one of only two such theaters in the state. A devastating fire in 1939 followed by earthquakes in 1954 led to its slight decline, but the theater was soon repaired, refurbished, and reopened to the delight of local citizens. The narrow building, with its thick plaster walls, Spanish-style arched ceilings and entryways, and dark-blue interior make the place a cool retreat, especially in summer. The theater has modern projection and sound equipment and was split into two rooms, giving moviegoers a choice of two screens.

Details: Call 775/423-4454 for show times. Movie tickets $6 adults, $4 ages 17 and under. (2 hours)

★★★ LATTIN FARMS
1955 McLean Rd., Fallon, 775/867-3750
www.lattinfarms.com

Fallon is in farm country, and it's famous for its super-sweet Hearts o' Gold cantaloupes. At Lattin Farms you can buy fresh-picked cantaloupes as well as watermelons, tomatoes, corn, and other vegetables that are in season. The top crop at Lattin is the berries—strawberries and raspberries. You can buy the whole fruits or opt for the jams and jellies, which are made at the farm. The Lattin family also started a new attraction at the farm—a maize maze. A cornfield has been cut into the shape of the state of Nevada and has a maze inside. Before you enter the three-acre field, you receive a flag, which you can send up if you can't find your way out. The farm also has volleyball, picnic tables, and a petting zoo on selected weekends.

Details: Maze open Aug–Oct daily 10–8 (closed Sun and Mon in Aug for irrigation). Maze $6 adults, $4 under 16. (1 hour)

★★★ WELLINGTON MERCANTILE
NV 208, Wellington, 775/465-2552

This old-fashioned country store and historic landmark is a great place to stop for a piece of pie and for soaking up the slow pace of a rural farming town. The big, red mercantile was originally called the Hoyes Store when it was built in 1873 in a nearby canyon. Later it was moved to downtown Wellington where it serves as the centerpiece and main gathering spot in town. Inside you'll find a hodgepodge of groceries, plants, candy, farm-fresh eggs, hardware, and antiques. Out front is a wide covered porch where you can enjoy a soda pop and one of the mercantile's deli sandwiches.

Details: 20 miles south of Yerington on NV 208. Open Mon–Sat 8–6, Sun 10–4. Free. (30 minutes–1 hour)

★★ HILLYGUS GAS STATION
201 S. Main St., Yerington
775/463-2640

It's easy to forget what decade you're living in when you pull into this tiny two-pump station in Yerington. Ed Hillygus darts out from his tiny office and promptly asks, "Fill 'er up?" While the tank is filling he grabs a rag and washes all your windows, then pops the hood and checks the oil, all the while cheerfully chatting about the weather or how he'd rather be on the golf course. This is one of Nevada's last throwbacks to a simpler time. The station has been in the Hillygus family since 1939. Ed's mother, Clara, ran the one-woman show until she died a couple of years ago. "She wouldn't let me come down because I didn't do a good enough job on the windows," the retired school-teacher says. The price of gas is a few cents higher than at the big stations on the highway, but the service is worth it—and Ed sends you off with a piece of candy and a smile and wave.

Details: Open 8:30–6, closed Wed–Sun. Free. (30 minutes)

★★ WORKMAN FARMS
4990 Reno Hwy., Fallon, 775/867-3716

The fruits of Fallon's fertile valley are also offered at Workman Farms' roadside stand. The family-operated market offers produce from area farms, including tomatoes, corn, cucumbers, and

YERINGTON

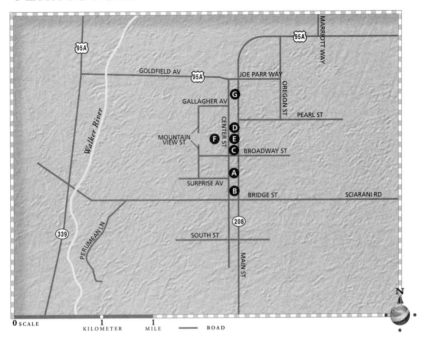

SIGHTS
Ⓐ Hillygus Gas Station
Ⓑ Lyon County Museum

FOOD
Ⓒ Casino West
Ⓓ Dini's
Ⓔ Greenfield Espresso
Ⓓ Guiseppe's

LODGING
Ⓕ Arbor House
Ⓒ Casino West
Ⓖ Copper Inn

Note: Items with the same letter are located in the same area.

---

cantaloupes. You'll also find a selection of shrubs and flowers as well as pickles, olives, and jams.

Details: *About 3 ¹/2 miles west of Fallon on Alternate U.S. 50. Open daily 8–5. Free. (30 minutes)*

★ CHURCHILL COUNTY COURTHOUSE
Fallon, 775/423-6028
You can't miss this stately old courthouse, prominently perched on the town's busiest intersection at Maine and U.S. 50. The white

neo-classical building with Tara-like columns and an entry resembling a schoolhouse was built in 1930 at a cost of $7,300. The wooden building remains the longest continuously operating courthouse in Nevada.

Details: *Free. (30 minutes)*

★ FALLON NAVAL AIR STATION
775/426-2880

Don't be alarmed if you hear a low-flying jet overhead—it's just the Top Gun fighter pilots cruising back to their home base at the Fallon Naval Air Station. The Top Gun Navy Fighter Pilot School, made sexy by Tom Cruise, is based in Fallon, so expect to see a lot of residents with short haircuts and aviator sunglasses while you tour town. It's not unusual to see the jets performing maneuvers on the outskirts of town. Groups of 10 to 50 people can tour the Fallon NAS, although you have to make reservations six months in advance (no drop-ins allowed).

Details: *Tours offered weekdays only, with the exception of the first and third Fri of the month. Call 775/426-2880 for reservations and rates. (30 minutes–1 hour)*

★ TOP GUN RACEWAY
U.S. 95, 775/423-0223 or 800/325-7448

In a town populated by Top Gun jet fighter pilots, it's not surprising that you'd find a motor raceway where speed is the name of the game. This quarter-mile drag strip stationed in the desert amid the sagebrush is sanctioned by the NHRA, so the racing action is top level. The track has a 3,500-seat spectator area.

Details: *15 miles south of Fallon on U.S. 95. Mar–Nov; call for race schedule. Tickets $7–$15. (1 hour minimum)*

★ YERINGTON PAIUTE COLONY
**171 Campbell Lane, Yerington, 775/463-3301
or 775/883-3895**

Take a quick drive to this quiet little colony where you should stop and check out the monument to Wovoka, the famous Paiute prophet who lived here in the early 1900s. He preached about peace, and started the Ghost Dance Movement. Unfortunately, his message was misinterpreted and led to the death of many soldiers and Indians at Wounded Knee in South Dakota.

Details: *Free. (30 minutes)*

FITNESS AND RECREATION

Stillwater National Wildlife Refuge, 775/423-5128, about 17 miles east of Fallon, surrounded by desert and low-lying mountain ranges, is a surprising oasis that offers some of the state's most diverse wildlife. As you drive along the dirt roads through the refuge, great blue herons scan the marshes for fish while golden eagles and hawks circle overhead. Great horned owls watch the action from the limbs of cottonwood trees while deer, quail, and chipmunks wander through the thick scrub. Bird-watchers should not leave home without the binoculars and bird guide—these wetlands are a nesting and migration site for hundreds of species, including tundra swans, pelicans, numerous types of ducks and geese, and hundreds of shorebirds. Native Americans found abundant food and materials among the dense marsh and cattails, but in more recent years the water was drained to supply irrigation to nearby farms. Fortunately, the emphasis in the past 10 years has been more toward preserving the wetlands.

The adobe-skeleton remains of Fort Churchill State Historic Park, 775/577-2345, 30 miles west of Fallon at Silver Springs, provide a hauntingly peaceful place to picnic and relive a piece of Nevada's history. Constructed as Nevada's first military base in 1860, Fort Churchill was designed to protect visitors passing through on the Overland Trail. The remains have been preserved in a state of arrested decay, and the visitors center map reveals the identities of the buildings that you see along the walking trail. Photogenic Fort Churchill also was once a stop for the Pony Express—the visitors center houses a few artifacts. The park, which comprises 710 acres, is perched on the banks of the Carson River, and a dirt road leads to a picnic area as well as a campground.

Sand Mountain, 775/885-6000, 25 miles southeast of Fallon by U.S. 50, is Nevada's answer to the Sahara Desert. The sword-shaped dunes provide a giant sandbox for dune buggy and ATV enthusiasts or visitors who just like to feel the sand between their toes. The sands are continually shifting and moving and are also said to "sing." In reality they make a booming noise that is created by the grains of sand rubbing together. Nature lovers can explore the Sand Springs Study Area, a short loop with interpretive signs that point out the more than 70 species of plants and wildlife. You can also explore the preserved ruins of a Pony Express Station.

At the Grimes Point Archaeological Site, 775/423-3677, 12 miles east of Fallon, visitors can see the drawings on the rocks left by Native Americans about 8,000 years ago. The one-mile Hidden Cave Interpretive Trail located 1.2 miles east of Grimes Point has about a dozen points of interest, the most notable of which is Hidden Cave. Bureau of Land Management rangers lead tours to this significant archaeological cave on the fourth Saturday of each month, starting at 9:30 a.m. at the Churchill County Museum in Fallon.

Lahontan State Recreation Area, 775/867-3500, 18 miles west of Fallon, offers a vast amount of recreational opportunities. This is a huge lake with 69 miles of shoreline and 12,000 surface acres, so there's plenty of room to stretch out on the beach or atop the water. Not surprisingly, fishing is big here as is boating and water-skiing. Several picnicking, swimming, and beach-lounging sites are spread out along the shoreline. There aren't any tall trees to hide under during the summer, so make sure you bring your own shade. One of the most intriguing places to explore at the lake is the Lahontan Dam, which also serves as a bridge. Bird-watching is popular, too—the lake is on the Pacific Flyway.

FOOD

The best place to grab a bite in Fallon is **Bob's Root Beer**, 4150 Reno Hwy., 775/867-2769, three miles west of Fallon, an authentic drive-in built in 1960 by retired navy man Francis "Gunner" Signore. He recently sold the orange-and-white burger stand to fellow Fallon residents George and Sharon Hansen who still make the root beer from scratch at the drive-in. Carhops serve the root beer, floats, and shakes in frosty mugs pulled right out of the freezer. Dogs (that arrive with paying customers) get free ice cream. The drive-in is open April to November.

At the railroad-themed Fallon Depot Casino, you'll find good food inside the **Depot Diner**, 875 W. Williams, 775/423-3233. Both Stockman's and the Fallon Nugget have restaurants. **Heidi's**, 855 W. Williams Ave., 775/423-0558, part of a local chain that has restaurants in Carson City, Reno, and Lake Tahoe, serves hearty breakfasts and lunches.

In downtown Fallon you'll find a mini-concentration of Mexican restaurants. The most established is **La Cocina**, 125 S. Main St., 775/423-6166, which serves humongous tostadas and other Mexican dishes. **El Comedor**, 66 W. Center St., 775/423-3070, serves killer tamales. **La Fiesta**, 60 W. Center St., 775/423-1605, a few doors down from the El Comedor, is in an attractive red-brick building. Also near downtown, the **Apple Tree Grille and Tavern**, 40 E. Center St., 775/423-4447, serves American fare—the burgers are delicious.

Coffee lovers won't feel neglected in Fallon, which has two high-octane cafés: **Cafe Nations**, 960 A Auction Rd., 775/423-6828, and **Java World**, 775/428-2400, downtown near the theater at 55 S. Main St.

In Yerington, the gourmet restaurant of choice is **Guiseppe's** inside Dini's Lucky Club, 45 N. Main St., where you'll find steak, seafood, and pasta dishes. **Dini's** also has a coffee shop. The café inside **Casino West**, 11 N. Main St., 775/463-2481, has a buffet in its spacious coffee shop. On the menu, the

WELLINGTON/MASON REGION

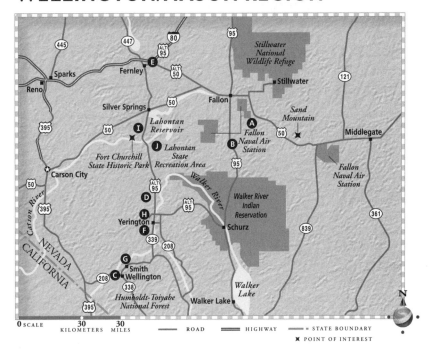

SIGHTS

- **A** Fallon Naval Air Station
- **B** Top Gun Raceway
- **C** Wellington Mercantile
- **D** Yerington Paiute Colony

FOOD

- **E** Wigwam Cafe

LODGING

- **F** Hoye Mansion
- **G** Smith Valley Bed and Breakfast
- **H** Walker River Resort

CAMPING

- **I** Fort Churchill Campground
- **J** Lahontan State Recreation Area

---

burgers with home-cut fries are worth sampling. **Greenfield Espresso**, 37 N. Main St., 775/463-3330, next to Casino West has coffee drinks, ice cream, muffins, and sandwiches as well as gifts. The cafe is located inside a former bank building—take a gander at the old safes. You can sit at the counter, at tables, or on the comfortable sofas that look out onto the main drag.

A drive to the **Wigwam Cafe** in Fernley, 255 W. Main St., 27 miles west of Fallon, 775/575-2573, is a popular locals' spot crammed with an intriguing collection of Native American artifacts. You'll also find a **Pizza Factory** at 1320 Highway 40 East.

LODGING

Nevada's greenbelt is also home to a cluster of cozy bed-and-breakfasts. The newest old home to open its doors to travelers is the **1906 House** in Fallon, 10 S. Carson St., 775/428-1906. With its gables, spires, and welcoming front porch, the bright-pink mansion on the town's main drag still looks today much as it did when it was built by Nevada State Senator Robert L. Douglass for his wife Eleanor. The home was later bought by Dr. F. E. Nichols who turned it into the town's only hospital. In 1996, Suzanne and Jerry Noonkester bought and restored the home, which offers guests two bedrooms with a shared bath. Another place to relax in the country lifestyle amid beautiful surroundings is in Wellington, 20 miles south of Yerington, at the **Hoye Mansion**, 2827 Hwy. 208, 775/465-2959. Situated next door to the Wellington Mercantile, the two-story B&B will make you feel as though you've been transplanted back 100 years. Guests choose from five bedrooms (which share two baths) in the stately old home, most of which are decorated with an old movie theme such as *Gone With the Wind*. Yerington also has a small inn called the **Arbor House**, 39 N. Center, 775/463-2991 or 800/891-6982, which is surrounded by beautiful gardens. In Smith, 15 miles south of Yerington, you'll find the remote **Smith Valley Bed and Breakfast**, 2400 NV 208, 775/465-2222, the former home of the valley's late famous female physician, Dr. Mary Fulstone. At this inn with three rooms and one bath, guests make their own breakfasts.

In Fallon you'll find several good motels, too. At **Stockman's Holiday Inn Express**, 1560 W. Williams St., 775/428-2588 or 800/HOLIDAY, is a good option. The **Best Western Fallon Inn**, 1035 W. Williams St., 775/423-6005 or 800/528-1234, recently expanded. Other good choices include the **Comfort Inn**, 1830 W. Williams St., 775/423-5554, and the **Oxbow Motor Inn**, 60 S. Allen Rd., 775/423-7021, next to McDonald's.

In Yerington, **Casino West**, 11 N. Main St., 775/463-2481 or 800/227-4661, has 79 rooms adjacent to its casino. Another good option is the **Copper Inn**, 307 N. Main St., 775/463-2135.

Sportsmen congregate 20 miles west of Yerington at the **Walker River Resort**, 1 Awora Rd., Smith, 775/465-2573 or 800/446-2573. It has five cabins and excellent fishing and hunting opportunities.

CAMPING

You can camp amid the tall cottonwoods, sagebrush, and historic parks at **Fort Churchill Campground**, 775/577-2345, next to the state historic area. You'll find 20 campsites with water, vault toilets, and fire pits that can accommodate tents as well as RVs up to 24 feet.

Visitors can take advantage of the fishing, swimming, boating, and water-skiing at **Lahontan State Recreation Area**, 775/867-3500. The state park campground has 40 sandy campsites for tents as well as RVs up to 30 feet. It also features flush toilets, water, and picnic tables.

For camping that's a little closer to civilization, the **Fallon RV Park**, 5787 U.S. 50, 775/867-2332, is a scenic park with lots of trees and 44 spaces for RVs (including 20 pull-throughs).

SPECIAL EVENTS

Fallon has two special events that are worth the trip. In the spring, the Fallon Naval Air Show features the aerobatics of the Blue Angels and other military jets. In fall, the season is ripe for the Fallon Hearts o' Gold Cantaloupe Festival. The event includes produce stands as well as cantaloupe-eating contests, a carnival, and camel rides (and be sure not to pass up the booth selling cantaloupe-flavored ice cream).

7
RENO

It's only natural to want to compare Reno, the Biggest Little City in the World, to Las Vegas, the Brightest Big City in the World. On the surface they both appear to be built on gaming, bright lights, and attractive showgirls. And it's not difficult to see that Las Vegas has a lot more wattage than Reno. But scratch Reno's surface and you'll see the roots of modern Nevada. You'll find the excitement and big-city attractions, but you'll also encounter small-town feeling—it's much more intimate than its big sister down south. But above all, you'll see a place that is nestled in some of the West's most beautiful country.

In the 1920s and 1930s, Reno beat Las Vegas to the punch in establishing Nevada's reputation for fun and frivolity, becoming a playground for celebrities and other adults seeking the glamour and glitz that only an up-and-coming casino town can provide. Defying social mores and risking bad public relations, Reno also capitalized on something that was drawing patrons from every slice of society—easy divorce. All the soon-to-be-divorced visitors had to do was establish six weeks' residency, and then they could toss their wedding rings into the Truckee River. While they waited, divorcees would occupy their days at dude ranches and their nights in the fabulous downtown casinos, clubs, and restaurants.

Reno weddings are more popular these days than divorces, and the casinos continue to be a draw. But unlike Las Vegas, where the casinos create attractions like volcanoes and pirate ships, Reno comes by them naturally. The Truckee River rolls right through the heart of downtown, and visitors can follow it right

DOWNTOWN RENO

N

O

395

MILL ST

ODDIE BLVD

395

80

647

9TH ST

COMMERCIAL ROW

2ND ST

KUENZLI ST

Pickett Park

KIRMAN AV

LOCUST ST

Washoe County Fairgrounds

MORRILL ST

WELLS AV

MILL ST

RYLAND ST

STEWART ST

HOLCOMB AV

6TH ST

HIGHLAND AV

Taylor Memorial Park

C

PINE ST

EVANS AV

LAKE ST

L

CENTER ST

D

E

PLUMAS ST

University of Nevada-Reno

B F

VIRGINIA ST

A

J

M N K

H

ISLAND ST

LIBERTY ST

I

CALIFORNIA AV

SIERRA ST

6TH ST

ARLINGTON AV

647

Riverside Park

11TH ST

RALSTON ST

G

WASHINGTON ST

Rancho San Rafael Regional Park

12TH ST

RIVERSIDE DR

P

COLEMAN DR

4TH ST

7TH ST

80

Idlewild Park

KEYSTONE AV

Truckee River

WYOMING AV

HIGHWAY

ROAD

0   1   MILE

0   1   KILOMETER

SCALE

into the mountains to become surrounded by skiing, hiking, biking, kayaking, windsurfing, golfing, and a myriad of other activities.

A PERFECT DAY IN RENO

A good place to start for breakfast is the Rotisserie Buffet at John Ascuaga's Nugget in Sparks. You can swing over to the nearby Reno Hilton where you can hit golf balls onto the floating islands on the small lake in the shadow of the hotel. Then rent some mountain bikes or in-line skates at Snowind Sports at the Reno Hilton and jump on the riverwalk trail that winds through urban and wild attractions. Park your bike next to the river and stop at the National Automobile Museum to learn about vehicles on four wheels. Next, you should spend the afternoon in downtown Reno, where you can do some casino hopping (check out the Silver Legacy's mining rig and the midway at Circus Circus). Pause for a refreshing Parisian-style lunch at Bistro Roxy. Then it's time to head over to the Wilbur D. May Museum and Arboretum, with a side visit to Great Basin Adventure's log ride and petting zoo. Top off the evening at Harrah's Reno, which always has an excellent production show playing in Sammy's Showroom.

SIGHTS
- **A** Circus Acts and Carnival Midway
- **B** Fleischmann Planetarium
- **C** National Automobile Museum
- **D** National Bowling Stadium
- **E** Nevada Museum of Art
- **F** University of Nevada, Reno Walking Tour
- **G** Wilbur D. May Museum

FOOD
- **A** Art Gecko's (Circus Circus)

FOOD *(continued)*
- **H** Bistro Roxy (Eldorado)
- **H** Brew Brothers (Eldorado)
- **H** Chef's Buffet (Eldorado)
- **I** Deux Gros Nes
- **J** Fairchild's Oyster Bar (Silver Legacy)
- **K** Fresh Market Square (Harrah's Reno)
- **H** Golden Fortune (Eldorado)
- **H** La Strada (Eldorado)
- **L** Louis' Basque Corner
- **J** Silver Legacy
- **J** Sterling's Steakhouse (Silver Legacy)

FOOD *(continued)*
- **J** Sweetwater Cafe (Silver Legacy)
- **M** Top of the Hilton at the Flamingo Hilton Reno (Silver Legacy)

LODGING
- **A** Circus Circus
- **H** Eldorado
- **N** Fitzgeralds
- **M** Flamingo Hilton Reno
- **K** Harrah's Reno
- **O** Reno Hilton
- **J** Silver Legacy

CAMPING
- **P** Chism's Trailer Park
- **O** Hilton Camperland

Note: Items with the same letter are located in the same area.

SIGHTSEEING HIGHLIGHTS: RENO

★★★★ WILBUR D. MAY MUSEUM
Rancho San Rafael Park, 1502 Washington St., 775/785-5961
Wilbur D. May (1898–1982), a well-known Renoite and the son of
a wealthy May Department Store magnate, had a lust for travel.
While his father pined that his son would never be a businessman
and join him in the company, May wanted to see the world, visit
exotic locales, and experience many cultures. The results of his
adventures, which ranged from African safaris to Asian excursions,
are housed at the Wilbur D. May Museum, which is a replica of May's
Double Diamond Ranch in Reno. May actually turned out to be a
good businessman—he had sold all his stocks before his travels and
returned after the stock market crashed. He had cash and was able
to buy up several stocks for a fraction of their worth. His fortunes
allowed him to become a pilot, collector, big-game hunter, and Reno
rancher while he honed his skills as a philanthropist. The replicated
ranch house is filled with his big-game prizes, including rhinos, zebras,
and several others. Visitors also can marvel at the numerous exotic
collectibles, such as a shrunken head and a collection of Tang
Dynasty horse sculptures. Next to the museum is a beautiful arboretum, which has more than 15 different gardens featuring plants found
at various locations in Nevada. Kids will enjoy the Great Basin
Adventure, which has a log-flume ride, a petting zoo with goats and
other critters, and pony rides.
    Details: *Open Mon–Sat 10–5, Sun 12–5 (closed Tue during winter).*
Museum $2.50 adults, $1.50 children, extra charge for special exhibits.
Great Basin Adventure, 775/785-4319, $3 adults, $2 kids (closed Mon).
(1–3 hours)

★★★ NATIONAL AUTOMOBILE MUSEUM
10 Lake St., 775/333-9300
This collection of more than 200 cars will rev the hearts of motor-
heads—it's undoubtedly the premiere museum for fans of the automotive age. The collection, which consists of about a thousand cars,
was owned by the late William F. Harrah—a man who obviously
loved to drive. His legacy is housed in this shiny, mauve museum, which
has the cars carefully labeled and lovingly exhibited in creative displays.
In one section you'll find the cars from the 1890s, and in the next are
autos from the 1910s, '20s, and '30s. Of course, there are Cadillacs,

Chevrolets, Mercedes, Jaguars, and other cars of various ages and manufacture, as well as Edsels and Volkswagens. The museum offers occasional lectures as well a multimedia presentation on cars. There's a coffee shop and, of course, a gift shop crammed with everything on four and two wheels.

Details: *Open Mon–Sat 9:30–5:30, Sun 10–4. $7.50 adults, $6.50 seniors, $2.50 ages 6–18. Free parking. (1–2 hours)*

★★ CIRCUS AND CARNIVAL MIDWAY
Circus Circus, 500 N. Sierra St.
775/329-0711

Pack up the kids and head for Circus Circus, the main kid-friendly attraction in downtown Reno. This is a slightly smaller version of the midway at Circus Circus in Las Vegas. Kids and grownups alike will enjoy the clowns, juggling, trapeze artists, and teeter-totter acrobats at the midway stage. One of the most popular acts is J. R. Johns and his Canine Companions—Johns has trained a group of mutts rescued from the animal shelter to perform amazing feats. You also can try your skills at Whack-A-Chicken and other carnival games on the midway.

Details: *Circus acts 11 a.m.–12 a.m. Free. (1 hour)*

★★ FLEISCHMANN PLANETARIUM
775/784-4812, www.scs.unr.edu/planet/

Folks who have their eyes on the skies can get a closer look at the stars at Fleischmann Planetarium. The public observatory has a 12-inch telescope trained on planets and other heavenly bodies. The planetarium also has a space museum, gift shop, and a theater that shows nature-themed double features often coupled with star lectures.

Details: *On the University of Nevada-Reno campus, just off N. Virginia Street north of Lawlor Events Center. Open Mon–Fri 8–9, Sat–Sun 10–9. Free building admission. Show tickets $6 adults, $4 seniors and children. Observatory open Fri evenings; free. (1–2 hours)*

★★ NATIONAL BOWLING STADIUM
300 N. Center St., 775/334-2634

That silver geodesic dome shimmering in downtown Reno is the centerpiece of the high-tech National Bowling Stadium. Visitors can't bowl here (unless they're competing), but you can sit in the stadium and watch professional bowlers vie for trophies on the national bowling circuit and in big-name tournaments. You'll find IMAX movies shown inside the 177-seat Stadium Theater. The stadium also has a pro shop and another unusual claim to fame—the lanes were featured in the bowling-themed movie *Kingpin*.

Details: *Open daily 8–5. Stadium admission free. Theater $6 adults, $4 seniors 60 and older and children 12 and under. (1–2 hours)*

★★ UNIVERSITY OF NEVADA-RENO
775/784-4865
www.unr.edu/tour/

In the fall, the campus of the University of Nevada gives you the feeling you've been transported to the grounds of an early New England school. The grounds feature ivy-covered buildings, numerous aging trees, and attractive ponds. It's no wonder, since the campus was modeled after Thomas Jefferson's design of the University of Virginia lawn. On the Quad, visitors will find a number of intriguing buildings that are worth a visit, including the Mackay School of Mines Building, dedicated in 1908 in honor of John Mackay, one of the Comstock silver barons who had the foresight to contribute some of his riches to education. The school has extensive book and map libraries as well as the W. M. Keck Museum, which has more than 6,000 mineral samples, fossils, and mining artifacts. At the other end of the Quad is Morrill Hall, the first building constructed on campus (in 1885) and home of the venerable University of Nevada Press. Nearby, scenic Manzanita Lake and other campus buildings were popular sites for Hollywood to make use of. Scenes from such films as *Mr. Belvedere Goes to College* were filmed here.

Details: *On the north end of Virginia St. near downtown. Free. (1–2 hours)*

★ NEVADA MUSEUM OF ART
160 W. Liberty St., 775/329-3333

Some visitors may be surprised to find a strong arts scene thriving in the heart of Reno, but you'll find art, theater, and music amid the downtown casinos. One of the best places to soak up the arts in the Biggest Little City is the Nevada Museum of Art, which attracts world-class exhibits and traveling shows from Rodin to Westin. The gift shop here is worth a tour as well.

Details: *Open Tues, Wed, Fri 10–4, Thu 10–7, Sat–Sun 12–4. $5 adults, $3 seniors and students, $1 children 6–12, free on Sun. (1 hour)*

SIGHTSEEING HIGHLIGHTS: RENO AREA

★★★ ANIMAL ARK
775/969-3111

The emphasis at this peaceful animal place is education and conservation. Situated amid the rolling juniper hills north of Reno, the Animal Ark has taken in animals that no longer could be returned to the wild. Diana Hiibel, who opened the site in 1994, gives informative tours of the animals. You'll learn about many animals such as the star of the place, Whoopi, a peregrine falcon who is blind in her left eye. Other animals include Yogi, a black bear who was raised in a home nearby, a pair of raccoons, and a group of kit foxes. The most popular animals at the sanctuary are the three wolves, Annie, Raven, and Nischa, who show visitors how to howl during the Wolf Howl Nights held during full moons. The two striped tigers have a huge savannah in which to roam, and visitors can watch them from a shaded observation area.

Details: 10 miles north on U.S. 395 to Red Rock Rd. (exit 78), 11.5 miles east to Deerlodge Rd., turn right and look for the signs. Open April–Oct daily 10–4:30. $6 adults, $5 seniors, $4 children 3–12. (1–2 hours)

★★★ BOOMTOWN FAMILY FUN CENTER
Boomtown Casino, Verdi, 800/648-3790

Kids can leave the parents behind in the casino and have their own fun at this extensive play area. It offers nine-hole miniature golf, an indoor Ferris wheel, more than 200 redemption games, and several arcade games. One of the best features is the 1908 antique carousel. For more extreme thrills you can try the Dynamic Motion Theaters, which offer virtual racing, haunted houses, and other attractions.

Details: 10 miles west of Reno on I-80. Open Mon–Thu and Sun 10–10, Fri–Sat 10 a.m.–12 a.m. Prices vary. (1–2 hours)

★★★ SIERRA SAFARI ZOO
775/677-1101

Kids love this place thanks to the large enclosure at the center of the zoo that has a curious assortment of goats, potbellied pigs, and deer that try to untie shoelaces while they're being petted. With more than 200 exotic creatures, this locally run zoo is Nevada's largest. Due to its location a few miles north of town, it is somewhat undiscovered. But visitors often are pleasantly surprised by the variety and surroundings of the animals, which include hyenas, wallabies, fainting goats, ring-tailed lemurs, a sloth, and Japanese snow monkeys. A large section of the zoo is devoted to a romping area for the big cats, such as Tasha the Siberian tiger and Hobbs, the zoo's rarest cat—he is a "liger," half lion, half tiger.

Details: 10 miles north on U.S. 395 at Red Rock Rd. (exit 78). Open Apr–Oct daily 10–5. $7 adults, $5 ages 3–12. (1–2 hours)

★ SPARKS HERITAGE MUSEUM
820 Victorian Ave., Sparks, 775/355-1144

This museum on Victorian Square in Sparks, just east of Reno, tells the story of the Rail City's roots as a railroad town. In the early 1900s, the Southern Pacific Railroad established a stop at this wide spot in the road. The place flourished once the railroad arrived. The museum occupies a two-story brick building that is listed on the National Register of Historic Places. It is filled with artifacts from Sparks's early days, such as old buggies and an extensive collection of railroad lanterns. Next to the museum you'll find historic Southern Pacific rolling stock such as a 1911 Pullman superintendent's car as well as the cute one-room Glendale School, dating to 1864. The volunteers and workers at the museum are eager to share tales from Sparks's early days.

Details: Tue–Fri 11–4, Sat–Sun 1–4. Donation. (30 minutes–1 hour)

FITNESS AND RECREATION

The Truckee River slices right through Reno, and a pedestrian path that offers jogging, walking, and bicycling winds right alongside it. In the downtown area you can soak up the sights of the Raymond I. Smith Truckee River Walk, 775/334-2077, a silver-and-purple architectural area that lends itself to afternoon strolls. The seven-mile path is a narrow strip of natural habitat where you'll encounter beavers, geese, and ducks. You can rent mountain bikes at Snowind Sports, at the Reno Hilton, 775/323-9463, which is on the far eastern edge of the trail.

Golfers shouldn't dare leave home without the clubs—the Reno area has eight public courses. Contact the Reno-Sparks Convention and Visitors Authority, 800-FOR-RENO, for a list of courses. One of Reno's most unusual golf experiences is at the Hilton Bay Aqua Driving Range, 775/789-2000, where you tee off toward holes on islands floating in the lake next to the Reno Hilton. A bucket of 90 floating balls costs $7, and club rentals are $2.

Idlewild Park near downtown on the Truckee River is packed with several activities. In the winter you can lace up your ice skates for figure eights on the

Rink by the River, 775/334-2262. In the summer Idlewild has a pool as well as several scenic picnic sites. Kids will enjoy the small Playland, which has carnival rides. One of the most aromatic areas of the park is the rose garden, which blooms throughout the summer and fall.

Anglers and bird-watchers shouldn't miss a trip to Pyramid Lake, about 30 miles north of Reno. Named by explorer John C. Frémont for its pyramid-shaped tufa formation, Pyramid is 27 miles long and 9 miles wide. Situated on the Pyramid Lake Paiute Indian Reservation, the lake lures fishermen to its cut-throat trout. Pyramid-Tahoe Fishing Charters, 775/852-3474, takes fishermen to the best spots on the lake. The other attraction here, besides the scenery, is the bird-watching because the lake's Anaho Island is a nesting site for the white pelican.

Hikers will enjoy the views atop 10,778-foot Mount Rose, a strenuous 11-mile-round-trip hike into the pines and wildflowers of the Mount Rose Wilderness. The trailhead is located on the north side of the Mount Rose Highway, about 15 miles south of Reno. Nearby is Galena Creek Regional Park, which offers another strenuous hike up the 9.6-mile Jones Creek–Whites Creek Loop Trail.

FOOD

Reno's hotel-casinos offer some excellent buffets. The Eldorado's **Chef's Buffet**, 345 N. Virginia St., 800/648-5966, has an Italianate feel with ivy painted on walls, a patina bronze trellis under a painted sky, and huge rotisseries with several chickens roasting over flames. **Toucan Charlie's**, 3800 S. Virginia St., 775/825-4700 or 800/723-6500, is the extremely popular buffet at the Atlantis Resort. The specialties here are made-to-order omelettes and hot spinach salads as well as the Mongolian barbecue for which you pick your Asian vegetables, meats, and spices, which are then cooked together while you wait and salivate. The copious salads—antipasto, crab, pasta—will fill you up before you even find the entrées, which include steaks that are grilled to order. At the Peppermill's **Island Buffet**, 2707 S. Virginia St., 775/826-2121 or 800/648-6992, you'll find a compact but superb assortment of salads and entrées. The Friday-night seafood buffet is worth the wait (try to avoid the peak times of 6 to 8 p.m.). It is so popular that patrons are issued beepers to notify them when a table is ready. Harrah's Reno's **Fresh Market Square**, 219 N. Center St., 775/788-3232 or 800/427-7247, is huge and even includes a make-your-own cappuccino section. In Sparks, the **Rotisserie Buffet**, 1100 Nugget Ave., 800/648-1177, at John Ascuaga's Nugget is a local favorite. The entrées are always fresh, and you'll often find an unusual one thrown in, such as sausage and

GREATER RENO

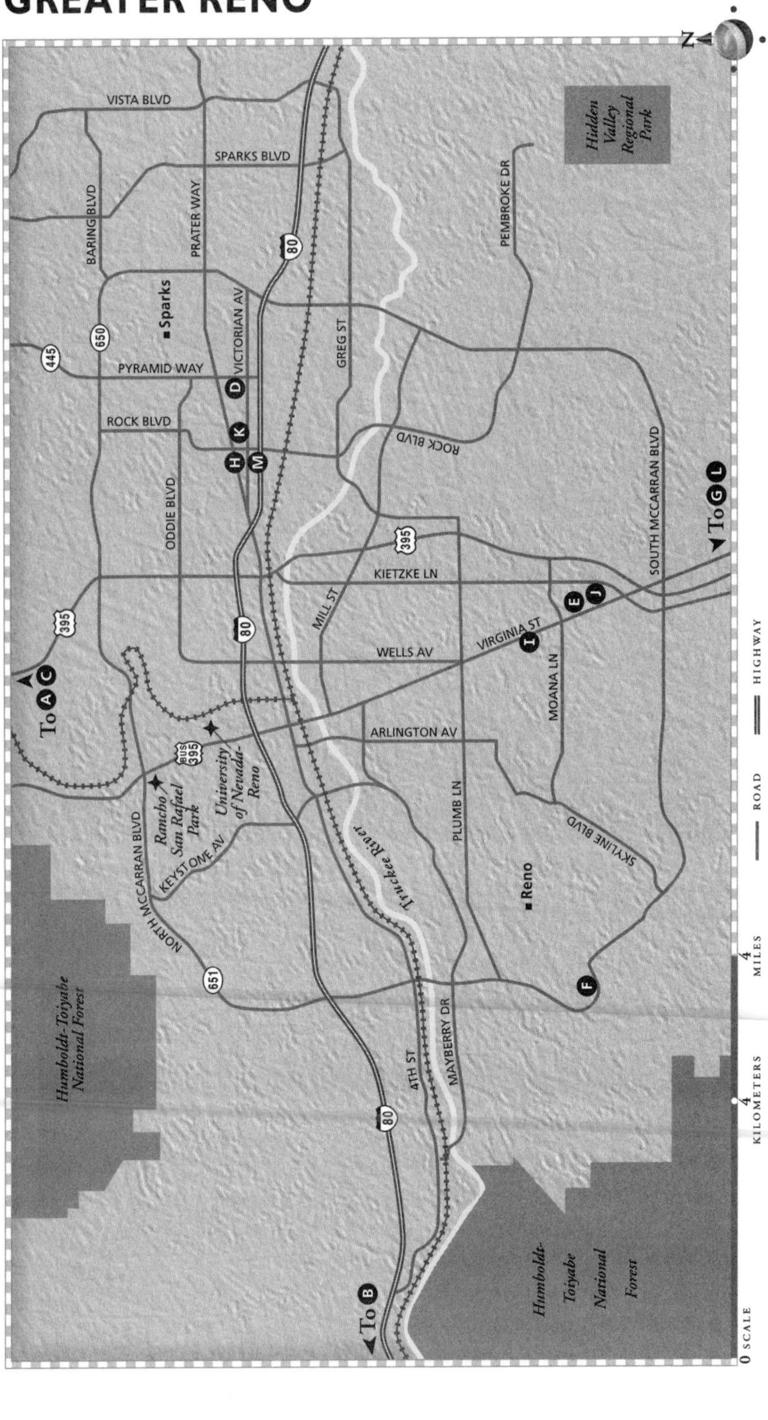

VISTA BLVD

SPARKS BLVD

PRATER WAY

BARING BLVD

Hidden Valley Regional Park

80

PEMBROKE DR

Sparks

VICTORIAN AV

GREG ST

650

445

PYRAMID WAY

D

ROCK BLVD

ROCK BLVD

H K

M

ODDIE BLVD

SOUTH McCARRAN BLVD

To G L

395

395

KIETZKE LN

MILL ST

E J

To A C

WELLS AV

VIRGINIA ST

I

80

MOANA LN

ARLINGTON AV

Humboldt-Toiyabe National Forest

395/305

University of Nevada-Reno

Rancho San Rafael Park

KEYSTONE AV

PLUMB LN

SKYLINE BLVD

Reno

Truckee River

NORTH McCARRAN BLVD

651

F

Humboldt-Toiyabe National Forest

4TH ST

MAYBERRY DR

80

To B

0 SCALE

4 MILES

4 KILOMETERS

━━━ ROAD   ═══ HIGHWAY

N

peppers. The buffet also has theme nights—don't miss Wednesdays, which are Chocolate Nights. Some of the desserts, salads, and entrées are so popular that the Nugget printed up recipe cards, which you can pick up on your way out. The **Silver Screen Buffet** at Boomtown in Verdi, 10 miles west of Reno, I-80 west, Exit 4, 800/648-3790, offers a weekend king crab and steak buffet in a colorful, Western-movie-themed room.

Beyond the buffets, the Eldorado, 345 N. Virginia St., 800/648-5966, has Reno's best variety of restaurants. At the top of its food chain is **La Strada**, a gorgeous Italian restaurant with murals from the Italian countryside painted on the walls. The specialty here is Northern Italian cuisine (heavy on the seafood) as well as some mouthwatering homemade raviolis. The wine list here is as thick as *War and Peace*—this list has won *Wine Spectator's* Award of Excellence. The scene is decidedly hip at the **Bistro Roxy** at the mezzanine area next to the Fountains of Fortune. You can dine alfresco next to the fountains or inside, through the French doors, where the warm, red lighting and copper accents give you a cozier feel. Before your table is ready, you can lounge in the bar and enjoy the live piano music while you sip martinis—Bistro Roxy has more than 100 choices that can be shaken or stirred. The cuisine is French, but the bistro atmosphere makes it elegant yet not pretentious. The newest addition to the Eldorado's restaurant lineup is the **Golden Fortune**, a fabulous Asian restaurant. **Brew Brothers** is a lively brewpub with great beer and dueling pianos and other entertainment.

SIGHTS

- Ⓐ Animal Ark
- Ⓑ Boomtown Family Fun Center, Boomtown Casino
- Ⓒ Sierra Safari Zoo
- Ⓓ Sparks Heritage Museum

FOOD

- Ⓔ Atlantis Steakhouse (Atlantis)
- Ⓕ Cafe Soleil
- Ⓖ Christmas Tree Restaurant
- Ⓗ Great Basin Brewery

FOOD *(continued)*

- Ⓘ Island Buffet (Peppermill)
- Ⓙ Liberty Belle
- Ⓚ Orozko (John Ascuaga's Nugget)
- Ⓛ Peppermill
- Ⓔ Purple Parrot (Atlantis)
- Ⓛ Rapscallion
- Ⓚ Rotisserie Buffet (John Ascuaga's Nugget)
- Ⓑ Silver Screen Buffet (Boomtown)
- Ⓔ Toucan Charlie's (Atlantis)

FOOD *(continued)*

- Ⓚ Trader Dick's (John Ascuaga's Nugget)

LODGING

- Ⓔ Atlantis
- Ⓚ John Ascuaga's Nugget
- Ⓛ Peppermill

CAMPING

- Ⓛ Mount Rose Campground
- Ⓜ River's Edge Park

Note: Items with the same letter are located in the same area.

You'll also find good restaurants at the **Silver Legacy**, 407 N. Virginia, 800/687-8733, which is owned by both the Eldorado and Circus Circus. Highly rated are **Fairchild's Oyster Bar** (the chioppino is worth the trip) as well as **Sterling's Steakhouse**. The **Sweetwater Cafe**, which gives diners the sense that they are dining alfresco overlooking the 120-foot-tall mining rig, is one of the best casino coffee shops around.

The scene is hip at **Art Gecko's**, 500 N. Sierra St., 775/329-0711 or 800/648-5010, a Circus Circus restaurant located on the skyway next to Silver Legacy. The restaurant serves nouvelle Southwest cuisine and several types of margaritas.

The best place to take a date is the **Top of the Hilton**, on the 21st floor of the Flamingo Hilton Reno, 255 N. Sierra St., 775/785-7080. The cuisine is continental, and the view of the twinkling lights of Reno is stunning. The elegant atmosphere is complemented by the piano bar.

About four miles south of downtown, the **Atlantis Steakhouse** at the Atlantis Casino Resort, 3800 S. Virginia St., 775/825-4700 or 800/723-6500, specializes in seafood, which it serves in a blue-lit room with a floor-to-ceiling saltwater fish tank at the room's center. The Atlantis's **Purple Parrot** is a 24-hour restaurant with a good salad bar and a wide range of entrées, from burgers to shrimp Louis.

The Peppermill, 2707 S. Virginia St., 775/826-2121 or 800/648-6992, has several restaurants. The gourmet room is the **White Orchid**, and the **Coffee Shop** has numerous choices that include Asian and other dishes that rise above the standard 24-hour restaurant.

John Ascuaga's Nugget, 1100 Nugget Ave., 800/648-1177, in Sparks has good eateries, the most exotic of which is the Basque-Mediterranean **Orozko**. The lamb, seafood, pasta, and steak dishes are excellent, and the Mediterranean decor with murals painted on the walls and ceiling make the room warm and inviting. For Polynesian cuisine **Trader Dick's** can't be topped—try some of the exotic drinks, some of which produce smoke.

Not all of Reno's great restaurants are in the casinos. Meat lovers who also enjoy a little gambling history should visit the **Liberty Belle**, 4250 S. Virginia St., 775/825-1776, fjfey@aol.com. Here you'll find the city's best prime rib and steaks as well as a museum of slot machines. Marshall Fey, who owns the restaurant, is the grandson of Charles August Fey, who invented the original slot machine.

Business folks generally congregate at **Cafe Soleil**, 4796 Caughlin Pkwy., 775/828-6444, but even if you've no deals to discuss you'll enjoy this restaurant's nouveau cuisine and the view of downtown Reno. It's a bit off the main drag, but the creative dishes are worth the side trip. Also off the beaten path is the **Christmas Tree Restaurant**, 20007 Mount Rose Hwy., 775/849-0127, which keeps diners in the holiday spirit year-round. This is a great place to go after hiking or skiing in the Sierra when you're searching for a cozy, lodgelike setting. In the summer you can dine outdoors, and in the winter patrons are entertained by the little train that chugs overhead through the restaurant. The bar has a good view and offers a pleasant spot next to the rock fireplace for snuggling.

For a great blueberry frappe and other exotic coffee and non-coffee drinks, the coffee house of choice is **Deux Gros Nes**, 249 California Ave., 775/786-9400. French for "two big noses," this irreverent eatery on the second floor of a rickety building has lots of character and great desserts.

In Sparks, one of the liveliest spots on Victorian Square is the **Great Basin Brewery**, 846 Victorian Ave., 775/355-7711. The award-winning beer goes well with the bleu-cheese hamburger or the spicy sausage sampler. A mural depicting Nevada's Great Basin Desert decorates one wall.

For seafood, you can't miss with **Rapscallion**, 1555 S. Wells Ave., 775/323-1211, which offers about 20 varieties of fish daily. Among the favorites are the shrimp scampi and the king crab legs. The San Francisco-style decor includes dark accents, brass, and stained glass.

You can eat with the Basques at **Louis' Basque Corner**, 301 E. Fourth St., 775/323-7203, which brings the traditions and cuisine handed down through generations of the Basque family of Louis and Lorraine Erreguible. Several Basques immigrated to northern Nevada from their homeland between Spain and France, and they brought with them their tradition of Basque boarding-houses, a forerunner to today's Basque restaurants. You don't order—just sit there and wait for plate after plate of salad, beans, and bread to be delivered to your table. You generally have a choice of entrées, including steaks, lamb, or chicken.

LODGING

You'll find a variety of hotel-casinos packed into Reno's small downtown, which means that even if you choose one hotel, others are usually within walking distance. My top picks are the Silver Legacy and the Eldorado, which are connected via a skywalk. Both are elegant and have plenty of gaming and good restaurants. The **Silver Legacy**, 407 N. Virginia St., 775/329-4777 or 800/687-8733, has a big, white dome that covers a giant moving mining rig, the centerpiece of the hotel. This place connects you, albeit very distantly, to the area's mining history—and the feel here is that you're a guest of a rich silver baron. The **Eldorado**, 345 N. Virginia St., 775/786-5700 or 800/648-5966, is a bit older but is still elegant. If you can splurge, request one of the recently renovated

SIDE TRIP: BLACK ROCK DESERT

The Black Rock Desert, about 120 miles north of Reno on NV 447, is one of Nevada's most enigmatic places. A wide-open desert playa mostly devoid of vegetation, the Black Rock Desert is a curious place— and it's even more curious that people are so drawn to this stretch of flat space and nothingness. But the lack of people, buildings, and other human trappings provides a calm, unearthly escape.

So what do people do here? They bring their tents, bicycles, land-sailers, race cars, four-wheel drive vehicles, model rockets, and lounge chairs. They hold weird festivals like Burning Man, a San Francisco–based Labor Day celebration during which there's dancing in the desert amid a communelike setting. The event culminates in the paganesque burning of a 40-foot wooden structure.

And true to the Nevada spirit, people also come here to participate in a golf tournament. This isn't just any golf game—the Black Rock Self-Invitational is a work of outdoor art. Yes, golfers aim for greens, but these greens are spray-painted with an environmentally safe paint. The themes change from year to year, but you might find a mock-up of a living room, complete with sofas, a burned-out TV, and a spray-painted rug. Even if you're not a golfer you'll enjoy the sights.

This area has naturally attracted some independent spirits, including the late DeWayne "Doobie" Williams who created and etched philosophical poems and diatribes on rocks along the road near his home in Gerlach, 100 miles north of Reno on the edge of the Black Rock. Known as Guru Road, the lane lined with Doobie's rock-art inscriptions reveals his take on the world.

suites. Of course, kids will prefer **Circus Circus**, 500 N. Sierra St., 775/329-0711 or 800/648-5010, on the other side of the Silver Legacy's skywalk, which recently renovated and upgraded its circus theme. Gone are the bright pinks in favor of purples and more of a harlequin theme rather than clowns. The best advantage to this place is that you can save a little money on the room and splurge on the restaurants at the Eldorado.

Harrah's Reno, 219 N. Center St., 775/786-3232 or 800/HARRAHS, has been a Reno favorite for close to 60 years since it was opened by Nevada gambling pioneer William F. Harrah. His joint had a long-running reputation for offering the very best service, which it continues to this day, more than 20 years after Harrah's death. Patrons always give it high marks for customer service and above-average rooms. Also clustered in the downtown casino core are the reputable **Fitzgeralds**, 255 N. Virginia St., 775/785-3300 or 800/648-5022, and the **Flamingo Hilton Reno**, 255 N. Sierra St., 775/322-1111 or 800/648-4882.

If you want to escape the more congested downtown, the **Peppermill**, 2707 S. Virginia St., 775/826-2121 or 800/648-6992, has exquisite suites as well as an attractive pool with an animatronic howling wolf. **Atlantis**, 3800 S. Virginia St., 775/825-4700 or 800/723-6500, about one mile south of the Peppermill, recently completed an expansion that includes a larger casino and another hotel tower, making it a formidable hotel-casino at Reno's south end. The place is attractive and has a great glass elevator that offers a view of Reno.

In Sparks, the best option is **John Ascuaga's Nugget**, 1100 Nugget Ave., 775/356-3300 or 800/648-1177, a family-owned and operated casino. Patriarch John Ascuaga started with a tiny coffee shop in Sparks and built it into a huge, 1,600-room resort. The Nugget offers some unusual attractions, including an elephant named Angel who serves as an official mascot, showroom performer, and diplomat at special events. Visitors can watch her taking a bath at her circus-tent home adjacent to the casino or taking her daily stroll through Sparks (look for the "Elephant Crossing" signs). The Nugget also has one of northern Nevada's most relaxing indoor pools. It's covered by Plexiglas and looks into the Reno sky—snowy nights are best spent here.

The **Reno Hilton**, 2500 E. Second St., 775/789-2000 or 800/648-5080, near the Reno/Tahoe International Airport is Reno's largest hotel with 2,001 rooms. Popular with business travelers and convention attendees, the sprawling hotel has shopping, a massive sports book, several good restaurants, an arcade, and even a movie theater.

CAMPING

Reno is at the foothills of the Sierra Nevada, so you can sneak away for camping without having to travel very far. One of the closest is the **Mount Rose Campground**, 775/882-2766, which has 24 campsites on a lofty summit for tents and RVs up to 16 feet. The campground, near the trailhead for the Mount Rose hiking trail, is open from Memorial Day to Labor Day.

If you'd prefer not to leave town, you'll find a few campgrounds next to the Truckee River in town. **Chism's Trailer Park**, 1300 W. Second St., 775/322-2281 or 800/638-2281, has been open since 1926 and offers a pleasant campground with big shade trees right on the river. At the Reno Hilton, RVers are close to the river at the **Hilton Camperland**, 775/789-2147 or 800/648-5080, which also offers the amenities of the nearby hotel. In Sparks, the **River's Edge Park**, 1405 S. Rock Blvd., 775/358-8533 or 800/621-4792, has 164 sites (98 are pull-throughs, no tents) near the Truckee River, and the bike path winds next to it.

NIGHTLIFE AND THE ARTS

Several of the hotels, such as the Reno Hilton, Eldorado, Flamingo Hilton, and Harrah's Reno offer production shows in their showrooms. You'll find big-name headliners such as Don Rickles, the Righteous Brothers, and the Captain and Tennille (who live nearby) at the Eldorado, Harrah's Reno, John Ascuaga's Nugget, Peppermill, Reno Hilton, and Silver Legacy. The Reno Hilton also has the Improv Comedy Club as well as an outdoor summer concert series.

For boogying late into the night, try Dick Clark's American Bandstand Club, 236 N. Virginia St., 775/786-2222, where a young crowd tends to congregate. Atlantis Nightclub at the Atlantis Resort has a giant, undulating octopus over its dance floor.

The arts scene is alive and well in Reno, where you can catch performances of the Nevada Opera, Reno Chamber Orchestra, Reno Philharmonic, and the Reno Little Theater at the Pioneer Center for the Performing Arts and other concert halls.

8

RENO REGION

Activities and attractions abound just beyond the bright lights of Reno, so if time permits you should schedule trips to nearby Carson City, Dayton, Genoa, and Minden-Gardnerville, all of which are filled with history and small-town charm. This little corner of Nevada is the cradle of the state's history. Two years after the California gold rush, prospectors began to explore this area and put down stakes, establishing both Genoa and Dayton in the mid-1800s. The lure here is obvious—mountains, lakes, history, ranches—and visitors are less than an hour from Lake Tahoe and Reno.

The biggest and closest to Reno is Carson City, the state's capital, which has excellent museums as well as gambling and good restaurants. Dayton, 15 miles east, is a tiny historic community with a pleasant state park on the Carson River.

Situated in the lush Carson Valley is Genoa, a quaint village tucked in the foothills of the Sierra Nevada. The pace here is laid-back—there are no traffic lights and there is only one stop sign. But visitors will find antique shops, a country store, and enough picture-perfect Victorian homes and gardens to be the envy of Martha Stewart. Also in Carson Valley are the twin towns of Minden-Gardnerville, a sprawling farm community that is a mecca for soaring.

A PERFECT DAY IN GREATER RENO

The day should begin early with a cappuccino and a scone at Java Joe's in downtown Carson City. From there it's an easy jaunt across Carson Street for

CARSON CITY

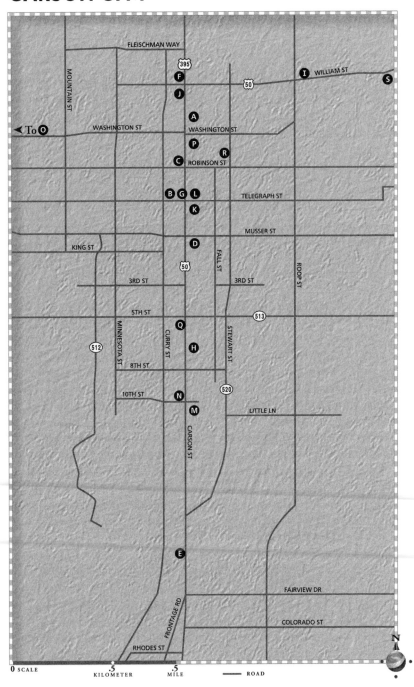

FLEISCHMAN WAY

MOUNTAIN ST

395
F
I WILLIAM ST
S
50
J

WASHINGTON ST
To O
WASHINGTON ST
A
P
R
C ROBINSON ST

B G L
TELEGRAPH ST
K

MUSSER ST

KING ST
D

50
FALL ST
ROOP ST

3RD ST
3RD ST

5TH ST
513

MINNESOTA ST
Q
CURRY ST
512
H
STEWART ST

8TH ST
520

10TH ST
N
M
LITTLE LN

CARSON ST

E

FAIRVIEW DR

FRONTAGE RD
COLORADO ST

RHODES ST

N

0 SCALE   .5   .5
        KILOMETER   MILE   ———— ROAD

a quick walking tour of the historic homes on the Kit Carson Trail. You can end the tour with a visit to the Nevada State Museum. Then jump in the car and head to Sharkey's Casino in Gardnerville for gambling and a glimpse at Nevada's boxing, ranching, and gaming history. After a hearty prime-rib lunch in Sharkey's coffee shop, it's time to amble north to Genoa to stroll through the antique shops, the Genoa Courthouse Museum, and Mormon Station. Weary travelers can end the day there with a long soak at David Walley's Hot Springs.

SIGHTSEEING HIGHLIGHTS: CARSON CITY

★★★★ NEVADA STATE MUSEUM
600 N. Carson St., 775/687-4810

Housed in a former U.S. Mint, the Nevada State Museum has exhibits on just about everything you'd want to know about the state. The location itself is historic—a U.S. Mint operated in the building from 1870 to 1895. The museum houses remnants of the mint, including a coin collection and Coin Press No. 1, which visitors can watch as it presses silver and bronze medallions every last Friday of the month to be sold in the museum store. The museum has a natural history section that shows Nevada's earliest history, including prehistoric times when the state was covered by an ancient sea. There are dioramas that reveal how the earliest human inhabitants lived as well as a collection of baskets by Nevada's most famous Washoe Indian basketmaker, the late Dat So La Lee. Dinosaur fans should check out the woolly mammoth exhibit. The ghost town exhibit captures the isolation and spooky ambiance of a Nevada ghost town. Even the museum's exit is intriguing—it resembles the interior of a mine shaft

SIGHTS
- **A** Children's Museum of Northern Nevada
- **B** Curry Street Antique Shops
- **C** Kit Carson Trail
- **D** Nevada State Capitol
- **C** Nevada State Museum
- **E** Nevada State Railroad Museum

FOOD
- **F** Adele's
- **G** B'Sghetti's
- **H** City Cafe Bakery
- **I** Cracker Box
- **J** Heidi's
- **K** Java Joe's
- **L** Nick's
- **M** Station Grille and Rotisserie

LODGING
- **N** Best Western-Carson Station
- **O** Bliss Mansion
- **P** Hardman House
- **Q** Ormsby House
- **R** Nugget Motel
- **S** Piñon Plaza

Note: Items with the same letter are located in the same area.

with miners and ore carts at work. The museum also has a well-stocked gift shop, which has one of the state's best collections of Nevada books. On the last Tuesday of the month, the museum hosts a historical lecture series.

Details: *Open daily 9–5:30; winter 8:30–4:30. $3 adults, $2.50 seniors, free for children under 18. (2 hours)*

★★★ KIT CARSON TRAIL
800/NEVADA-1

The Kit Carson Trail is a self-guided walking tour of Carson City's historic westside neighborhood. The trail is a blue stripe painted on the sidewalk and is easy to follow with the map-brochure that points out the homes and attractions of interest and provides some historical background. On selected weekends historians dressed in period attire lead visitors on tours of the homes. One of the most popular tours is the Ghost Walk, which is held on the weekend close to Halloween (which, incidentally, is also Nevada Day, the state's admission day). Some of the stately old Victorian homes are said to be haunted, and tour leaders tell ghost stories along the way. The neighborhood is known for its notable residents. The governor resides on Mountain Street (kids can trick-or-treat there, too). Orion Clemens, who served as secretary of Nevada Territory in the 1860s and was the brother of Samuel Clemens, lived in one of the homes. The Krebs-Peterson House is where John Wayne's last movie, *The Shootist*, was filmed.

Details: *Tour and brochure are free and available at the Carson City Convention and Visitors Bureau, 1900 S. Carson St., 800/NEVADA-1. (1–2 hours)*

★★ CHILDREN'S MUSEUM OF NORTHERN NEVADA
813 N. Carson St., 775/884-2226

This fledgling museum (founded in 1988) has a well-rounded group of exhibits, most of which seem best oriented for children under age 12 or so. There's a pretend grocery store, a giant piano keyboard, a kid-sized fire station, and other educational exhibits.

Details: *Open Mon–Fri 10–4:30, Sat–Sun 10–5:30; closed Sun during winter. Admission $3 adults, $2 ages 3–13. (1–2 hours)*

★★ CURRY STREET ANTIQUE SHOPS

Curry Street, one block west of Carson Street, is Carson City's Antique Row. You can begin your stroll at Third and Carson Streets. The antique and gift shops carry vintage clothing, old china, collectibles, and rare books. Frontier Antiques on Third and Curry Streets has a large collection of antique radios. At the far north end is the Abell House, 1114 N. Curry St., where you'll find antiques as well as gifts in the historic home.

Details: *Free. (1–2 hours)*

★★ NEVADA STATE CAPITOL
Carson St. and Musser St., 775/687-4810

The striking silver-domed capitol building peeks out among the trees in downtown Carson City, attracting visitors to its small, park-like grounds. The building has floors made from Alaskan marble, displays of Nevada-made products, an exhibit of the capitol's history, and Nevada photographs. Guided tours are available. Spring and summer, when the peonies and roses are in bloom, are the best times to stroll the grounds, which neighbor the legislative building and the Nevada State Library and Archives.

Details: *Open daily 8–5. Call ahead for tours. Free. (1 hour)*

★★ NEVADA STATE RAILROAD MUSEUM
2180 S. Carson St., 775/687-6953

Rolling stock from the old V&T have been meticulously restored and placed on display here. One of the centerpieces of the museum is the *Dayton*, an 1873 steam engine that sits on tracks inside the museum where visitors can see, touch, and smell the old trains. The *Dayton* is attached to a boxcar and V&T coach car No. 4, an ornate, restored passenger car that appeared in a few Paramount Pictures movies. The museum houses more than 50 pieces of railroad equipment (including five steam trains) as well as railroad photos, equipment displays, artwork, and a gift shop. On selected weekends a couple of the engines are steamed up for rides on the one-and-a-half-mile loop of track that surrounds the museum complex—one of the most popular is the Santa train.

Details: *Open daily 8:30–4:30. Admission $2, free for children under 18. Rides during steam-ups $2.50 adults, $1 ages 6–11. (1–2 hours)*

★★ STEWART INDIAN CULTURAL CENTER
5366 Stewart Ave., 775/882-1808

This museum, located on the south end of town on the Carson Indian Colony, offers a peek into the lives of Nevada's Native Americans. The

HOT-AIR BALLOONS (Carson Valley)

Nevada Commission on Tourism

buildings, listed on the National Register of Historic Places, include the former Stewart Indian School. The museum features baskets, grinding stones, and artwork, as well as a trading post and other vestiges of Native American life.

Details: *Open daily 9–4. Free. (1 hour)*

SIGHTSEEING HIGHLIGHTS: GENOA

★★★ GENOA COURTHOUSE MUSEUM
2304 Main St., 775/782-4325

This two-story brick building was built in 1865 as a courthouse when Genoa was the county seat. Later it was used as a school, until 1956. This museum has thoughtfully prepared exhibits and offers a glimpse into the lives of early Carson Valley residents. The Snowshoe Thompson exhibit honors famous resident John "Snowshoe" Thompson, the man who skied across the snowy Sierra Nevada to transport mail and other necessary items between Genoa and Placerville, California.

Details: *Open May–Oct 10–4:30. Donation. (1 hour)*

★★ GENOA COUNTRY STORE
Foothill Rd., 775/782-5974

The Genoa Country Store has essentials such as videos and groceries as well as a crafter's attic with homemade quilts and dolls. You can also get sandwiches, ice cream, and cappuccino in addition to bags of peanuts in the shell for 99 cents.

Details: *Open daily 8:30–6. Free. (30 minutes)*

★★ MORMON STATION STATE HISTORIC PARK
775/782-2590

Mormon Station is a shady picnic area with a replica of the original Mormon trading post that burned down in 1910. Inside the trading post you'll find historic relics and exhibits relating to the town's origins. The Candy Dance, the town's big event and fund-raiser that originated in the early 1900s, is held on the grassy lawn at Mormon Station. You'll find divinity, fudge, and other homemade confections as well as crafts and games during the Candy Dance. It's held on the last weekend of September.

Details: *Museum open May–Oct 10–5. Free. (1 hour)*

★ GENOA BAR
2282 Foothill Rd., 775/782-3870

You can't miss the sign pointing to Nevada's oldest saloon, the Genoa Bar, located right in the heart of town. You'll find a pool table, a good jukebox, and relics on the wall. It's worth a stop just so you can say you had a beer in Nevada's "oldest thirst parlor."

Details: *Open daily. Free. (30 minutes)*

SIGHTSEEING HIGHLIGHTS: MINDEN-GARDNERVILLE

★★★★ SHARKEY'S NUGGET
1440 Hwy. 395 S., 775/782-3133

Sharkey's is more than just a smoky casino with slots and a bar. This place is a living museum. The walls of the casino, arcade, and restaurant are plastered with posters and photographs of Western and boxing lore. Owner and local legend Sharkey Begovich has amassed a huge collection of photos of famous Nevada boxing matches. The bar features one of the state's best saddle collections—some of the barstools are even made from saddles. Each January Sharkey holds a

Serbian Christmas dinner for which he cooks up a huge feast and feeds as many visitors as he can for free.

Details: Open 24 hours. Free. (2–3 hours)

★★★ CARSON VALLEY MUSEUM AND CULTURAL CENTER
1477 U.S. 395 N., 775/782-2555

This eclectic museum and gallery is housed in the former Douglas High School, built in 1915 and designed by prominent Nevada architect Frederic De Longchamps. When the building fell into disrepair, a grassroots group of former classmates and residents decided to resurrect the downtown Gardnerville landmark. The museum houses exhibits on the Washoe Indians, Basques, ranchers, and pioneers. A collection of taxidermied animals, including a polar bear, jaguar, cobra, and assorted animal heads was donated by the late Red Swift, a longtime Carson Valley resident. The museum also offers a changing gallery, a visitors center, and the East Fork Gallery, which features works by local artists.

Details: Open daily summer 10–5; winter 10–4. Donation. (1–2 hours)

★ DREAM WEAVERS HOT-AIR BALLOON RIDES
800/386-2563

Hot-air ballooning is a lofty way to explore the scenery of northern Nevada. Dream Weavers launches its hot-air balloon rides at Lampe Park in Gardnerville and floats over the Carson Valley with views of Lake Tahoe and beyond. The company specializes in rides for couples and wedding excursions.

Details: Open year-round. Flights depart after sunrise. Cost is $145 per person for a one-hour ride, including a traditional champagne ceremony and a flight certificate. (half day)

★ MILKY WAY DAIRY FARM
Airport Road, Minden, 775/782-5305

Kids clamor for the chance to meet the cows at the Milky Way Dairy Farm, which offers tours for classrooms and adult groups during the spring, summer, and early fall. After the tour, you can peruse the country- and milk-themed merchandise at the Country Gift Showroom. During the summer one of the fields is planted with sunflowers, making it a popular spot for photographers.

Details: Located north of Minden off Airport Rd. Open Apr–Oct.

Prices vary for tours, which are available for groups of children or adults. (half day)

★ SOAR MINDEN
Douglas County Airport, Minden, 775/782-7627 or 800/345-7627

The atmosphere above the Carson Valley attracts soar-plane pilots from around the world. Novices can experience the famous thermals—the winds that give the engineless planes their lift—at Soar Minden based at the Douglas County Airport. Passengers soar above Carson Valley, Lake Tahoe, and anywhere else the thermals and the skilled pilot carry them. Rides for one or two passengers are available, or your can try the Top Gun aerobatic ride. Lessons also are available.

Details: One-person rides $55–$75, two-person $99–$145, Top Gun ride $125. (half day)

FITNESS AND RECREATION

Golf is the premier recreational activity in northern Nevada. A number of hotels, such as the Carson Valley Inn in Minden, offer room and tee-time packages. On every course golfers will find spectacular scenery and well-manicured greens.

In Carson City you'll find three public golf courses, Eagle Valley, 775/887-2380, Empire Ranch, 775/885-2100, and Silver Oak, 775/841-7000. Two miles south of Carson City is the Sunridge Golf Club, 775/267-4448. The Carson Valley Golf Course, 775/265-3181, is in Gardnerville. Genoa has the Golf Club at Genoa Lakes, 775/782-4653, and the Sierra Nevada Golf Club, 775/782-7700. Even Dayton has joined the swing with its Dayton Valley Country Club, 775/246-PUTT, designed by Arnold Palmer and Ed Seay.

Scenic Washoe Valley, midway between Carson City and Reno, holds several recreational opportunities. On the east side below the towering Sierra, the grassy park at Bowers Mansion, 775/849-0201, is a good spot for kite-flying, picnicking, and goofing off. Tours of the mansion, built by Comstock millionaire Sandy Bowers, are available during the summer. The park also has a swimming pool. Just north of the mansion is Davis Creek Park, 775/849-0684, a county park that is crisscrossed with several hiking and equestrian trails and has a small pond that is used by ice skaters during the winter. Bicyclists like to pedal Franktown Road (begin at the parking lot at Bowers Mansion), which meanders into the foothills past ritzy mansions and farmland.

RENO REGION

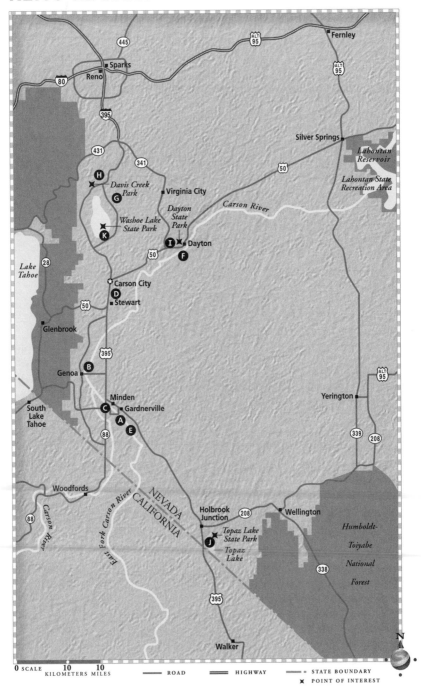

Fernley

445

ALT 95

Sparks

80   Reno

ALT 95

395

Silver Springs

Lahontan Reservoir

431

341

50

Lahontan State Recreation Area

H

Davis Creek Park

G   Virginia City

Carson River

Dayton State Park

Washoe Lake State Park

K

I   Dayton

50   F

Lake Tahoe   28

Carson City

D

Stewart

50

Glenbrook

395

B

Genoa

Minden

Yerington

C   Gardnerville

A

South Lake Tahoe   E

339   208

88

Woodfords

Carson River

East Fork Carson River   NEVADA
CALIFORNIA

Holbrook Junction   208   Wellington

Humboldt-

88

J   *Topaz Lake State Park*

Toiyabe

Topaz Lake

National

338   *Forest*

395

N

Walker

0 SCALE   10   10
KILOMETERS MILES   ROAD   HIGHWAY   STATE BOUNDARY
                                                    ✕ POINT OF INTEREST

On the east side of U.S. 395 in the valley is Washoe Lake State Recreation Area, 775/687-4319. After wet winters the shallow lake often laps up against the highway. Bird-watchers will find a menagerie of waterfowl, including pelicans, cranes, and geese. The lake is also a haven for such watersports as water-skiing, catamaran sailing, and windsurfing—the breezes are strong and steady in Washoe Valley.

Near Dayton, visitors will find hiking trails and picnicking at Dayton State Historic Park, 775/687-5678, along the Carson River.

At David Walley's Hot Springs, 775/782-8155, two miles south of Genoa, you can follow a rigorous workout in the gym with a massage. Then there's nothing better than a long soak in one of the hot-springs pools. The views here are sublime—the Sierra Nevada casts its shadow over soakers to the west and the Carson Valley sprawls to the east.

Straddling the Nevada-California state line 35 miles south of Gardnerville,. Topaz Lake Park, 775/266-3343, attracts anglers and water-skiers. Topaz is fed by the East Walker River, one of the few rivers in North America that flows north on its meandering path to the lake. Either a Nevada or California license is required for both shore and boat fishermen. There isn't a lot of vegetation—the lure here is less the scenery and more the trophy trout. You can read about and see some of the prized catches at the Topaz Lake Lodge and Casino, 775/266-3338, which overlooks the lake on U.S. 395. Trophy-sized trout are mounted on the wall, and you can see photographs of others that were destined for the dinner table. The

SIGHTS

- Ⓐ Carson Valley Museum and Cultural Center
- Ⓐ Dream Weavers Hot-Air Balloon Rides
- Ⓑ Genoa Bar
- Ⓑ Genoa Country Store
- Ⓑ Genoa Courthouse Museum
- Ⓒ Milky Way Dairy Farm
- Ⓑ Mormon Station State Historic Park
- Ⓐ Sharkey's Nugget
- Ⓒ Soar Minden
- Ⓓ Stewart Indian Cultural Center

FOOD

- Ⓔ Carson Valley Country Club
- Ⓒ Fiona's
- Ⓑ Inn Cognito
- Ⓐ J.T. Basque Bar and Dining Room
- Ⓒ Katie's
- Ⓕ Mia's Swiss Restaurant
- Ⓐ Overland Hotel
- Ⓐ Rib Room at Sharkey's Nugget
- Ⓕ Roadrunner Cafe

LODGING

- Ⓒ Best Western–Minden
- Ⓒ Carson Valley Inn

LODGING (continued)

- Ⓑ David Walley's Hot Springs
- Ⓖ Deer Run Ranch B&B
- Ⓑ Genoa House Inn
- Ⓐ Nenzel Mansion
- Ⓑ Snowshoe Thompson Lodge
- Ⓑ Wild Rose Inn

CAMPING

- Ⓗ Davis Creek Park
- Ⓘ Dayton State Park
- Ⓙ Topaz Lake Lodge
- Ⓚ Washoe Lake State Park

Note: Items with the same letter are located in the same area.

lodge has a restaurant and lounge (with live music on occasional weekends) with slot machines. On the lake you'll find camping, picnicking, and a boat launch.

FOOD

Carson City offers a wide range of restaurants. For breakfast, locals cram into the **Cracker Box**, 402 E. William (U.S. 50), 775/882-4556, for their "soon-to-be-famous spuds" and green chile, tomato, bacon, and cheese omelette. For giant pancakes, omelettes, and sandwiches, another popular haunt is **Heidi's**, 1020 N. Carson St., 775/882-0486, a local chain that has restaurants in Reno, Lake Tahoe, and Gardnerville, and is open for breakfast and lunch. On the lighter side is **City Cafe Bakery**, 701 S. Carson St., 775/882-2253, which has a vast selection of muffins (some oil-free), scones, bagels, and danishes. The sandwiches are piled high and can be made from more than a dozen fresh-baked breads. **Java Joe's**, 319 N. Carson St., 775/883-4004, located downtown near the Carson Nugget, has tasty coffee drinks and sandwiches. The place has good atmosphere, too—the tall ceilings and creaky wood floors are original to the building, which was formerly a funeral parlor. A visit to downtown **Nick's**, 303 N. Carson St., 775/885-8008, is a requisite stop for pizza lovers. The atmosphere is a little rustic, but the owners, who emigrated from Greece, know their pizzas and salads. Across the street at **B'Sghetti's**, 318 N. Carson St., 775/887-8879, you'll find good pastas. On the south end of town, the **Station Grill and Rotisserie**, 1105 S. Carson St., 775/883-8400, lures hungry patrons with its mesquite grill, the aroma of which permeates the restaurant. Carson City's most upscale offering is **Adele's**, 1112 N. Carson St., 775/882-3353, owned by local legendary restaurateur Adele Abowd. Adele's has a chic French dining room that often becomes a home away from home for celebrities, high rollers, and state legislators.

Prime rib is the specialty of the **Rib Room at Sharkey's Nugget**, 1440 U.S. 395 S., 775/782-3133, in Gardnerville. The huge slab of beef ribs comes with a slice of history—while you dine you can scope out the handmade tables, inlaid with items ranging from National Finals Rodeo belt buckles to rare casino chips. Along the walls are portraits of celebrities when they were children (check out Tom Jones and Liberace as kids). The adjacent coffee shop also serves prime rib, as well as round-the-clock eggs Benedict. The room is wall-papered with vintage Ringling Brothers and Barnum and Bailey Circus posters.

The Basque influence is strong in the Carson Valley, where several Basques emigrated from their tiny region bordering France and Spain to herd sheep in the hills of Nevada. Basque restaurants are still going strong, and you'll find three in Gardnerville: the **Carson Valley Country Club**, 1029 Riverview Dr. (two miles south of Gardnerville), 775/265-3715, **J. T. Basque Bar and Dining Room**, 1426 U.S. 395, 775/782-2074, and the **Overland Hotel**, 691 Main, 775/782-2138. The hearty meals of steak or lamb smothered in garlic, in addition to shrimp, beans, salads, and bread, are often served family style, and you don't order from a menu. Make sure you arrive hungry—no one leaves a Basque restaurant without having to let out the belt a notch or two.

The Carson Valley Inn, 1627 U.S. 395 N. in Minden, serves excellent fare at its coffee shop, **Katie's**, 775/782-9711, as well as at its gourmet room, **Fiona's**, 775/782-4347. In Genoa, **Inn Cognito** on Genoa Lane, 775/782-8898, is a gourmet restaurant situated inside an old Victorian home. Its eclectic menu items range from duck ravioli and elk to seafood pasta and baby back ribs.

Dayton has two local standouts, the **Roadrunner Cafe**, 130 Douglas St., 775/246-0205, a popular locals' breakfast spot, and **Mia's Swiss Restaurant**, 65 Pike St., 775/246-3993, which features live accordion music with its gourmet dinner menu.

LODGING

Lodging in Carson City and the Carson Valley is less expensive than in Reno or Lake Tahoe, and it's centrally located to both.

In Carson City, the **Ormsby House**, 600 S. Carson St., 775/882-1890 or 800/622-1890, is the place to stay on the Fourth of July because the hotel puts on a huge fireworks display in its parking lot. **Piñon Plaza**, 2171 U.S. 50 E., 775/885-9000, is off the beaten path but it's new—the casino opened in 1995, and the rooms were added in the summer of 1998. **Best Western-Carson Station**, 900 S. Carson St., 775/883-0900 or 800/501-2929, is close to downtown, as is the **Nugget Motel**, across the street from the Carson Nugget casino at 651 N. Stewart St., 775/882-7711 or 800/948-9111. The **Hardman House**, 917 N. Carson St., 775/882-7744 or 800/626-0793, doesn't have a casino but is popular among business travelers.

The stately **Bliss Mansion**, 710 W. Robinson St., 775/887-8988 or 800/320-0627, on Carson City's west side was the largest home in Nevada when it was built by lumber magnate Duane Bliss in 1879. Renovated as a bed-and-breakfast in 1994, the Bliss Mansion is one of Nevada's fanciest inns. The four rooms (each is $170 per night) are furnished with gorgeous antique beds and have mahogany fireplaces.

In bucolic Genoa, B&Bs are the only lodging choice. The **Genoa House Inn**, 180 Nixon, 775/782-7075, built in 1872, is a romantic old home with Victorian furnishings and a striking stained-glass window in the upstairs Rose Room. In the Garden Room, the cottage attached to the main house, guests will

SIDE TRIP: DAYTON

Dayton is one of Nevada's oldest settlements (it's neck-and-neck with Genoa), and a few reminders of its early days remain. The **Bluestone Building***, which houses county offices, was built on Main Street in the early 1870s. The* **Dayton Cemetery***, perched up on the hill west of the Bluestone Building, was established in the 1850s, and it is the final resting place for some of Nevada's earliest pioneers.* **Odeon Hall** *in downtown Dayton is now a restaurant and appeared in the movie* The Misfits *starring Clark Gable and Marilyn Monroe. The* **Dayton Historic Society Museum** *recently brought its exhibits and photographs to the 1865 schoolhouse, which is open on weekends during summer. Of course, just because Dayton is a historic community doesn't mean it doesn't have modern amenities. The* **Dayton Depot** *has a casino and restaurant, and the* **Dayton Valley Country Club** *is one of northern Nevada's most scenic and popular golf courses.*

find a clawfoot bathtub and a pull-chain toilet that was manufactured in 1905. The **Snowshoe Thompson Lodge**, 2260 Main St., 775/782-7286, on the south end of town is another cozy outpost. The **Wild Rose Inn**, 2332 Main St., 775/782-5697, just north of town is a two-story B&B furnished with antiques. At **David Walley's Hot Springs**, 2001 Foothill Rd., 775/782-8155, one-and-a-half miles south of Genoa, you can soak during the day at the recently renovated mineral pools and sleep at night in one of the cozy cabins.

In Minden, you'll find the **Carson Valley Inn**, 1627 U.S. 395, 775/782-9711, (with a motor lodge attached) and the **Best Western-Minden**, 1795 Ironwood Dr., 775/782-7766. In Gardnerville, the **Nenzel Mansion**, 1431 Ezell, 775/782-1644, is a three-story 1910 colonial-style building that could easily have been transplanted from the Deep South.

The **Deer Run Ranch B&B**, 5440 Eastlake Blvd., 775/882-3643, on the east side of Washoe Valley north of Carson City, is a peaceful retreat. Owners Muffy and David Vhay prepare breakfast from the fruits and vegetables they cultivate from their prolific garden.

CAMPING

Davis Creek Park, 12 miles north of Carson City on the west side of Washoe Valley, 775/849-0684, is a county park that offers several hiking and equestrian trails as well as campsites for tents and RVs. **Washoe Lake State Park**, 775/687-4319, has 49 well-developed sites. The Carson River rolls right through **Dayton State Park**, 775/687-5678, 15 miles east of Carson City, where you'll find campsites for tents and RVs. The RV park at **Topaz Lake Lodge**, 775/266-3338, 35 miles south of Gardnerville, has full hookups and showers.

NIGHTLIFE AND THE ARTS

Carson City doesn't bombard the visitor with too many flashy casinos, but it does have enough to keep downtown looking lively. The Carson Nugget is one of the most popular, and while you're tempting Lady Luck you also can check out the small gold-nugget display. Nearby, both the Ormsby House and Carson Station have slots and live gaming. Cactus Jacks is also downtown. It's a tiny casino with an excellent snack bar. In Minden-Gardnerville you'll find gambling at Sharkey's and the Carson Valley Inn. On weekends and most weekdays you can expect to hear live musicians in casino lounges.

You'll find a full schedule of concerts, plays, and musicals at both the Brewery Arts Center and the Community Center in Carson City.

Scenic Route: Virginia City via Reno or Carson City

There are two ways (via paved road) to get to Virginia City—one from Reno (NV 341 via U.S. 395) and the other from Carson City (NV 342 via U.S. 50). Both are scenic, but make sure you have a good clutch and brakes if you're headed up from U.S. 50.

On 50 you'll pass old and new homesteads, mines, and deep canyons as you head into tiny Silver City. Devil's Gate, once a toll area, leads to a steeper uphill climb. The last couple of turns are real hair-raisers. At Gold Hill, the V&T Railroad crosses the roadway to reach the depot, so cars often have to stop to allow the train to pass. The last turn, known as Greiner's Bend, is a doozie of a hairpin. During winter, although it's a little longer, the truck route (NV 341) is often the best way to enter town.

From Reno, the highway isn't quite as treacherous and the vistas are spectacular. You can see Washoe Valley and the mountains beyond as well as the twinkling lights of Reno. But the road does have several twists and turns, and wild horses and other animals can pose a hazard.

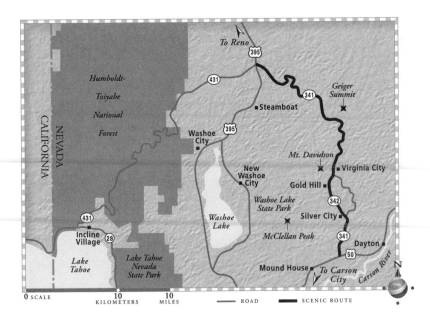

9

VIRGINIA CITY

Gold, silver, prostitutes, saloons, churches—what more could you ask for in a Wild West town? Virginia City had it all—and still has some of it. With its antiquated storefronts, old bars, and wooden sidewalks, Virginia City gives visitors the sense that any second a drunken miner could come swaggering into the street, guns drawn, ready for a fight. You half expect to see horses clopping down the main drag, pulling ornate carriages with passengers wearing beaver hats and carrying parasols.

Once one of the richest towns in the West, Virginia City, perched atop massive deposits of gold and silver, still retains its Old West charm. Despite the souvenir shops and trinket-filled tourist traps, the experience here is authentic. Virginia City was born in the 1850s, when some of the 49ers wandered into the hills of Nevada hoping to find the same fortunes that had been found in California. First gold was discovered, then silver, and the rush to the famed Comstock Lode began. Numerous saloons, banks, churches, a famous red-light district, opera houses, and hotels began to sprawl out amid the sagebrush-covered canyons and hills. In the 1860s, a curious young prospector named Samuel Clemens visited the area and soon began to cut his journalistic and literary teeth at the *Territorial Enterprise* newspaper. There he penned his nom de plume, Mark Twain.

In 1875, more than 30 blocks were destroyed by fire—the first blow to this major metropolitan city. By the early 1900s, the gold and silver were beginning to play out, and the town began to decline. New faces, many of them follow-

VIRGINIA CITY

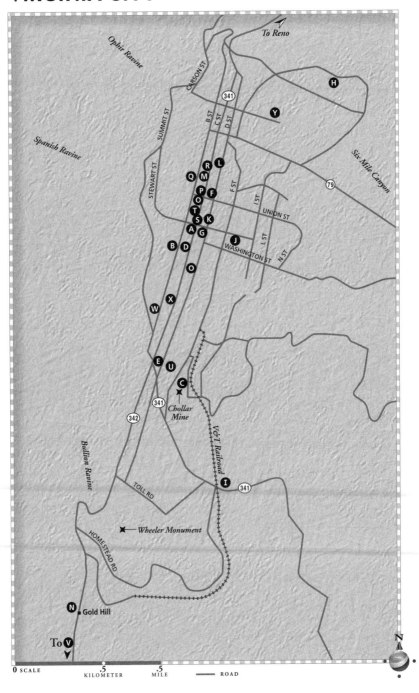

To Reno

Ophir Ravine

CARSON ST

341

B ST
C ST
D ST

Y

Spanish Ravine

SUMMIT ST

Six-Mile Canyon

STEWART ST

79

Q
R
L
M
P
F
O
T
S
K
A
G

F ST

I ST

UNION ST

L ST

N ST

J

WASHINGTON ST

B
D

O

X

W

E
U

C

★ Chollar
Mine

341

342

V&T Railroad

I 341

Bullion Ravine

TOLL RD

★ Wheeler Monument

HOMESTEAD RD

N ★ Gold Hill

To V

N

0 SCALE   .5   .5
        KILOMETER   MILE   —— ROAD

ing in the literary footsteps of Mark Twain, began to appear in Virginia City, and the indomitable spirit of the Comstock refused to die. A few enterprising souls opened museums and turned to tourism to keep the town alive. In the 1970s, the TV show *Bonanza* helped revitalize Virginia City. Some of the scenes were filmed nearby at Lake Tahoe (a replica of the ranch and studio later opened in Incline Village), and Hoss, Adam, Little Joe, and Ben Cartwright would make frequent fictional trips to Virginia City in the show. The town capitalized on the new-found fame (note the Ponderosa Saloon and other throwbacks), and visitors still see remnants of the Cartwright Boys in the gift shops.

A PERFECT DAY IN VIRGINIA CITY

A day in Virginia City should begin aptly at the Mark Twain Bookstore on C Street. You can peruse the shelves and whet your appetite for Comstock history. Here you can learn about the famous—and not so famous—folks who roamed the Virginia City boardwalks, such as silver baron John Mackay, celebrated courtesan Julia Bulette, and author Mark Twain. The whistle of the Virginia and Truckee Railroad will lure you downhill to the depot where you can climb aboard the train and prepare to ride into another century, a time when the Comstock was at its peak. Belly up to the gorgeous old back bar at the Bucket of Blood Saloon and order a Bucket of Blood beer. Try to duck into a few other saloons such as the Delta or the

SIGHTS

- Ⓐ Best and Belcher Mine
- Ⓑ The Castle
- Ⓒ Chollar Mine
- Ⓓ Comstock Firemen's Museum
- Ⓔ Fourth Ward School Museum
- Ⓕ Julia Bulette Red Light Museum
- Ⓖ Mark Twain Bookstore
- Ⓗ Silver Terrace Cemeteries
- Ⓘ Virginia and Truckee Railroad
- Ⓙ Virginia City Radio Museum

SIGHTS *(continued)*

- Ⓚ Territorial Enterprise Mark Twain Museum
- Ⓛ Way It Was Museum

FOOD

- Ⓜ Comstock Cookie Company
- Ⓝ Crown Point Restaurant at the Gold Hill Hotel
- Ⓞ Delta Saloon's Sawdust Corner Restaurant
- Ⓟ Grandma's Fudge Factory
- Ⓠ Mandarin Garden Chinese Restaurant
- Ⓡ Red Dog Saloon

FOOD *(continued)*

- Ⓢ Red's Old-Fashioned Candies
- Ⓣ Walden's Coffee Company

LODGING

- Ⓤ Chollar Mansion
- Ⓝ Gold Hill Hotel
- Ⓥ Hardwicke House
- Ⓦ Spargo House
- Ⓧ Sugarloaf Mountain Motel

CAMPING

- Ⓨ Virginia City RV Park

Note: Items with the same letter are located in the same area.

Bonanza, which are filled with character—and characters. Grab a slice of pizza at the Red Dog Saloon and head down to the Chollar Mine, where the guided tour will place you in the shoes of the miners who searched for riches under the earth. After meandering along the boardwalk, ducking into the saloons, museums, and shops, you can end your day with a twilight tour of the Silver Terrace Cemeteries, where some of the famous folks you read about are buried.

SIGHTSEEING HIGHLIGHTS

★★★★ V&T RAILROAD
F St., 775/847-0380

The Virginia and Truckee Railroad had chugged its last gasp of steam in the 1950s after nearly 100 years of hauling miners, residents, and gold ore from the Comstock Lode to Carson City, Minden, and Reno. Then, in 1976, enterprising railroad buff Bob Gray bought the railroad and revived it as a tourist train. Today folks can climb aboard for a 35-minute ride, narrated by a guide wearing an engineer's cap, to the Gold Hill Depot and back. Visitors will pass trestles, narrow canyons, and old mines, and get a snootful of soot as the train chugs through a tunnel.

Details: Depot at F Street east of C Street. Daily runs May 23–Oct 18, weekends through Nov, 10:30–5:45. Fares $4.75 adults, $2.50 children, $9.50 all-day pass. Tickets available at the visitor center in the railroad car on C Street or at the depot on F Street. (1 hour)

★★★ MARK TWAIN BOOKSTORE
111 S. C St., Virginia City, 775/847-0454

If you're looking for books about Nevada, the Mark Twain Bookstore is a good place to peruse the shelves. Proprietors Joe and Ellie Curtis keep their shelves well stocked with Nevada books as well as titles by local authors. The "Archives of Antiquities" section is a good place to find rare volumes, including some early editions of Mark Twain's classics. His classic *Roughing It* is based on his experiences in Nevada and the West. The bookstore was once the Mark Twain Museum of Memories, and a Mark Twain mannequin greets visitors as they enter the store. The place is filled with antiques, including a couple of nickelodeon pianos that visitors can prompt to play a tune for a quarter.

Details: Open summer daily 10–5; winter Tue–Sun 11–4. (30 minutes–1 hour)

★★★ SILVER TERRACE CEMETERIES
**C St., 775/847-0281, or the Chamber of Commerce
775/847-0311**

One of the best ways to learn about the people who lived in Virginia City during its high-spirited mining boom days is to visit the cemeteries located on the north end of town. Some of the headstones and grave sites have suffered from neglect, wild-horse tramplings, and the ravages of time—an effect that adds a spooky element. Various community organizations are working to repair the damage at this scenic area, which has nine cemeteries, including Catholic, Mason, Miner's Union, and others. You'll find walking-tour guides at the V&T boxcar (the Virginia City Visitors Bureau) on C Street.

Details: *Located at the north end of town on the east side of C St. Open daily dawn to dusk. Free. (30 minutes–1 hour)*

★★★ VIRGINIA CITY RADIO MUSEUM
**109 S. F St., Virginia City, 775/847-9047
www.tek-majic.com/radio**

Museums nearly outnumber saloons in Virginia City. The quality varies at the museums, but visitors rarely walk away feeling as though they didn't get to see some unusual artifacts. One of the best museums for the buck is the Virginia City Radio Museum where radio buffs can tune into the displays of crystal sets and the more than 80 radios on display. Old tunes piped through the speakers add to the vintage atmosphere.

Details: *Corner of F and Taylor Sts. behind St. Mary's Catholic Church. Hours vary. $2 adults, $1 children under 12. (30 minutes–1 hour)*

★★ BEST AND BELCHER MINE
Ponderosa Saloon, C St., 775/847-0757

Visitors can take the 30-minute tour of the Best and Belcher Mine, the entrance to which is located at the back of the Ponderosa Saloon. It's a chilling experience to relive the claustrophobic, dangerous working conditions of the miners.

Details: *Open daily 10–5:30 (11–5 in winter). $3.50 adults, $1.50 children. (30 minutes)*

★★ THE CASTLE
775/847-0275

One of the spookiest residences in Virginia City, the 1868 Castle appears as though it could have hosted the cast of *Psycho*. The mansion has been

maintained in its original state right down to the French wallpaper and marble fireplaces. The 16-room home contains its original furnishings and is a remarkable lesson in architecture and history. Visitors can examine such nineteenth-century antiques as a fainting couch and Dutch vases.
Details: *Open daily 11–5. $3.50. (30 minutes)*

★★ CHOLLAR MINE
775/847-0155

The Comstock is honeycombed with old mines from its gold-boom days, and the safest way to view them is to take one of the guided tours into the depths. The Chollar Mine, established in 1861, was one of the original mines as well as the fifth largest producing mine on the Comstock.
Details: *Just off Truck Route. Open May–Sept. $5. (1 hour)*

★★ FOURTH WARD SCHOOL MUSEUM
C St., 775/847-0975

The Fourth Ward School, built in 1875, was a schoolhouse until 1936. For its time, the imposing red-and-white building had modern conveniences not available at most schools, including indoor water fountains. Today visitors can see the classrooms as well as tour the changing exhibits and the gift shop. On the bottom floor you'll also find exhibits about mining history, women, and immigrants, among others.
Details: *South end of C St. Open May–Oct daily 10–5. Donation. (30 minutes–1 hour)*

★ COMSTOCK FIREMEN'S MUSEUM
S. C St., 775/847-0717

Firefighting was a crucial occupation in Virginia City during its early years, especially after the entire town nearly went up in flames in 1875. You'll find relics of early firefighting technology, including old fire engines, extinguishers, equipment, and photographs.
Details: *Open May 15–Oct 31 daily 10–5. Donation. (30 minutes)*

★ JULIA BULETTE RED LIGHT MUSEUM
5 C St., 775/847-9394

This musty museum below the Julia Bulette Saloon honors Virginia City's most famous courtesan, and her profession, with displays of old contraceptive methods, medical devices, and medicines used to cure all sorts of ailments. The life of Bulette, who was especially revered by the local Comstock firefighters, became the stuff of legend after she

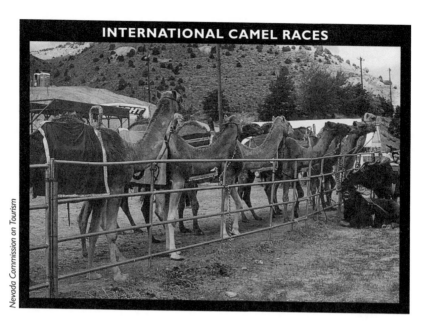

INTERNATIONAL CAMEL RACES

Nevada Commission on Tourism

was murdered in 1867. Remnants of Virginia City's once-thriving red-light district are still visible, and visitors can learn more about prostitution on the Comstock in the 1800s and the folklore surrounding Bulette at this museum.

Details: *Open daily 10–9. $1 adults. (30 minutes)*

★ TERRITORIAL ENTERPRISE MARK TWAIN MUSEUM
47-53 C St., 775/847-0525

This museum contains relics from the days when the *Territorial Enterprise* was the main rag in town. In the newsroom museum you'll find an 1894 linotype machine as well as the desk where Mark Twain worked while writing for the newspaper.

Details: *Open daily 10–5. $1.50 admission. (30 minutes–1 hour)*

★ THE WAY IT WAS MUSEUM
113 N. C St., 775/847-0766

One of the town's biggest museums is the Way It Was Museum. It houses mining artifacts, photographs, a doll collection, and more. The scale models that show the mines that wind through and around town are intriguing. You'll also find an assortment of mining equipment and wagons outside.

Details: *Open daily 10–6. Adults $2.50, ages 11 and under free.* *(1 hour)*

FITNESS AND RECREATION

If you venture beyond C Street, you'll find several side streets and trails that wind into the hillsides and offer great views that reveal the impact that mining has had on the area. One of the best trails is the hike up Mount Davidson, home of the whitewashed "V." You'll find the trailhead at Taylor Street near the water tanks. The trail to the "V" and the flagpole gets steep toward the top—make sure you pack water if you're in it for the long haul. Despite the hilly countryside, you will find some good mountain-bike trails. There's a relatively flat stretch along the old railroad grade beginning at the Gold Hill Depot, two miles south of Virginia City. After tramping about in the desert, you can enjoy a dip in the public pool situated in the town's grassy little park overlooking the canyons.

FOOD

Virginia City has a surprisingly good lineup of restaurants. The **Crown Point Restaurant** at the Gold Hill Hotel, 1540 Main St., two miles south of Virginia City, has French continental cuisine that is often paired with lectures by local historians.

You'll find sandwiches, salads, and pastries at **Walden's Coffee Company**, 58 S. C St., 775/847-7277, as well as coffee drinks in this attractive building—check out the rock walls and the Western mural. At the Delta Saloon's **Sawdust Corner Restaurant**, 18 C St., 775/847-0789, you'll find sandwiches as well as unique attractions, such as the Suicide Table. At the **Red Dog Saloon** you can munch on freshly baked pizza amid the old music posters and memorabilia. If you're hankering for something a little more exotic, try the **Mandarin Garden Chinese Restaurant** at 40 B Street, next to the Storey County Courthouse, 775/847-9288. The Chinese cuisine is served inside a beautifully restored Victorian mansion complete with tall ceilings and huge windows.

You won't have any trouble satisfying a sweet tooth along C Street. You'll be tempted by such places as **Red's Old-Fashioned Candies**, 68 S. C St., 775/847-0404, or **Grandma's Fudge Factory**, 20 N. C St., 775/847-0770, both of which prepare fresh fudge and caramel apples right before your eyes, piping the aromas directly into the nostrils of passersby. Or, try the snickerdoodles and ice cream at the **Comstock Cookie Company**, 38 N. C St., 775/847-9500.

Also Worth a Look

Mansions

Mackay Mansion, 775/847-0173, built in 1860 as a mining office and owned by Comstock millionaire John Mackay, is open daily for tours and is a popular wedding spot. **Piper's Opera House**, 775/847-0433, open in the summer for tours, is currently undergoing a renovation and will soon return to its former glory as a concert hall. On B Street, one block west of the main drag, the 1877 **Storey County Courthouse**, 775/847-0969, is an unusual site. Still a working courthouse and home of county government offices, the building features a statue of Justice that is unblindfolded.

Churches

St. Mary's in the Mountains on E Street, open 9 to 5 daily, with its Victorian architecture and spires reaching toward the heavens, is an often-photographed Virginia City landmark. **St. Paul's Episcopal** on F Street (open to the public summer months) and the **Presbyterian Church** on C Street are also havens of history. All three still have Sunday services. St. Mary's is open to visitors during the day.

Saloons

Bucket of Blood, **Old Washoe Club**, **Silver Queen**, and **Delta**—the colorful old saloons along Virginia City's C Street boardwalk—haven't changed much since the days they served hard-working miners in the 1880s. Today the saloons are packed with modern slot machines, but the floors, barstools, back bars, and decor are in most cases original. At the Silver Queen Saloon visitors can marvel at the huge mural of the Silver Queen, a tribute to Virginia City's celebrated silver mines, inlaid with 3,261 silver dollars. The Bucket of Blood has a beautiful old back bar and a panoramic view of Sun Mountain and Six-Mile Canyon as well as its own beer label and occasional live music. The Delta has the "world-famous Suicide Table," a bizarre attraction that is pure tourist trap, although the club is an interesting place to meander through. The **Red Dog Saloon** is a modern-day tribute to the original, which was founded in the 1960s and was a mecca for musicians from the Bay Area. Today you'll find live music, open-mike nights, and old posters from the Grateful Dead as well as a group called the Charlatans who lived above the Red Dog during its heyday.

LODGING

Gold Hill Hotel, 1540 Main St., 775/847-0111, in Gold Hill, two miles south of Virginia City, is Nevada's oldest hotel. Despite its age, the hotel has been restored and is quite luxurious, although it is said to be haunted by a ghost named Rosie who leaves a lingering scent of roses when she is present.

In Virginia City, you can't miss the bright-blue **Sugarloaf Mountain Motel**, 434 S. C St., 775/847-0551, as you enter from the west end of town. Well-to-do mine owners and business people built cozy Victorian homes on the Comstock in the late 1800s, a few of which have been converted into bed-and-breakfast inns. Choices include the **Chollar Mansion**, 565 S. D St., 775/847-9777, **Hardwicke House**, 99 Main St., 775/847-0215, and **Spargo House**, 395 S. B St., 775/847-7455.

CAMPING

It's not easy to find a flat spot on which to camp in the rolling hillsides surrounding Virginia City, but on the Comstock, RVers congregate at the well-maintained **Virginia City RV Park**, 355 N. F St., 775/847-0999. The scenic park has a grocery store, showers, full hookups, and great views.

SPECIAL EVENTS

If you time your visit to Virginia City in the fall, you can catch one of the most bizarre spectacles in Nevada: the Virginia City International Camel Races. Not surprisingly, the races began in 1959 as a hoax, and locals and visitors alike have been drawn to the dromedaries ever since. Since camels are not bred—or designed—for racing, the competitors, usually a group of crazed local residents and celebrities, hold on for dear life as they bounce and bumble their way to the finish lines. The weekend usually includes a parade, ostrich races, and a Camel Hump Ball. On a more dignified note, the Comstock Historic Preservation Weekend, held during May and throughout the summer weekends, usually consists of high teas, tours of local mansions, and a 1860s ball. Both are worth the trip.

TOWN TOURS

Visitors will find a number of options for touring Virginia City. A&M Horse-Drawn Carriage Tours, 775/246-0322, is an old-fashioned way to see the sights. The Virginia City Tram Tour, 916/587-5742, offers a 20-minute narrated ride. For a more detailed trek, Detours, 775/847-9233, guided by Virginia City resident and geologist Becky Purkey, offers half- and full-day tours covering geology, history, and the flora and fauna of the Comstock.

10
LAKE TAHOE

In reference to Lake Tahoe, the oft-quoted Mark Twain said it best: "It's the fairest picture the earth affords." A bright-blue oasis amid the rugged, snow-capped Sierra that surrounds it, Lake Tahoe is the largest alpine lake in North America—22 miles long and 12 miles wide. Created millions of years ago by massive ice floes, the waters of the lake were trapped when the boulders and other debris blocked the exits. Whether you're looking down on it from one of a dozen ski slopes or from the deck of a paddle wheeler, the vision of Lake Tahoe stretching out before you forces you to take a deep breath of pine-scented air to rejuvenate your spirit. The Washoe Indian tribe considered this area to be sacred, and its mystic qualities still permeate visitors. But don't think it's all about resting on your laurels—the slopes, hiking trails, afternoon tradewinds, and even the casinos beckon you to answer the call of exploration.

A PERFECT DAY IN LAKE TAHOE

The best way to spend the day at Lake Tahoe is to drive leisurely around its 72-mile circumference, pausing to gamble, eat, shop, hike, or gaze upon the beauty of the water and mountains whenever the mood strikes. If you're coming from Reno, the drive up the Mount Rose Highway will serve as a warm-up to the vistas to come. If you're traveling from Carson City, when you first see the lake, your reaction will be an instantaneous "wow." The best approach is to go clockwise because you're always guaranteed to have the closest view of the lake

LAKE TAHOE

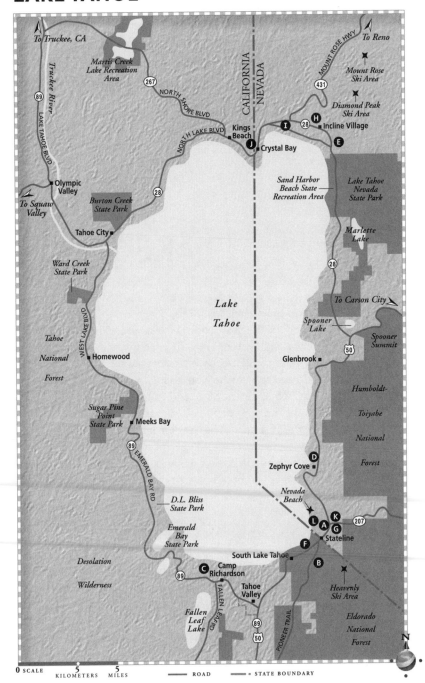

To Truckee, CA

Martis Creek
Lake Recreation
Area

To Reno

Mount Rose
Ski Area

MOUNT ROSE HWY

431

Diamond Peak
Ski Area

H

Incline Village

E

NORTH SHORE BLVD

267

Truckee River

89

LAKE TAHOE BLVD

NORTH LAKE BLVD

Kings
Beach

I

J

Crystal Bay

CALIFORNIA
NEVADA

28

Sand Harbor
Beach State
Recreation Area

Lake Tahoe
Nevada
State Park

Olympic
Valley

To Squaw
Valley

Burton Creek
State Park

28

Tahoe City

Marlette
Lake

Ward Creek
State Park

WEST LAKE BLVD

*Lake
Tahoe*

28

To Carson City

Spooner
Lake

Spooner
Summit

Tahoe

National

Forest

Homewood

50

Glenbrook

Humboldt-

Toiyabe

National

Forest

Sugar Pine
Point
State Park

Meeks Bay

89

EMERALD BAY RD

Zephyr Cove

D

D.L. Bliss
State Park

Nevada
Beach

Emerald
Bay
State Park

L **A** **K**
G

207

Stateline

Desolation

South Lake Tahoe

F

Wilderness

C

Camp
Richardson

B

FALLEN LEAF RD

Tahoe
Valley

Heavenly
Ski Area

89

Fallen
Leaf
Lake

89

50

PIONEER TRAIL

Eldorado

National

Forest

N

0 SCALE   5   5
KILOMETERS MILES

——— ROAD   ▪ ▪ STATE BOUNDARY

from your passenger window. If you can, begin with breakfast at the Forest Buffet atop Harrah's Tahoe—the room has one of the casino core's best views of the lake. Along the way you will want to stop at the Emerald Bay scenic overlook, occupied by an island with a now-vacant summer house. By the time you reach Crystal Bay on the north end of the lake it'll be lunch time—plan to partake at the restaurant at the Cal-Neva Lodge. In the summer the beaches at Lake Tahoe Nevada State Park are irresistible—pack your swimsuit and sunscreen. You should plan to end your tour at Zephyr Cove where you can catch either a dinner-dance evening cruise aboard the paddle wheeler *M.S. Dixie II* or a champagne sunset cruise on the *Woodwind II*.

TRAVELER'S WARNING

In the winter, be sure to keep an eye on the weather. Strong snowstorms can catch you by surprise and leave you stranded. Check out www.tahoe.com/weather/index.html for weather conditions or call 775/793-1313 for road conditions.

SIGHTS

- **A** Borges Family Carriage Rides, Horizon Casino
- **B** Heavenly Aerial Tram
- **C** Lake Tahoe Stream Profile Chamber
- **D** M.S. Dixie II
- **E** Ponderosa Ranch
- **F** Tahoe Queen
- **D** Woodwind Sailing Cruises

FOOD

- **G** American River Cafe (Harrah's Tahoe)
- **H** Cafe 333
- **G** El Vaquero (Harveys)
- **G** Forest Buffet (Harrah's Tahoe)

FOOD (continued)

- **G** Friday's Station Steak and Seafood Grill (Harrah's Tahoe)
- **G** Garden Buffet (Harveys)
- **G** Hard Rock Cafe (Harveys)
- **G** Llewellyns (Harveys)
- **H** Lone Eagle Grille (Hyatt)
- **I** Mofo's Pizza and Pasta
- **G** Planet Hollywood (Caesars Tahoe)
- **G** Primavera (Caesars Tahoe)
- **G** Sage Room Steak House (Harveys)
- **G** Seafood Grotto (Harveys)

FOOD (continued)

- **G** Summit (Harrah's Tahoe)

LODGING

- **G** Caesars Tahoe
- **J** Cal-Neva Resort
- **K** Embassy Suites
- **G** Harrah's Tahoe
- **G** Harvey's
- **H** Haus Bavaria
- **G** Horizon
- **H** Hyatt Regency Lake Tahoe
- **J** Tahoe Biltmore

CAMPING

- **D** Zephyr Cove
- **L** Nevada Beach

Note: Items with the same letter are located in the same area.

SIGHTSEEING HIGHLIGHTS

★★★ HEAVENLY AERIAL TRAM
**Top of the Ski Run Blvd., 775/586-7000
or 530/544-6263**

You can get a lofty view of the lake and the surrounding Sierra Nevada by catching a ride on the tram. The five-minute tram ride eases up to an elevation of 8,250 feet and drops you off at Monument Peak Restaurant. At the top you'll also find the trailhead for the Tahoe Vista Trail, a 2.1-mile nature walk.

Details: *Open daily 10–9. Rides depart every 15 minutes. $12.50 adults, $9 children 12 and under. (1–2 hours)*

★★★ *M. S. DIXIE II*
**775/588-3508 or 775/882-0786
www.tahoedixie2.com/Dixie1.html**

One of the best ways to see the lake is aboard the *M. S. Dixie II*, a paddle wheeler that chugs out of Zephyr Cove. Aboard the old-fashioned riverboat replica you'll be able to get a great view of such spectacular sights as Emerald Bay and the south shore of the lake. The boat offers breakfast, sightseeing, and dinner-dance cruises.

Details: *Sightseeing cruises mid-June–Labor Day daily 11, 2, 5; after Labor Day–Oct 15 daily 11, 2; rest of year daily 12 p.m. Fares $17 adults, $15 seniors, $5 ages 3–11. Reservations recommended. Call for schedules, which vary with the season. (2 hours)*

★★★ PONDEROSA RANCH
**100 Ponderosa Ranch Rd., Incline Village
775/831-0691**

Fans of the TV show *Bonanza* will enjoy a visit to the Ponderosa Ranch in Incline Village. For avid *Bonanza* watchers, the highlight is the ranch house, where a few of the scenes for the series were filmed. The house, which appears much smaller than it did on TV, has the familiar fireplace and, hanging next to the door, you'll see the coats and hats that belonged to Hoss, Ben, Adam, and Little Joe Cartwright. The ranch also has an Old West town with a saloon and shops as well as staged gunfights throughout the day. Hoss's Mystery Mine will test your skills of perception and balance. The petting zoo is another popular place, as is the shooting gallery. Adventurous couples can tie the knot at the authentic 1870s Church of the Ponderosa Wedding Chapel.

Details: *Open May–Oct daily 9:30–5. $9.50 adults, $5.50 children 5–11. (1–2 hours)*

★★★ TAHOE QUEEN
530/541-3364

In winter, you can combine a ski trip with a cruise on the *Tahoe Queen*. Skiers can hop aboard the paddle wheeler docked at the Marina Village on Ski Run Boulevard and ride across the lake to Squaw Valley. The round-trip ski shuttle tickets include a lift ticket to Squaw as well as bus transportation to and from your hotel. A ski shuttle breakfast package is also available. In both the winter and summer, the *Tahoe Queen* offers two-hour cruises to Emerald Bay as well as three-hour dinner-dance cruises. The heritage tour features a short history of Lake Tahoe. In summer, visitors can opt for the two-and-a-half-hour early sunset cruise.

Details: *Ski Run Marina, South Lake Tahoe, CA. Emerald Bay cruise $18 adults, $8 children. Dinner-dance cruise $45 adults, $28 children. Call for cruising schedule. (2 hours)*

★★★ WOODWIND SAILING CRUISES
Hwy. 50 at Zephyr Cove, 775/588-3000 or 888/867-6394

You can feel the wind in your hair if you opt for a cruise aboard the *Woodwind II*, a 55-foot, 50-passenger catamaran. Sailors can relax while the wind takes them either across the lake or along the shores—the views are breathtaking no matter where you end up. The cruises are great for sunbathing, but one of the most popular cruises is the daily sunset champagne cruise. The boat has a glass bottom that gives you a view of what's going on below—and due to the lake's clarity, you can see down several feet. A similar cruise is offered aboard the *Woodwind I*, docked at Camp Richardson, just north of Stateline on the California side.

Details: *Departs Zephyr Cove 9:30, 11:30, 1:30, 3:30. Cruises are 1 hour and 45 minutes. $18 adults, $16 seniors, $9 children 3–12. Woodwind I departs from Camp Richardson Resort at 11:30, 1:30, and 3:30. (2 hours)*

★★ BORGES FAMILY CARRIAGE RIDES
775/588-2953 or 800-726-RIDE

A carriage ride pulled by horses is probably the most romantic way to soak up the views and ambiance of the south shore at Lake Tahoe. In the summer, the Borges family operates carriage rides pulled by the big Belgium draft horses or one of the family's Baskir Curlies. The rides begin at the Horizon Casino and wind past the Edgewood Tahoe golf course and other scenic areas. Carriage and Western-style surrey rides are available. In winter you can ride in a one-horse open sleigh through snow-covered fields near Stateline.

Details: *Horizon Casino. Sleigh and carriage rides $15 adults, $7.50 children under 11; dinner rides $35 adults, $25 children; lunch rides $25 adults, $20 children. Call for schedule. (1 hour)*

★★ LAKE TAHOE STREAM PROFILE CHAMBER
530/573-2674

In the fall, it's worth the trek across the Nevada–California border to see the profile chamber. It gives you an underwater view of the kokanee salmon as they make their way up Taylor Creek to spawn. The salmon turn bright red during spawning season—a spectacular sight. The U.S. Forest Service Visitor Center, which recently renovated the chamber, also has interpretive exhibits about the ecosystem of the creek and the surrounding area.

Details: *U.S. Forest Service Visitor Center is three miles north of South Lake Tahoe on Hwy. 89. Free. (30 minutes–1 hour)*

FITNESS AND RECREATION

Ah, the skiing at Lake Tahoe—it simply can't be topped. More than a dozen downhill resorts surround the lake and provide an incomparable variety of verticals for all levels of skiers. The 1960 Olympics were held at Squaw Valley, 530/583-6955, www.squaw.com. The resort's 30 lifts and 2,850 vertical feet of skiing were good enough for Olympians and still provide some of the lake's most spectacular skiing. Heavenly, 775/586-7000, www.skiheavenly.com, perched right on the Nevada-California state line at the lake's south shore, ranks right up there, too. Even beginning skiers will find trails that offer views of the lake, a pleasing distraction while you're cutting turns and bouncing over moguls. The views are even better at Diamond Peak, 775/831-3211, www.diamondpeak .com, a resort favored by expert skiers for its numerous black-diamond runs. Mount Rose, 775/849-0704, www.mtrose.com, is a popular hill among locals thanks to its location 25 miles south of Reno. Snowboarding is an option at all the resorts, and a few, such as Boreal, 530/426-3666, www.skiboreal, have designated snowboard parks.

Cross-country skiing is probably the second most popular pastime at the lake. There are a half-dozen developed cross-country areas and several other areas where you can ski on your own. Spooner Lake Cross-Country Ski Area, 775/887-8844, NV 28 a half-mile north of the U.S. 50 junction, 12 miles north of Stateline, has 101 kilometers of trails that wind across meadows, with a challenging 18-mile round-trip up to Marlette Lake. The scenery is pretty, and you'll find a warming hut and rentals here. Diamond Peak, 800/GO-TAHOE or 775/831-3249, has 35 kilometers of well-developed trails, and on selected days you can invite your dog along.

There's plenty of snow frolicking to be had around the lake. You can grab your inner tube or toboggan and head for just about any place you see a relatively treeless hill with lots of snow. The hills around Spooner Lake are especially popular for snow play and cross-country skiing, as is the Incline Village Driving Range, 955 Fairway Blvd., at the golf course.

In summer, sunbathing and swimming are top priorities, and there are several places to stretch out your beach blanket. You'll find excellent sandy beaches at Zephyr Cove, 775/588-5021, which has volleyball courts, a pier, a marina, jet-skiing, parasailing, a restaurant and bar, and two cruise boats, the *M. S. Dixie II* and the *Woodwind II*. Across the roadway at Zephyr Cove Stables, 775/588-5664, you can take trail rides on gentle horses into the Sierra.

The next best beaches are at Sand Harbor and Lake Tahoe Nevada State Park, 775/831-0494, where huge pine trees creep up to the white-sand shores. Lake Tahoe Nevada State Park juts out into the lake and is decorated by huge boulders, deposited when a glacier formed Lake Tahoe millions of years ago. This beautiful area, which has barbecue pits, rest rooms, paved walkways, and a boat ramp, provides the spectacular backdrop for the annual Shakespeare at Sand Harbor Festival.

A trip to Tahoe would be incomplete without donning a backpack and exploring some of the country's best hiking trails. This area is stitched from meadow to hill to peak with places to explore, the most famous of which is the Tahoe Rim Trail, 775/588-0686. The 150-mile trail circles the lake along the ridge lines overlooking the Tahoe Basin. Construction on the trail, which encompasses two states and six counties, began in 1984 and has been the work of mostly volunteers, who complete major sections each summer. One of the easiest places to pick up the trail is near Spooner Summit—watch for signs pointing to the trail on U.S. 50 near the NV 28 junction. You can dig in and help build and maintain portions of the trail by joining the volunteer group. They'll loan you a hard hat and show you how to remove fallen trees and construct the trail. In the summer, the two-mile loop around Spooner Lake also makes a pleasant outing.

Mountain bikers should schedule a trip to the Flume Trail, a strenuous ride with views guaranteed to knock you off your seat. The ride begins at Spooner Lake where the route becomes a lung-crushing six-mile stretch up 800 feet to Marlette Lake. After another four miles you'll reach the Flume Trail, a narrow, single track that hugs the hillsides and overlooks the lake 1,600 feet below. The Flume is a rigorous workout and not for beginners or scaredy-cats—it's a long, bumpy shortcut down to the lake. The best time to tackle this trail is during the fall when the aspen leaves put on a show and temperatures are slightly cooler.

The calmer sport of golfing also lures visitors to the lake. The views will elevate your spirits—and the higher elevation makes your ball go farther, too. One of the most prestigious lake courses is Edgewood Tahoe, 180 Lake Parkway, 775/588-3566, which stands near the hotel-casinos at the south shore. Named one of *Golf Digest's* top 25 courses in the country, Edgewood is home to a celebrity golf tournament. At Incline Village, you'll find both a championship course and a mountain course, both of which were designed by Robert Trent Jones.

Tahoe has fishing, too, and you can pursue the coveted deep-water mackinaw trout by taking a fishing charter. Mickey's "Big Mack" Charters, 530/583-4602 or 800/877-1462, based at Tahoe City, California, and Mac-A-Tack, 530/546-2500, can take you where the lunkers lurk. You'll also find catch-and-release fishing at Spooner Lake.

FOOD

The **Forest Buffet** at Harrah's Tahoe, Hwy. 50, 775/588-6611, qualifies as having the state's best view from a buffet. Harrah's has other excellent eateries, including **Friday's Station Steak and Seafood Grill**, **American River Cafe**, and the **Summit**, a two-story gourmet room that was converted from a former star suite.

One of the best gourmet rooms at the lake is **Llewellyn's** at Harveys, U.S. 50 and Stateline Ave. Named after the wife of Harvey Gross, the resort's originator, the restaurant has superb views of the lake and food to match. For atmosphere you can dine to the music of pianist Ron Rose who has played at the hotel for 42 years. Harveys also has a **Hard Rock Cafe**, the **Seafood Grotto**, **Sage Room Steak House**, **Garden Buffet**, and Mexican restaurant **El Vaquero**.

For Italian food the best bet is **Primavera** at Caesars Tahoe, 55 U.S. 50, 775/588-3515. The hotel also has a **Planet Hollywood**.

The posh community of Incline Village is crammed with several excellent eateries. At the top is the **Lone Eagle Grille** at the Hyatt, 111 Country Club

LAKE TAHOE

Dr., 775/832-3250, which has a menu that includes spit-roasted entrées and a delicacy known to chocoholics as the six-layer Monster Cake. The room has two-story picture windows overlooking Lake Tahoe as well as two huge rock fireplaces. **Cafe 333**, 333 Village Boulevard, 775/832-7333, is a brightly decorated café that serves nouvelle cuisine. If you're looking for a refreshing change for breakfast, try the Cafe 333's breakfast strata, a bread pudding cooked with proscuitto spinach, mascarpone cream cheese, and other savory ingredients. **Mofo's Pizza and Pasta** at Christmas Tree Center, 868 Tahoe Blvd. #23, 775/831-4999, is a highly recommended local favorite.

LODGING

At Stateline, you'll find the big four: Harrah's Tahoe, Harveys, Caesars Tahoe, and the Horizon. My top recommendation is **Harrah's Tahoe**, Hwy. 50, 775/588-6611 or 800/427-7247, which offers numerous amenities, the best one being that each room has two bathrooms. The spacious rooms, a large nonsmoking area in the casino, and a dome-covered indoor pool and Jacuzzi are also good benefits. **Harveys**, U.S. 50 and Stateline Ave., 775/588-2411 or 800/HARVEYS, is no slouch when it comes to providing amenities. With more than 740 rooms, Harveys is the largest at the lake and was the first —Harvey Gross opened the Wagon Wheel casino in the mid-1940s, and the resort grew up from there. The huge, recently renovated casino has a woodsy decor that blends in well with its surroundings. **Caesars Tahoe**, 55 U.S. 50, 775/588-3515 or 800/648-3353, is also quite elegant—a small-scale version of its big-sister property in Las Vegas. The Roman theme isn't quite as pervasive here as it is in Las Vegas, but you can luxuriate in the rock-lined pool adjacent to the Primavera restaurant. The **Horizon**, 50 Hwy. 50, 775/588-6211 or 800/322-7723, is a pleasant resort, and it has some history for Elvis fans—the King performed here in the mid-1970s when the hotel was called the Sahara Tahoe. Just across the state line is the attractive **Embassy Suites**, 4130 Lake Tahoe Blvd., 530/544-5400.

In Incline Village, the resort of choice is the **Hyatt Regency Lake Tahoe**, 111 Country Club Dr., 775/885-1111 or 800/233-1234. The best benefit here

WEDDING BELLS

Lake Tahoe is wedding central with an instant honeymoon site built in. Several hotel-casinos, such as Caesars Tahoe and the Cal-Neva, have beautiful wedding chapels and can provide everything you need, from limo and cake to flowers and minister. Numerous wedding chapels are spread out around the lake, the majority of them clustered near Stateline and South Lake Tahoe, California. You can also opt for a ceremony on the shores of the lake or another scenic area outdoors. The *M.S. Dixie II*, *Tahoe Queen*, and the *Woodwind II* offer wedding cruises, or you can take a carriage or sleigh ride in a wedding chariot with Borges Sleigh, Hay, and Carriage Rides. An easy way to find out how to arrange a Tahoe wedding is to call a one-stop service such as the Lake Tahoe Weddings Service, 800/427-3148. No matter how you choose to tie the knot you will need a marriage license—and make sure you buy it for the appropriate state. In Nevada, acquiring a license is dangerously easy. You must be 18 years of age and provide a current ID such as a driver's license—a blood test is not required. You can pick up one at the Washoe County Clerk's Office in Incline Village, 865 Tahoe Blvd., 775/832-4166. Cost is $35. Licenses are also issued at the Douglas County Clerk's Office in Zephyr Cove, 175 Hwy. 50 at Kahle Dr., 775/588-7100. The cost is $42. Neither place accepts credit cards or personal checks.

is the private beach, located right across the highway from the hotel. Surrounded in every direction by tall pines and good scenery, the pool with adjacent bar is the best place to hang out during summer. You'll also find tennis courts, a health club, and hiking trails. The only bed-and-breakfast on the east shore of Lake Tahoe is **Haus Bavaria**, 593 North Dyer Circle, 775/831-6222, a German-style guest house with wood paneling and a wood-burning stove in the den. Each of the five rooms has a private bath and a balcony. The specialty for breakfast is fresh-baked breads and pastries.

On the north shore at Crystal Bay, lovers congregate at the romantic **Cal-Neva Resort**, 2 Stateline Rd., 775/832-4000 or 800/225-6382, which was owned for a short time in the 1960s by Frank Sinatra (the Nevada Gaming Control Board pulled his gaming license for his association with mobsters). The most fascinating feature of this cozy, lodge-style hotel, which was built in 1926, is that it sits right on the Nevada-California state line. You can swim back and forth between Nevada and California in the pool, which also straddles the line. Be sure to see the Indian Room (also half in Nevada and half in California) as well as the Circle Bar, which is accented by a huge glass dome made of more than 7,000 pieces of handcut German crystal. The gazebo overlooking the lake (and the rumors that Frank Sinatra shared dalliances with Marilyn Monroe here) has made this one of Tahoe's most popular places to tie the knot. The spa provides beauty treatments and massages. The rustic **Tahoe Biltmore**, on NV 28, 775/831-0660 or 800/BILTMOR, also has a casino and hotel rooms.

CAMPING

Surprisingly, camping on the Nevada side is fairly limited—and in the summer it can become a little crowded. But the scenery is perfect, and you can't top awakening to the smell of pine and having thousands of acres of recreation right out your backdoor (or tent flap). You'll find boating, swimming, horseback riding, and numerous other activities at **Zephyr Cove**, 775/588-6644, which has 170 sites for RVs up to 40 feet and tents; fees are $15 to $23 per day. Toward Stateline at **Nevada Beach**, 530/544-5994, you'll find 54 sites for RVs up to 24 feet for $14 to $16. California State Parks, 530/525-7277, and the U.S. Forest Service Lake Tahoe Basin Management Unit, 530/573-2600, oversee the campgrounds on the California side of the lake.

NIGHTLIFE

The nightlife is geared toward the young and active here, so bring your dancing shoes. Nero's, at Caesars Tahoe, 775/588-3515, is the hottest dance club in

Stateline. You'll find live bands that play everything from swing to disco. Watch for Mr. Hot Buns Night and other intriguing themes. Lily's Beach Club at the Horizon has similar themes, such as Studio 54 Night. Just across the state line, Turtles Sports Bar and Dance Emporium, 4130 Lake Tahoe Blvd., 530/543-2135, offers another happening spot where you can shake your bootie.

The hotel-casinos at Stateline also offer production shows and headliner entertainment. At Harrah's Tahoe's South Shore Room you'll usually find a production show alternating with a headliner, such as Ringo Starr or Ray Charles. Harveys' Emerald Theater hosts a production show as does the Horizon's Golden Cabaret. The Circus Maximus showroom at Caesars Tahoe brings in headliners such as Willie Nelson and Wynonna. At Incline, the Hyatt Regency hosts local lounge bands as well as the occasional headliner. The Cal-Neva at Crystal Bay also offers lounge entertainment.

11
COWBOY COUNTRY

Elko and Winnemucca probably have the state's highest concentration of Ford pickups with dogs in the back, buckaroos in cowboy hats, and Wrangler-clad residents. This is cowboy country. You'll see deep traces of ranch life in every aspect of the two towns, from the saloons to the museums.

Elko is a friendly small town that has experienced a population boom in recent years—partly due to a resurgence of mining and partly because the mountains and scenery here are irresistible for folks looking to settle down in a peaceful place. The Ruby Mountains, the ranches, the open spaces, and the evolving cultural scene make Elko a great place to visit, too. Although thoroughly modern in its hotels and businesses, Elko embraces and celebrates its cowboy culture through its museums, events, and historic preservation—a facet that takes travelers back to the Old West.

In Winnemucca, you'll find a similar frontier feel. A good stop on the long haul across Interstate 80, Winnemucca has surprisingly good attractions. Named for the famed Paiute Chief Winnemucca, this ranching and farming community also has plenty of mining activity that has kept the town fairly prosperous. But the small-town cowboy charm is what people will notice most here, whether they're perusing the Buckaroo Hall of Fame or carousing in the town's saloons.

A PERFECT DAY IN COWBOY COUNTRY

Breakfast should begin in Winnemucca at the Griddle. You'll find it hard to decide between the huge omelettes and even bigger pancakes. Then check out the

ELKO

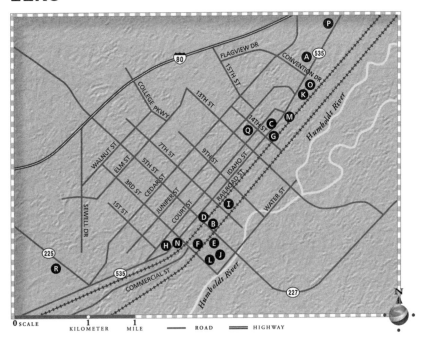

SIGHTS

- Ⓐ Elko Custom Carriage Tours
- Ⓑ J. M. Capriola Company
- Ⓒ Northeastern Nevada Museum
- Ⓓ Western Folklife Center

FOOD

- Ⓔ Biltoki
- Ⓕ Bull Penn at Stockmen's Hotel

FOOD (continued)

- Ⓓ Cowboy Joe's
- Ⓖ Dinner Station
- Ⓗ D'Orazio's
- Ⓘ La Fiesta
- Ⓙ Nevada Dinner House
- Ⓐ Red Lion
- Ⓚ Showboat Southern Kitchen
- Ⓛ Star Hotel
- Ⓜ Toki Ona
- Ⓝ Zapata's

LODGING

- Ⓞ Ameritel Inn
- Ⓟ High Desert Inn
- Ⓠ Once Upon a Time B&B
- Ⓐ Red Lion Inn and Casino
- Ⓡ Shilo Inn

Note: Items with the same letter are located in the same area.

Humboldt Museum and the Buckaroo Hall of Fame. In Elko, you should begin with a drive to Lamoille for a hike up to one of the lakes in the Ruby Mountains. If you picked up lunch meat and fresh-baked bread at Swisher's General Store in Lamoille, you can stop at the Terraces, a spectacular picnicking spot that is covered with wildflowers in the summer. Head back into town to tour the Northeastern Nevada Museum and the Western Folklife Center. A good way to top off a day of hiking and exploring is a hearty Basque meal—Elko has four equally excellent Basque restaurants. If there's time, take a horse-and-carriage tour of town before settling into one of the casinos for an evening of live music and two-stepping.

SIGHTSEEING HIGHLIGHTS: ELKO AREA

★★★★ LAMOILLE
775/738-4091 or 888/248-3556 (Elko Convention and Visitors Authority)

Ah, the cows, the freshly mown hay, the pastures of wildflowers—you won't find a community more removed from the hustle and bustle of the big city than Lamoille, a mountain retreat nestled in a canyon at the western foot of the Ruby Mountains. If you plan to visit Lamoille you should pack your hiking boots—you'll find spectacular hiking trails that overlook the ranchlands below. Skiers with the "No Fear" bumper stickers can opt for a trek with Ruby Mountain Heli-Ski, a company that delivers you to pristine snow in the Rubies where you can power through the powder. After a day of hiking or extreme skiing, you can bed down for the night at one of two bed-and-breakfasts, the Breitenstein House and Ruby Mountain Magic. For dinner the top recommendation is the Pine Lodge, a log-cabin style restaurant decorated with several taxidermied animals (the lodge also has four motel rooms). The Breitenstein House also has a small restaurant. If you'd rather pack your own picnic, you should drop by Swisher's General Store, which offers locally baked breads, groceries, fishing gear, and antiques.

Details: Ruby Mountain Heli-Ski, 775/753-6867; Breitenstein House, 775/753-6456; Ruby Mountain Magic, 775/753-9111; Pine Lodge, 775/753-6363; Swisher's General Store, 775/753-6489. (1 hour minimum)

★★★★ NORTHEASTERN NEVADA MUSEUM
1515 Idaho St., Elko, 775/738-3418

Among the extensive and varied exhibits at this fascinating museum, one of rural Nevada's best, you'll find Nevada's most bizarre pair of shoes. The shoes belonged to an Elko cattle rustler known as Crazy Tex, who was as clever as he was crazy—the shoes were fitted with cow hooves so he could steal cattle without leaving behind footprints. There's a collection of the intricate silver-accented saddles made by renowned saddlemaker G. S. Garcia as well as a large section devoted to the Basques who came to Elko in the late 1800s to herd sheep. And don't miss the denim tuxedo that was worn by Bing Crosby. He owned and lived at an Elko County ranch. The natural-history section of the museum has a wide array of mounted animals, including a bighorn sheep, several birds, and a big butterfly collection.

Details: Open Mon–Sat 9–5, Sun 1–5. Donation. (1 hour)

★★★ J. M. CAPRIOLA COMPANY
Elko, 775/738-5816

For dudes and dudettes wishing to blend in with Elko's intrinsic cowboy culture, a required shopping stop is the J. M. Capriola Company, a downtown fixture for buckaroos for several decades. Racks are filled with cowboy hats both black and white, made by Stetson and Resistol. The brim of your new hat can be curled to your specifications. Of course, you'll find Wrangler jeans as well as boots made from a variety of leathers, from cow to lizard. City slickers and buckaroos alike converge at Capriola's to shop for doeskin gloves, bridles, saddles, ropes, riding gear, and all other forms of cowboy tack imaginable. It's worth a stop just to step back in time, soak up the cowboy way, and fill your nostrils with the smell of rich leather.

Details: At the corner of Commercial and Fifth Sts. Open Mon–Sat 9–5:30. Free. (30 minutes–1 hour)

★★ ELKO CUSTOM CARRIAGE TOURS
336 Rustic Dr., Elko, 775/778-6969

Relive the Old West by taking a tour of Elko aboard an old-fashioned surrey. Elko Custom Carriage Tours offers morning and afternoon tours, beginning at the Red Lion Hotel. Your guide will point out the attractions along the way. The Amish-built horse-drawn carriage can hold up to 15 people and is usually piloted by local buckaroo Mike Golden. Choose a two-hour morning or afternoon tour, or an evening champagne ride.

Details: Daily tours available morning, afternoon, and dinner. $5–$15 adults, 10 percent senior discount, free for children under 6. (2 hours minimum)

★★ WESTERN FOLKLIFE CENTER
501 Railroad St., Elko, 775/738-7508

The offices for the Elko Cowboy Poetry Gathering are based inside this historic building, the former Pioneer Saloon and Hotel. A portion of the ground floor is occupied by a gift shop, stocked with cowboy poetry CDs, posters from past festivals, music, and other cowboy, cowgirl, and Indian items. During the gathering, some evening events are held here, and the restored back bar is put back into service.

Details: Open Tue–Sat 10–5:30. Free. (30 minutes)

SIGHTSEEING HIGHLIGHTS: WINNEMUCCA AREA

★★★ HUMBOLDT MUSEUM
Winnemucca, 775/623-2225

Visitors here can learn about one of the town's early famous residents, Edna Purviance. Born in 1896 in nearby Paradise Valley, Edna went to Hollywood in the early 1900s and was Charlie Chaplin's leading lady in more than 30 films. At the museum you can learn about her life and see the silk gown she wore in Chaplin's *The Adventurer*. The building was originally a 1907 Methodist Church that was moved to its current site in 1976. The well-stocked museum also houses Winnemucca's first piano as well as a good antique automobile collection.

Details: Maple Ave. and Jungo Rd. Open weekdays 10–12 and 1:30–4, Sat 1–4. Donation. (30 minutes–1 hour)

★★ BUCKAROO HALL OF FAME
Winnemucca, 775/623-2225

Winnemucca is a ranching town—you'll quickly learn this if you pay a visit to the Buckaroo Hall of Fame. You can find out about local ranching legends at the wall filled with photos and stories. The hall of fame also includes a collection of saddles, ropes, artwork, and other cowboy-related items and gear.

Details: Located inside the Winnemucca Chamber of Commerce, 50 Winnemucca Blvd. Open weekdays 8–12, 1–5. Free. (30 minutes)

★★ POKE AND PEEK SECOND HAND SHOP
Sage Heights Dr., Winnemucca, 775/623-2076

Bargain hunters can scour the racks at the Poke and Peek, an intriguing

COWBOY COUNTRY

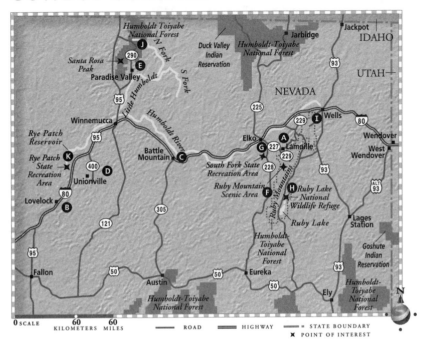

Humboldt Toiyabe National Forest · Jackpot · IDAHO · Jarbidge · Humboldt-Toiyabe National Forest · Duck Valley Indian Reservation · Santa Rosa Peak · Paradise Valley · UTAH · NEVADA · Winnemucca · Wells · Wendover · Rye Patch Reservoir · Elko · West Wendover · Rye Patch State Recreation Area · Battle Mountain · Lamoille · South Fork State Recreation Area · Unionville · Ruby Mountain Scenic Area · Lovelock · Ruby Lake National Wildlife Refuge · Lages Station · Ruby Lake · Humboldt-Toiyabe National Forest · Goshute Indian Reservation · Fallon · Austin · Eureka · Ely · Humboldt-Toiyabe National Forest · Humboldt-Toiyabe National Forest

0 SCALE 60 KILOMETERS 60 MILES ▬▬ ROAD ▬▬ HIGHWAY ▬ ▪ = STATE BOUNDARY ✕ POINT OF INTEREST

SIGHTS

- **A** Lamoille
- **B** Lovelock
- **C** Battle Mountain

LODGING

- **D** Old Pioneer Garden Country Inn
- **E** Stonehouse Country Inn

CAMPING

- **F** Ruby Mountains
- **G** South Fork State Recreation Area

CAMPING (continued)

- **H** Ruby Lake National Wildlife Refuge
- **I** Angel Creek and Angel Lake
- **J** Lye Creek Campground
- **K** Rye Patch State Recreation Area

second-hand shop operated by members of the hospital auxiliary. You'll find used clothing (check out the T-shirt collection), old suitcases, lamps, furniture, jewelry, toys, and other items that locals have donated.
   Details: *Call for hours. (30 minutes)*

★ LOVELOCK/BATTLE MOUNTAIN

Lovelock, a quiet community 72 miles west of Winnemucca on I-80, has a couple of attractions that are worth a closer look. The most prominent landmark is the Pershing County Courthouse. It is one of the country's few (and Nevada's only) round courthouses still in use. Built in 1921 by prominent Reno architect Frederick De Longchamps, the courthouse makes for a pleasant tour—the courtroom is round and has excellent acoustics. Because of Lovelock's romantic name, couples find the courthouse a perfect place at which to tie the knot.

In Battle Mountain, an even smaller town 53 miles east of Winnemucca, history buffs should stop at the Trail of the 49ers Interpretive Center. The center features exhibits from pioneers who crossed near here. This is the path that the infamous Donner Party took before they got trapped in the Sierra and had to resort to cannibalism to survive. The center offers maps, photographs, and a few artifacts from the numerous people who traversed Nevada and the West on the Emigrant Trail.

Details: *Pershing County Courthouse, Lovelock, free. Trail of the 49ers, 453 N. Second St., Battle Mountain, 775/635-5720, open Mon–Fri 10–5, Sat 10–4, Sun 12–4. Donation. (1 hour)*

FITNESS AND RECREATION

Northeastern Nevada has verdant mountains and valleys and several lakes and rivers, making it one of the best destinations for lovers of the great outdoors. The premiere scene for hikers is the Ruby Mountains, which have several trails that reach small lakes and phenomenal views. At the Ruby Mountain Scenic Area you'll find trailheads leading to a two-mile hike to Island Lake as well as one that begins the 40-mile Ruby Crest Trail. As you climb the Ruby Crest Trail, the vistas of jutting mountains, pine trees, and wildflowers can't be topped. The trail is dotted by several little scenic creeks and lakes, including Dollar Lakes, Lamoille Lake, and Liberty Lake. There's also prime picnicking near the end of NV 227 at The Terraces, which becomes a summer sea of wildflowers. Contact the U.S. Forest Service, 775/752-3357, for detailed maps and more information.

You'll find even more spectacular scenery, hiking, and camping at Angel Lake near Wells, a tiny town 50 miles east of Elko on I-80. This area in the East Humboldt Wilderness Area is some of the state's most scenic—the ranches in the valley are nearly as beautiful as the towering mountains, the tallest of which is 11,306-foot Hole in the Mountain Peak. The drive is worth the extra mileage and effort.

At the south end of the Rubies via NV 228 you'll find Ruby Lake National Wildlife Refuge, 775/779-2237. It has trails for hikers and bird-watchers as well

WINNEMUCCA

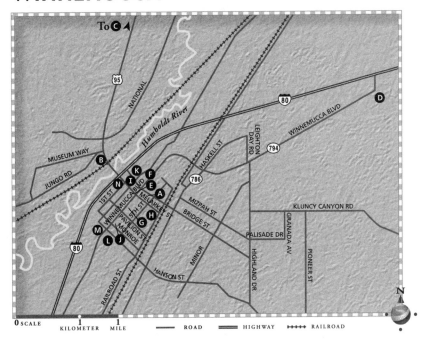

SIGHTS

- **A** Buckaroo Hall of Fame
- **B** Humboldt Museum
- **C** Poke and Peek Second Hand Shop

FOOD

- **D** Ardie's Steak House
- **E** Country Kitchen

FOOD (continued)

- **F** Grandma's House
- **G** Griddle
- **H** Martin Hotel
- **I** Ormachea's Dinner House
- **P** Pete's Coffee Shop at Winners Hotel
- **J** San Fermin
- **K** Winnemucca Hotel

LODGING

- **L** Best Western Gold Country Inn
- **M** Model T
- **N** Scott Shady Court
- **O** Winners Hotel and Casino

Note: Items with the same letter are located in the same area.

---

as camping. The peaceful and beautiful Ruby Marshes, as they're called, also offer excellent fishing.

Bass and trout fishing should be on your itinerary if you plan to visit the South Fork State Recreation Area, 16 miles south of Elko on NV 228, 775/744-2010. The scenic reservoir has a boat ramp as well as wildlife watching.

You'll find one of the state's best small-town ski hills at the Elko Snobowl,

775/738-6125. It boasts a rope tow as well as a chair lift. Skiers will find 650 vertical feet of skiing and one of the best lift-ticket prices—only $6.

Winnemucca locals find recreation in the Santa Rosa Mountains, about 50 miles north via U.S. 95 and NV 290, 775/623-5025. This area near Paradise Valley offers hiking, mountain biking, wildflower viewing, and even snowmobiling at 7,867-foot Hinkey Summit. Rye Patch State Recreation Area, about 50 miles west of Winnemucca, 775/538-7321, is a bit more desolate than the forested areas surrounding Elko but is nonetheless a haven for anglers seeking its trophy trout and bass.

For golfers, Elko has the Ruby View Golf Course (18 holes), 2100 Ruby View Dr., 775/777-7277, and Winnemucca has its Winnemucca Municipal Golf Course (nine holes), 1395 Mizpah St., 775/623-9920.

FOOD

Both Elko and Winnemucca became destinations for Basque sheepherders whose descendants still operate the state's highest concentration of Basque restaurants. There's no menu, you simply choose from a selection of entrées, which generally includes steak, lamb, chicken, and shrimp. You usually get salad, soup, french fries, beans, bread, dessert, and red wine—enough to feed an army of Basques at your table. You should sample a picon punch, a Basque potent potable.

In Elko you'll find the **Biltoki**, 405 Silver St., 775/738-9691, the **Nevada Dinner House**, 351 Silver St., 775/738-8485, the **Star Hotel**, 246 Silver St., 775/738-9925, and the **Toki Ona**, 1550 Idaho St., 775/738-3214. In Winnemucca the Basque restaurants include the **Martin Hotel**, Melarky and Railroad, 775/623-3197, **Ormachea's Dinner House**, 180 Merlarky St., 775/623-3455, the **San Fermin,** 485 W. Winnemucca Blvd., 775/625-2555, and the **Winnemucca Hotel**, 95 S. Bridge St., 775/623-2908.

Elko has several other restaurants. You'll find good buckaroo fare (steaks and other meat) at **D'Orazio's**, 217 Idaho St., 775/738-7088, as well as the **Dinner Station**, 1430 Idaho St., 775/738-8528. For gumbo, fried catfish, and other Cajun-style cuisine try the **Showboat Southern Kitchen**, 1900 Idaho St., 775/738-3936. The **Bull Pen** at Stockmen's Hotel, 340 Commercial St., 775/738-5141, also serves steaks and seafood.

The **Red Lion**, 2065 Idaho St., 775/738-2111 or 800/545-0044, has a combined buffet and coffee shop. The Mexican restaurants are a hit in Elko, too. Try **Zapata's**, 220 Idaho St., 775/753-9880, or **La Fiesta**, 780 Commercial St., 775/738-1622. Coffee drinkers can fuel up at **Cowboy Joe's**, 376 Fifth St., 775/753-5612, or 2140 Idaho St., 775/753-3900.

In Winnemucca you'll find two excellent breakfast places: the **Country**

SIDE TRIP: BORDERTOWNS

This northeastern corner of Nevada has two bordertowns where gambling is the main attraction. **Wendover**, perched right on the Nevada–Utah border 109 miles east of Elko, has a couple of big casinos that lure visitors from across the state line. But another draw is the massive stretch of salt flats that land-speed racers have used for several decades as a place to set speed records in super-speedy automobiles. You'll find several racing events, such as the World of Speed races, during which drivers zip across this 28-square-mile swath of nothingness. Exercise caution if you plan to visit the salt flats—it's frighteningly easy to get stuck in the mud. You can learn more about the area and the racers who've visited here at the Bonneville Speedway Museum, 801/665-7721, on the east (Utah) end of town. Wendover was also the site of the Wendover Air Force Base, established in 1940. The crew of the Enola Gay trained here. As for the casinos, you can't miss friendly Wendover Will welcoming you to the State Line Casino, 775/664-2221 or 800/982-3671, which was the town's first major hotel-casino. This is a bordertown, so expect superior quality rooms and bargain-basement prices. The State Line, as well as the Silver Smith, 775/664-2231 or 800/354-3671, and the Peppermill, 775/664-2255 or 800/648-9660, have large casinos, lounge entertainment, good hotel rooms, buffets, and restaurants.

On the northern end at the Idaho border you'll find the blossoming casino town of **Jackpot**. Other than an attractive golf course, the main reason for Jackpot's existence is the casinos. Cactus Pete's, 775/755-2321, is the largest and offers all of the gambling amenities—blackjack tables, lots of slots, and a buffet. The Horseshu (a sister property of Pete's), 775/755-2321, and the Red Garter, 775/664-2111 or 800/982-2111, offer pleasant places to gamble and relax.

Kitchen, 45 E. Winnemucca Blvd., 775/623-0800, and the **Griddle**, 460 W. Winnemucca Blvd., 775/623-2977. Idaho isn't the only place that grows good potatoes—Winnemucca produces its own major crop of tubers, and you'll find them on the menus of several restaurants. The Winners Hotel, 185 W. Winnemucca Blvd., 775/623-2511, serves them with steak and lobster at

Grandma's House and with coffee shop fare at **Pete's Coffee Shop.**
Ardie's Steak House, 5186 E. Winnemucca Blvd., 775/623-1444, also serves
Winnemucca-label "bakers" with its steaks and seafood.

LODGING

If you have time to wander off the beaten path, I highly recommend a weekend
at the **Old Pioneer Garden Country Inn,** 2805 Unionville Rd., Unionville,
a quiet, verdant little ghost town 50 miles south of Winnemucca via I-80 and NV
400, 775/538-7585. Lew and Mitzi Jones have renovated two old homes where
they have entertained such famous visitors as Sandra Bullock. Guests can relax
amid the rustic furnishings and peaceful surroundings. Mitzi prepares meals using
fruits, vegetables, and herbs from her prolific garden. At $75 per night, the R and
R is worth the dusty drive. You'll also find relaxing, out-of-the-way accommodations at the **Stonehouse Country Inn** in Paradise Valley, 35 miles north of
Winnemucca on U.S. 95 and NV 290, 775/578-3530. The house is at the base
of the Santa Rosa Mountains.

Elko has the **Once Upon a Time B&B,** 537 14th St., 775/738-1200, as well
as several hotels and motels. The largest is the **Red Lion Inn and Casino,** 2065
Idaho St., 775/738-2111 or 800/545-0044, www.redlioncasino.com. The 223-
room hotel has several amenities, including a pool. The **High Desert Inn,** 3015
Idaho St., 775/738-8425 or 888/EXIT303, and the **Ameritel Inn,** 1930 Idaho
St., 775/738-8787 or 800/600-6001, are both upscale and have indoor pools.
The **Shilo Inn,** 2401 Mountain City Hwy., 775/738-5522 or 800/222-2244, is
probably the swankiest in town, offering 70 suites and an indoor pool.

In Winnemucca, you'll find one of Nevada's most intriguing indoor pools at
Scott Shady Court, 400 First St., 775/623-3646, which has a grassy com-
pound and beautiful surroundings with basic rooms. **Winners Hotel and
Casino,** 185 W. Winnemucca Blvd., 775/623-2511 or 800/648-4770,
www.winnerscasino.com, is Winnemucca's largest with 123 rooms. Both the
Model T, 1130 W. Winnemucca Blvd., 775/623-2588, and the **Best Western Gold Country Inn,** 921 W. Winnemucca Blvd., 775/623-6999 or
800/346-5306, offer good rooms in Winnemucca.

CAMPING

The Ruby Mountains are covered with excellent campgrounds. In the Ruby
Mountain Scenic Area off NV 227 you'll find the beautiful **Thomas Creek
Campground,** 775/738-5171, which is open May through September. Off
NV 228 you'll find 25 sites at **South Fork State Recreation Area,**

SIDE TRIP: JARBIDGE

*Without a doubt, the tiny town of Jarbidge, population 30 or so, is Nevada's most remote town. Most travelers without a snowplow or snowmobile wouldn't even dare to try to reach the mountain town during the winter, when snowdrifts cover the two main entrances. But in the summer there's no place finer. The folks are friendly to a fault, and everyone gathers at one of the two saloons in town, the **Red Dog**, which has resident red dogs but no phone, and the **Outdoor Inn**, 775/488-2311. Visitors come here to hike, see abundant wildflowers, hunt, fish in the spectacular Jarbidge River, camp, and totally escape from civilization. Next to the Outdoor Inn is the **Tired Devil Cafe,** which has excellent sandwiches, burgers, soups, and pies. The Outdoor Inn is more or less the nerve center of town—several community events are staged here. Just down the road you'll find the **Tsawhawbitts B&B**, 775/488-2338, a rustic hunting lodge, as well as the **Barn Motel**, 775/488-2311, which, you guessed it, is in a barn. For supplies and lively conversation, drop in on Rey Nystrom at the **Trading Post**, 775/488-2315. It has everything from worms and tackle to soda pop and Oreos (in addition to a few camping supplies).*

775/744-2010, where you also can fish. **Ruby Lake National Wildlife Refuge**, 775/779-2237, has a 35-site campground at the northern tip of the marshes. To the east just south of Wells on NV 231 are two campgrounds: **Angel Creek** and **Angel Lake**. Both are beautiful and are close to superb hiking and views.

Near Winnemucca you can camp in the Santa Rosas at the **Lye Creek Campground**, 55 miles north of town, 775/623-5025, near Hinkey Summit. Reservations are recommended at the attractive campground—it has 13 sites. **Rye Patch State Recreation Area**, 45 miles west of Winnemucca, 775/538-7321, has two campgrounds, one with 44 sites and the other with 25.

NIGHTLIFE

Expect to find plenty of buckle-shining (two-stepping) in these cow-county towns. Stockmen's Casino, 775/738-5141, is one of the best places to hang out during Elko's Cowboy Poetry Gathering in January, when fiddlers, guitar pickers, and other talented musicians are in town and jam sessions become spontaneous. The Red Lion, 775/738-2111, has a casino as well as a show-room where performers appear. The Commercial Hotel, 775/738-3181, is a quirky and intriguing place to gamble—be sure to check out White King, the giant white polar bear that reigns over the casino. The Commercial has a comedy night on Wednesday.

In Winnemucca you'll find live music and dancing at the Winners Hotel, 775/623-2511.

SPECIAL EVENTS

In Elko, Basque families come together during the National Basque Festival, usu-ally held near the Fourth of July. These colorful celebrations include dancing, lots of food, and games of strength and endurance. You can't help but hear the con-tests to find out who's got the best *irrintzi*, a loud yell that borders on a con-trolled scream. You'll also find a sheepherders' bread auction and a Catholic mass during the event. In the winter, fans of the buckaroo way should check out the Cowboy Poetry Gathering. Cowboy poets come to recite heartfelt poems about ornery cattle, the best cowdog ever, and lonely nights on the range. The talent is truly topnotch.

In Winnemucca you'll be inspired to become a photographer at the high-caliber photography seminar in March called Shooting the West. The event includes seminars by National Geographic photographers and other shutter-bugs who have their eyes on ranch life, cowboying, and other aspects of the West. Salt Lake City, Utah, photographer Richard Menzies is the event's hilarious host—this event is worth the trip even if you've never shot with any-thing but a Polaroid.

12
BOOMTOWNS: AUSTIN AND EUREKA

The two small outposts of Austin and Eureka are welcome sights for travelers crossing U.S. 50, a highway that *Life* magazine cheekily labeled America's Loneliest Road. But being lonely isn't a curse out here; rather, it's a blessing. The communities revel in the solitude—and even capitalize on it. Besides, it's the beauty, isolation, and independent spirit of these bright beacons amid the sagebrush and mountains that draw visitors to the communities on this road less traveled.

Like many towns across Nevada, Austin and Eureka have deep roots in mining—silver was discovered in 1862 in Austin and in 1864 in Eureka. And both were stops on the Pony Express, the man-and-horse method of delivering mail in the Old West.

In Austin, you can still see the remnants of its mining-boom days in the clapboard buildings and old churches. Landmarks such as Stokes Castle and the Gridley Store entice visitors into exploring the town's colorful history and legends. Austin is isolated—it's 170 miles to Reno, the closest major city—so residents are prone to being independent sorts. But visitors will find a welcoming spirit here as they explore the rock shops, relax in the local cafés, and ride bikes amid the surrounding mountains.

Eureka has been experiencing a mining boom in recent years, and this has helped fund the rescue of several of the town's historic buildings. Travelers lured here discover history and small-town charms.

A PERFECT DAY IN AUSTIN AND EUREKA

The day should begin in Austin with a morning mountain-bike ride on the Castle Loop (rentals and maps are available at T-Rix Mountain Bikes), an easy, 4.5-mile loop that winds past Stokes Castle. The crisp morning air is ripe with the smell of juniper and the sounds of chirping birds.

After a quick tour of the turquoise shops it's time to get on the road to Eureka, where you'll be ready for a salami sandwich at Luigi's Deli. Follow your meal with a walking tour of Eureka that will take you past historical buildings and quaint antique shops.

Early afternoon is the best time to stroll into the Jackson House for a glass of wine before dinner. If you time your visit just right, you can catch a performance by cowboy singer Ian Tyson on the venerable stage of the Eureka Opera House.

SIGHTSEEING HIGHLIGHTS: AUSTIN

★★★ TYRANNOSAURUS RIX MOUNTAIN BIKE AND SPECIALTIES
Austin, 775/964-1212

Oddly juxtaposed against the backdrop of historic buildings is the bright blue T-Rix mountain-bike shop. The rolling hills and panoramic vistas in the area inspired young entrepreneur Rick Crawford to develop trails and maps. Crawford opened the shop in 1996 and today offers mountain bikes as well as equipment, maps, T-shirts, tourist information, and frozen cappuccino.

Details: Located on the east end of town. Closed during winter. In summer open daily 10–6. Free. (30 minutes)

★★ AUSTIN WALKING TOUR
775/964-2200

Visitors should pick up a copy of the "Austin Walking Tour Guide" at the chamber of commerce or other businesses. The guide points out places of interest, such as the early home of Emma Nevada, the famous nineteenth-century opera star who was the daughter of an Austin doctor. The map also points out Nevada's oldest bank building (now the Austin library) as well as the Masonic-Odd Fellows Hall, built in 1867.

Details: Chamber office located inside the Lander County Courthouse. Free. (1 hour)

AUSTIN

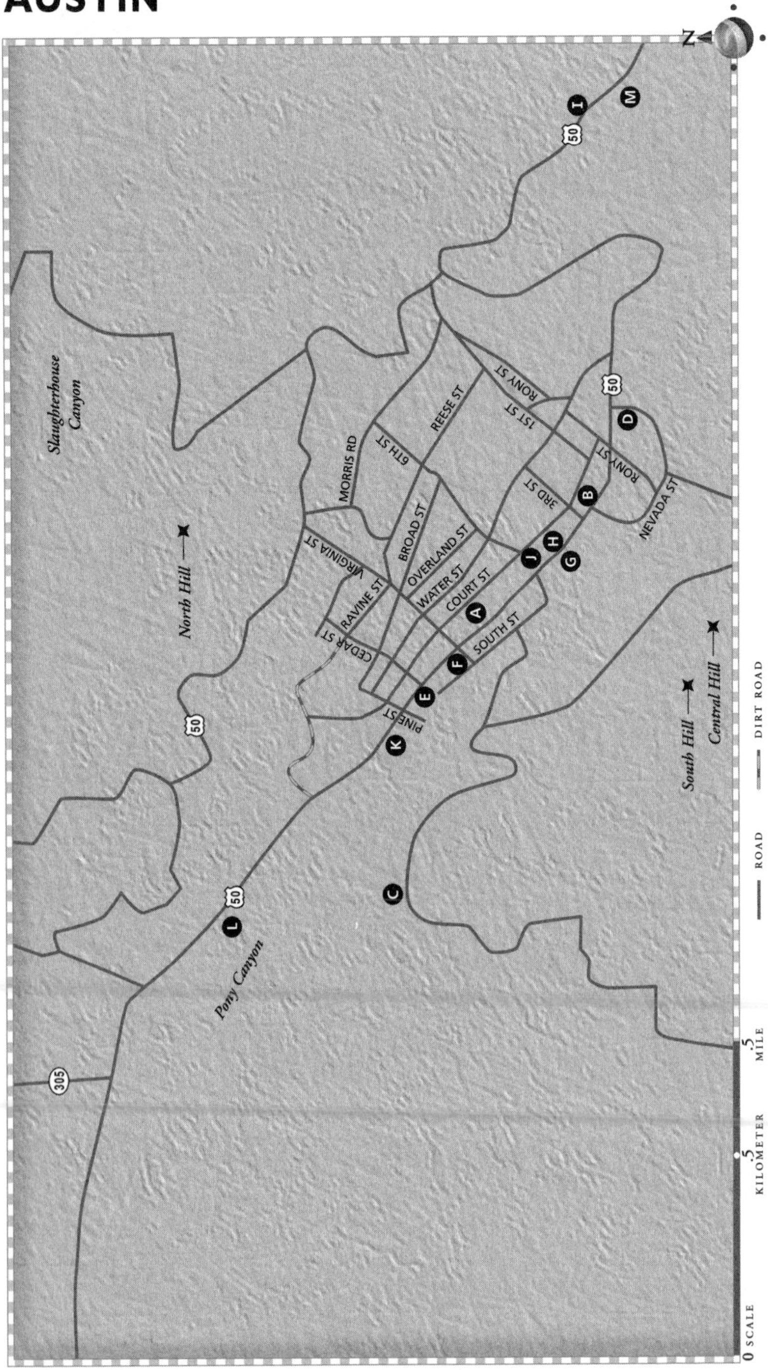

Slaughterhouse Canyon

North Hill →

Pony Canyon

South Hill →

Central Hill →

MORRIS RD

RESE ST

RONY ST

1ST ST

6TH ST

3RD ST

RONY ST

NEVADA ST

BROAD ST

OVERLAND ST

WATER ST

COURT ST

SOUTH ST

VIRGINIA ST

RAVINE ST

CEDAR ST

PINE ST

N

ROAD
DIRT ROAD

0 SCALE

5
KILOMETER

5
MILE

★★ STOKES CASTLE
Austin, 775/964-2200

A skeletal reminder of Austin's wealthy mining days, the Stokes Castle is a good place to have a picnic while you absorb some history and soak up views of the Reese River Valley. Perched atop a hill a half-mile off U.S. 50, the native-granite castle was built in 1897 by mining and railroad magnate Anson Phelps Stokes as the family's summer home. The three-story, skinny castle, made to resemble a tower near Rome, is now surrounded by a chain-link fence and watched over mostly by buzzards and jackrabbits.

Details: *On the west end of town off U.S. 50, turn on Castle Road and follow the dirt road about a half-mile. Free. (30 minutes)*

★ GRIDLEY STORE
Austin, 775/964-2200

Austin certainly has its share of offbeat historical markers. The Gridley Store, built in 1863, earned its notoriety through a famous sack of flour. The story began in 1864 when store owner Reuel C. Gridley lost an election bet. His penance was to carry a 50-pound sack of flour through Austin. The sack was covered with ribbons and banners, and Gridley was made to march through town to the tune of "John Brown's Body." In the spirit of the moment, Gridley decided to auction off the sack of flour to help raise money for the Sanitary Fund, the forerunner of the Red Cross, which was helping victims of the Civil War. The generous spirit caught on, and soon the sack of flour was auctioned several times during the day. The lowly sack of flour earned more than $6,000. The sack eventually toured the country, raising $275,000. In honor of the famous fund-raiser, folks in Austin hold

---

SIGHTS
- Ⓐ Austin Walking Tour
- Ⓑ Gridley Store
- Ⓐ Lander County Courthouse
- Ⓒ Stokes Castle
- Ⓓ Tyrannosaurus Rix Mountain Bike and Specialities

FOOD
- Ⓔ International Cafe
- Ⓕ Mary's Owl Club
- Ⓖ Toiyabe Drive-In

LODGING
- Ⓗ Lincoln Motel
- Ⓘ Mountain Motel

LODGING (continued)
- Ⓙ Pony Canyon Motel
- Ⓚ Pony Express House

CAMPING
- Ⓛ Austin RV Park and Baptist Church
- Ⓜ Bob Scott Summit Campground

Note: Items with the same letter are located in the same area.

Gridley Days and flour-sack races. Folks can still peek into the little stone store on Main Street where the famous sack of flour originated.

Details: *At the east end of town on U.S. 50. (30 minutes)*

★ LANDER COUNTY COURTHOUSE
Court St., Austin, 775/964-2447

Austin was the county seat from 1863 to 1979 (when it was moved to Battle Mountain), but the courthouse still holds county offices as well as the chamber of commerce. Built in 1869, the small courthouse is simple by design but oozes with history. Inside you can see old safes that are still in use as well as the old jail cells, used as storage areas. Tours of the jail are available by request.

Details: *Free. (30 minutes)*

SIGHTSEEING HIGHLIGHTS: EUREKA

★★★★ EUREKA OPERA HOUSE
U.S. 50, Eureka, 775/237-6006

The Eureka Opera House, built in 1880 and restored in 1993, strikes a prominent pose downtown. Visitors can stroll in and see the unusual horseshoe-shaped balcony as well as the stage curtain, painstakingly restored to its original design. In 1915, the opera house became the Eureka Theatre where silent movies and later "talkies" entertained Eurekans. Today, the Eureka Opera House is used as a convention hall, and performers ranging from cowboy poets and comedians to African dance groups and puppeteers appear on the venerable stage.

Details: *Mon–Fri 8–5; tours by appointment. (30 minutes–1 hour)*

★★★ DOWNTOWN EUREKA WALKING TOUR
775/237-5484

Eureka's buildings and houses are filled with history, and one of the best ways to absorb some of it is to take the self-guided walking tour of town. You can pick up the booklet at the Eureka Opera House and explore the 47 historical buildings, such as the Eureka County Courthouse. Some of the buildings have been restored to peak form while others appear on the verge of collapse. Visitors will see evidence of the town's mining-boom days in former saloons, schools, shops, and churches, many of which are still standing and in use. The old Wells

Fargo Bank, the Masonic Building, the Tannehill Log Cabin, and Mary Isles-Wattles's home all have interesting tales to reveal. Downtown you can't miss Crew Car No. 29, the only piece of rolling stock in Eureka County from the Eureka and Palisade Railroad (a narrow gauge line that carried ore to the nearby town of Palisade in the late 1800s).
Details: Free. (1 hour)

★★★ EUREKA SENTINEL MUSEUM
Monroe St., 775/237-5010
Newspaper buffs will be able to read all about the history of the town's newspaper, published in the building from 1870–1960. The walls of the museum are plastered with old playbills, public notices, and clippings that were printed on the newspaper's flat-bed cylinder press. Scattered about the desks and tables are ink bottles, typewriters, and lead type, and visitors can almost imagine the reporters and pressman scurrying about to get the paper out on time. The three-room museum also has exhibits dedicated to mining as well as the town's fire department.
Details: Take Ruby Hill Avenue south to Monroe. Apr–Oct daily 10–5, Nov–Mar Tue–Sat 10–5. Donation. (1 hour)

★★ RAINE'S MARKET
U.S. 50, Eureka, 775/237-5296
Shoppers may feel as though they're being watched while they buy milk, bread, and other sundries—Raine's is one of the few grocery stores in the world that is also a museum of taxidermy. The heads of deer and other animals peer down on shoppers as they stroll down the aisles in this historic building. This place survived a devastating fire in 1879. Formerly F. J. Schneider's Drugstore, the store has been a restaurant, shoe store, and assay office. The market has creaky wood floors and pressed-tin ceilings.
Details: Open Mon–Sat 9–7, Sun 9–6. Free. (30 minutes)

FITNESS AND RECREATION
Mountain biking is taking off in Austin. Visitors can rent bikes at T-Rix, pick up the "Austin-Toiyabe Mountain Bike Trail Guide," and tackle one of the six designated trails. The trails range from easy 4.5-mile loops to lung-splitting 27.5-mile treks that traverse canyons and peaks. T-Rix sponsors races on the trails—check with bike-shop owner Rick Crawford for details.

EUREKA

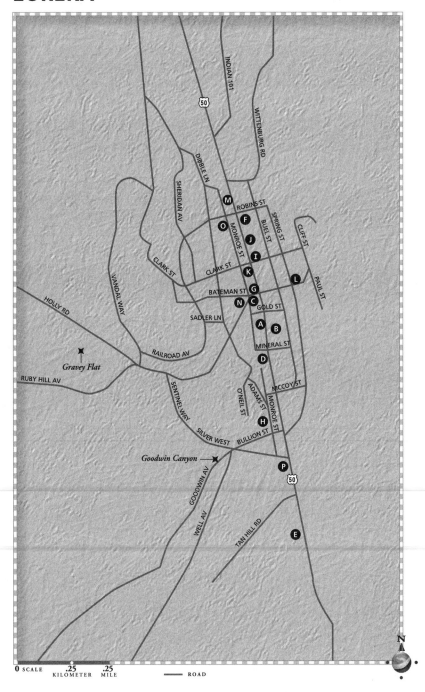

Gravey Flat

Goodwin Canyon

Streets and roads (labeled on map):
INDIAN 101
50
WITTENBURG RD
DIBBLE LN
SHERIDAN AV
ROBINS ST
SPRING ST
BUEL ST
CLIFF ST
MONROE ST
CLARK ST
CLARK ST
PAUL ST
BATEMAN ST
GOLD ST
SADLER LN
VANDAL WAY
HOLLY RD
RAILROAD AV
MINERAL ST
RUBY HILL AV
McCOY ST
ADAMS ST
O'NEIL ST
MONROE ST
SENTINEL WAY
SILVER WEST
BULLION ST
GOODWIN AV
WELL AV
TAN HILL RD
50

Markers: M, F, O, J, I, K, L, G, C, N, A, B, D, H, P, E

0 SCALE .25 KILOMETER .25 MILE ——— ROAD

N

Hikers will find numerous trails in the Austin area, not the least of which is the Toiyabe Crest National Recreation Trail, 775/964-2671. The 65-mile trail winds through the Toiyabes, the mighty piñon-covered mountain range that dominates the geography of central Nevada.

Sportsmen have begun to discover Kingston Canyon, 28 miles south of Austin on NV 376. Here you'll find camping, fishing, hunting, and the Kingston Creek Lodge, which also has a restaurant. There are several scattered home sites in the area, occupied mostly by folks who like isolation and peaceful, scenic surroundings.

The Hickison Petroglyph Recreation Site, 24 miles east of Austin on U.S. 50, is overseen by the Bureau of Land Management, 775/635-4000, and is an excellent place to see early Native American rock art. The site features signs of prehistoric occupation and hunting that date to 10,000 B.C. Visitors can pick up the walking-tour guide. It points out the petroglyphs as well as vegetation and scenic overlooks along the short looped trail.

In Eureka, you can take aim at the targets at the Perdiz Sport Shooting Complex, two miles south of town in Windfall Canyon, 775/237-7027 or 775/237-5484. The sport shooting course has 10 stations with five rounds that simulate a variety of different game. You'll also find trap and skeet shooting as well as several events and competitions.

FOOD

In Austin, the **Toiyabe Drive-In**, 27 Main St., 775/964-2220, is one of the best places for a hot meal. You'll find anything from pancakes, burritos, and sandwiches to ice-cream cones and shakes. The service is friendly, and the dining room has signs such as "Free beer tomorrow" posted on the walls. The **International Cafe** on Main Street, 775/964-9905, was built in 1859–60 and is the

SIGHTS
- Ⓐ Eureka Opera House
- Ⓑ Eureka Walking Tour
- Ⓒ Eureka Sentinel Museum
- Ⓓ Raine's Market

FOOD
- Ⓔ Busy Bee Drive-In
- Ⓕ Eureka Cafe
- Ⓖ Jackson House

FOOD (continued)
- Ⓗ Luigi's Deli
- Ⓘ Owl Club and Steak House

LODGING
- Ⓙ Best Western Eureka Inn
- Ⓚ Colonnade Hotel
- Ⓖ Jackson House Bed and Breakfast

LODGING (continued)
- Ⓛ Parsonage House
- Ⓜ Ruby Hill Motel
- Ⓝ Sundown Lodge

CAMPING
- Ⓞ PITA RV and Rentals
- Ⓟ Silver Sky Lodge RV Park

Note: Items with the same letter are located in the same area.

oldest hotel in Nevada—although there are no rooms here. Portions of the building and bar were transported from Virginia City to make room for a larger International Hotel on the Comstock. Today you'll find a saloon and restaurant—burgers are your best bet here. **Mary's Owl Club**, 735 Main St., 775/964-2627, is a rustic bar that serves the only pizza in Austin.

In Eureka, the hottest spot in town is the **Jackson House**, 11 S. Main St., 775/237-5577, a gorgeously renovated restaurant with gourmet food and an attractive bar. The prices are higher than you usually find in rural Nevada, but the food is worth it. The fare includes such delectable dishes as the Crystal Parlor, tiger shrimp sautéed with mushrooms, pine nuts, and spinach served over angel hair pasta ($13.50); the Ruby, homemade manicotti ($9.95); and the Opera House, veal scaloppine marsala ($11.50). The **Owl Club and Steak House**, 61 N. Main St., 775/237-5280, is another excellent dining option, especially if you're hankering for steak or ribs. For a quick bite, **Luigi's Deli** on the corner of Monroe and Bullion, 775/237-5477, offers exceptional sandwiches. The **Busy Bee Drive-In**, 509 S. Main St., 775/237-5356, has some of Highway 50's tastiest burgers and shakes. The **Eureka Cafe**, 90 N. Main St., 775/237-7165, offers authentic Chinese cuisine.

LODGING

The **Lincoln Motel**, 28 S. Main St., 775/964-2698, the **Mountain Motel**, on U.S. 50, 775/964-2471, and the **Pony Canyon Motel**, on U.S. 50, 775/964-2605, are older and small but well-maintained. The **Pony Express House**, 115 N.W. Main St., 775/964-2306, is a bed-and-make-your-own-breakfast where guests rent the entire house. Rates are $35 if you use one room or $70 if you use both. The historic house, built on the Pony Express route, is furnished with old saddles and other Pony Express antiques. It's rustic—most people either love its charms or don't care for it. I'd suggest asking for a preview to see if it meets your needs.

In Eureka you'll find the new **Best Western Eureka Inn**, 251 N. Main St., 775/237-5247, which has a pool and Jacuzzi, exercise rooms, and spacious, modern rooms. For a more authentic mining-town experience, the **Parsonage House**, on Spring and Bateman, 775/237-5756, is a bed-and-breakfast fashioned out of an 1886 cottage making it a romantic and fascinating place. The one-bedroom home has a kitchen as well as a huge bathtub, antique furnishings, and a wine cellar for couples seeking libations for a celebration. Proprietors Carol and Frank Bleuss are longtime residents of Eureka who carved their home out of the church next door. They both poured their own sweat into restoring the church and parsonage house—to say Frank is a talented woodworker would be an understatement. The newest bed-and-breakfast offering is the **Jackson House Bed and Breakfast**, 10200 Main St., 775/237-5577. The romantic rooms are fabulously furnished in antiques (some with clawfoot bathtubs). Rates range from $30–$57. The **Colonnade Hotel**, Clark and Monroe Sts., 775/237-9988, **Ruby Hill Motel**, U.S. 50, 775/237-5339, and **Sundown Lodge**, Main St., 775/237-5334, also offer good accommodations at reasonable prices ($21–$31).

CAMPING

Austin is a great place for campers. One of the most scenic and popular spots is **Bob Scott Summit Campground** six miles east of town. There's plenty of space between the campsites, which overlook the juniper-covered hillsides. Camping here is free since there's no potable water, but you will find barbecue pits, picnic tables, and restrooms. In town, RVers can rest easy at the **Austin RV Park and Baptist Church**, 1.5 miles east of state road 305 on U.S. 50, 775/964-1011. There's no direct affiliation—the RV park is leased out from the church—but the RV office is also used as the Sunday school room. The campground has 26 sites, and the cost is $15 for RVers.

Eureka has a couple of RV parks, including the **Silver Sky Lodge RV Park**, 606 Commercial, 775/237-5034, which charges $15 per night, and **PITA RV and Rentals**, Monroe St., 775/237-5281, which charges $10.

AUSTIN'S CHURCHES

Austin is a town of steeples—the churches here are some of the state's most striking and historically significant. San Augustine's Catholic Church, just north of Main Street, opened its doors on Christmas Eve 1866 and is the state's oldest Catholic church. Worshipers were charged admission that night to help pay for a roof. The funds needed to build St. George's Episcopal Church were raised during a single passing of the collection plate on Easter Sunday in 1877, and the church was built on Main Street the following year. The Methodist Church, on Court Street, constructed in 1866, employed equally unorthodox fund-raising methods. When the church received several sizable donations of mining stock, the minister established the Methodist Mining Company and sold the stocks to investors back East. He raised enough to build a quaint but handsome church that today serves as town hall.

13
ELY

Copper mining gave birth to Ely, settled in late 1800s, and continued to help the small town grow over the next 100 years. The Nevada Northern Railway was established in East Ely in the early 1900s to deliver ore from the Ruth copper pit west of town to the smelter in McGill, 12 miles northeast of town. Unlike many of Nevada's boom-and-bust towns built by gold, Ely's copper mines sustained the town for several years, and new attractions, such as the revived Nevada Northern Railway and Great Basin National Park, helped it prosper.

Ely is an excellent base camp for visitors en route to some of Nevada's most intriguing attractions and spectacular scenic wonders. Ely has small-town charm—the townsfolk are friendly, and there's an old-fashioned soda fountain and drugstore downtown. But it also has lots to offer as a haven for history buffs, hikers, hunters, and fishermen. There are a number of good hotels and restaurants. You can even buy a cappuccino here—a claim not every small town in Nevada can make.

The Nevada Northern Railway forms a backbone through town and parallels Aultman Street, Ely's main drag. The city itself has a classic downtown dotted with historic buildings. Outside the city limits, Ely is sandwiched by mountain ranges on both sides. To the east, snowcapped Wheeler Peak stands as a reminder that the beauty of the great outdoors is this region's main attraction.

A PERFECT DAY IN ELY

If you had only one day to spend in Ely, you would have to cram in a visit to the area's two biggest attractions, Great Basin National Park and the Nevada Northern Railway Museum. You can begin the day early with a drive to the park and time it to catch a tour of Lehman Caves (advance tickets are available in summer). You should pause for a sandwich and a slice of homemade pie at the snack bar at the park visitors center. Then it's time to head back to Ely for a visit to the Nevada Northern Railway Museum. Hitch a ride on one of the sunset trains, which offer restful tours with wine and cheese. If you're not too tired you can play the penny slots at the historic Hotel Nevada and grab a graveyard special at the coffee shop.

SIGHTSEEING HIGHLIGHTS

★★★★ GREAT BASIN NATIONAL PARK
775/234-7331, www.great.basin.national-park.com

Bring your hiking boots. Great Basin National Park, which was designated in 1986 and is the nation's youngest park, has been blessed by spectacular scenery that is unspoiled and often very unpopulated. The park has trails galore, camping, fishing, guided spelunking, and great views. Nature lovers can choose from nine trails that range from an easy loop around the visitors center to a vigorous climb to the tallest peak in the park. The three-mile Bristlecone Pine-Glacier Trail passes a series of small lakes enroute to the bristlecone forest, containing some of the earth's oldest living things. The trail continues to the Wheeler Peak Cirque, Nevada's only glacier. The five-mile trail to the top of 13,063-foot Wheeler Peak requires a bit more effort, but hikers are rewarded with spectacular views. Spelunkers will enjoy the guided tours of Lehman Caves, a series of caverns and formations made of sculpted limestone.

Details: *74 miles east of Ely on U.S. 50. Cave tours $4 adults, $3 ages 6–15. (4 hours minimum)*

★★★★ NEVADA NORTHERN RAILWAY MUSEUM
1100 Avenue A, Ely, 775/289-2085

Train fever is rampant in Ely, and the only cure is a ride on one of the locomotives at the East Ely depot. In 1983, the Nevada Northern made its final run and appeared doomed to the scrap heap. But citizens formed the White Pine Historical Railroad Foundation to operate a railroad museum, and Kennecott, which owned the railroad, donated

ELY

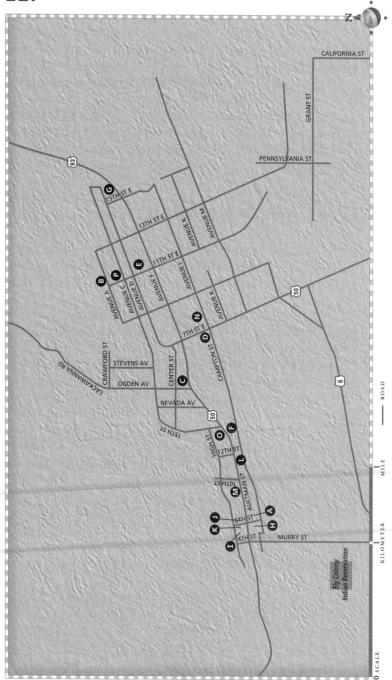

more than 32 miles of track, the roundhouse and railroad shops, and the rolling stock. The railway features a steam-powered excursion, the Ghost Train of Old Ely, a passenger train pulled either by No. 40, a 1910 Baldwin Steamer, or a 1909 American Locomotive. The Ghost Train ride is a 14-mile, round-trip excursion past the ghost town of Lane City and up to Robinson Canyon. Another route called the Hiliner is a 22-mile round-trip trek that follows the rail line built in 1908 to haul ore to the smelter at McGill. The Hiliner, pulled by a diesel engine, traverses scenic Steptoe Valley. The railway offers two additional diesel train rides, Ely after Dark, an evening train ride on the Keystone Route with wine and candlelight, and Sunset at Steptoe during which you can watch the sun go down in Steptoe Valley. The museum is worth a look, too, and you can explore the railroad yards on your own or on guided tours that take visitors to the blacksmith shops and depot offices. Train buffs can become engineers for a day by taking the museum's locomotive student engineer program. The museum also hosts a number of special events throughout the year, including the Christmas train (expect a visit from Santa Claus) and a Fourth of July fireworks train and barbecue.

Details: *Open May–Sept. Diesel train $12 adults, $10 seniors and ages 12–18, and $6 ages 5–11. Steam train $16, $14, and $8. Guided museum tours (45 minutes) twice daily except Mon; $2.50 adults, free for children under 10. Train rentals for the student engineer program $250 for diesel, $500 for steam. (half–full day)*

SIGHTS

Ⓐ Bristlecone Visitor Center
Ⓑ Nevada Northern Railway Museum
Ⓒ White Pine Public Museum

FOOD

Ⓓ Evah's Restaurant, Copper Queen
Ⓔ Flower Basket Espresso Depot

FOOD (continued)

Ⓕ Good Friends Chinese
Ⓖ Holiday Inn's Prospector Casino
Ⓗ Hotel Nevada
Ⓘ Jailhouse Cellblock
Ⓙ La Fiesta
Ⓚ Orient Express
Ⓛ Steptoe Drug

LODGING

Ⓛ Best Western–Main Motel

LODGING (continued)

Ⓜ Best Western Park-Vue Motel
Ⓝ Bristlecone Motel
Ⓞ El Rancho Motel
Ⓖ Holiday Inn and Prospector Casino
Ⓗ Hotel Nevada
Ⓘ Jailhouse Motel
Ⓓ Ramada Inn-Copper Queen
Ⓟ Steptoe Valley Inn

Note: Items with the same letter are located in the same area.

★★★ WHITE PINE PUBLIC MUSEUM
2000 Aultman St., Ely, 775/289-4710
This interesting little museum is packed with relics of early Ely, such as an antique bicycle, an old shoe that still contains the foot bones of some poor hapless soul, and, of course, photographs, railroad cars, and other items from the Nevada Northern Railway. History buffs can study the more than 300 mineral samples, the huge Hesselgesser doll collection, and the historic map with corresponding photos. The train depot that once greeted the Nevada Northern Railway in the nearby town of Cherry Creek was moved to Ely and is now preserved at the museum.
Details: Open Mon–Fri 9–4, Sat–Sun 10–4. Donation. (2 hours)

★★ BRISTLECONE VISITOR CENTER
150 Sixth St., Ely, 775/289-3720
Aside from brochures and maps to the area, the most unusual attraction at the Bristlecone Visitor Center is the slab from Prometheus, the 4,950-year-old bristlecone tree that was believed to have been the oldest living thing on earth. How much longer it would have lived is uncertain—sadly, the U.S. Forest Service cut down Prometheus in 1964 to study it and determine its age. Nevertheless, the slab is a fascinating slice of natural history and provides a lesson for future tree scientists.
Details: Mon–Fri 8–5, Sat 9–1. Free. (1 hour)

★★ ELY ELK VIEWING AREA
U.S. 93
Wildlife watchers should be sure to pack the binoculars for the drive out to the Ely Elk Viewing Area. Early morning and dusk are the best times to spy on herds of Rocky Mountain Elk as they move from their summer grazing area high in the Schell Creek Range to the sagebrush and grasslands near U.S. 93 in the fall. The peak time for elk viewing is winter.
Details: Six miles south of Ely on U.S. 93. Free. (1–2 hours)

★★ RUTH COPPER PIT OVERLOOK
This is one impressive hole in the ground. The massive Liberty Pit is more than a mile long and half a mile wide. The view and the perspective are amazing—earth movers and trucks with tires the size of small elephants look like Tonka trucks in a sandbox. History runs deep at this pit, too. The copper mine and the tiny town nearby were named by Daniel C. McDonald. He staked the claim in honor of his

WARD CHARCOAL OVENS

daughter Ruth, who was born in 1896. The overlook has a map of the pits and towns that occupied the area as well as giant tires for climbing on and big ore samples to examine. BHP, the copper company that now owns the mine, offers tours of its operations.

Details: *Seven miles west of Ely off U.S. 50. Tours Sat at 10. Call BHP, 775/289-7000, for tour information. (1 hour)*

★★ WARD CHARCOAL OVENS STATE HISTORIC SITE
775/728-4467

These giant beehive-shaped ovens are an odd sight but a good place for a picnic. The ovens are the only remains of the Ward Mining District. The ovens were constructed in 1876 by a master mason to produce charcoal for a nearby smelter. Most of the town burned in 1883, but the 30-foot-tall kilns are a photogenic reminder of another era.

Details: *Seven miles south of Ely via U.S. 50/6/93, then 11 miles southwest on Cave Valley Road. Free. (1–2 hours)*

★ GARNET HILL

The scenery here often is more rewarding than the garnet hunting—the hills have been picked pretty clean of the little red gems. But the drive up Garnet Hill is a local tradition and a popular spot for RV campers. The Bureau of Land Management, which oversees the area, detonates small explosives on the hill to bring the gems to the surface.

Details: *Turnoff seven miles west of Ely; hill is three miles up a dirt road. Free. (1–2 hours)*

FITNESS AND RECREATION

The scene at Cave Lake State Park, 12 miles east of Ely, 775/728-4467, is serene—canoeists silently glide across the olive-green lake where fish jump and squirrels dart and chatter on the shore. For fishermen, the elusive brown trout are the prized catch. The state's biggest brown was caught in Cave Lake and weighed a whopping 27 pounds, five ounces. The Nevada Division of Wildlife stocks this 32-acre reservoir with other fish, too, including German brown and rainbow trout. The lake and surrounding area are excellent for wildlife watchers who might see deer, elk, coyotes, badgers, snakes, and a variety of birds. Hikers and mountain bikers can explore the five-mile interpretive trail near the lake campground or the three-mile trail that meanders near Steptoe Creek.

Ward Mountain Recreation Area, six miles southwest of Ely, 775/289-3031, is another picturesque mountainous area managed by both the U.S. Forest Service and the Bureau of Land Management. Part of Humboldt National Forest, Ward Mountain offers scenic picnicking and numerous trails for hiking, horseback riding, and cross-country skiing.

Another largely undiscovered little gem of a lake in northeastern Nevada is Illipah Reservoir, 37 miles east of Ely on U.S. 50, which is known primarily for its trout. It's rather stark by comparison to Cave Lake—there are few shade trees—but it is peaceful and unpopulated.

Golfers can tee off at the White Pine County Golf Course, 775/289-4095, established in 1957, where an additional nine holes were added in the summer of 1998.

For dudes and dudettes, Bunk Out West offers ranch-style vacations at its Quarter Circle Five Ranch near the remote town of Lund, 32 miles south of Ely, 888/837-2382. Visitors can opt for a stay at the bunkhouse and participate in such activities as making pioneer crafts, spending evenings around the campfire, swimming in the hot springs, and saddling up for one of the two- or five-day cattle drives.

FOOD

Ely's casinos offer a number of decent coffee shops and steak houses, but the **Jailhouse Cellblock**, Fifth and Aultman Sts., 775/289-3033, next door to the

ELY REGION

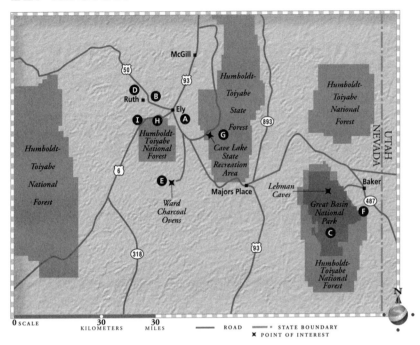

SIGHTS

- **A** Ely Elk Viewing Area
- **B** Garnet Hill
- **C** Great Basin National Park
- **D** Ruth Copper Pit Overlook
- **E** Ward Charcoal Ovens State Historic Site

FOOD

- **E** Lehman Caves Cafe
- **F** Outlaw Bar and Restaurant

LODGING

- **G** Hidden Canyon Guest Ranch-Great Basin
- **G** Silver Jack

CAMPING

- **G** Cave Lake State Park
- **C** Great Basin National Park
- **H** Humboldt National Forest
- **I** Ward Mountain Campground

Note: Items with the same letter are located in the same area.

Jailhouse casino and motel, steals the honor as most unique. Diners become jail-birds as they enjoy their steaks and ribs inside small jail cells. The result is an inti-mate, if not surreal, ambiance, and the Old West feel will have you asking for a deputy rather than a waitress when you need a coffee refill.

Another standout is **La Fiesta**, 612 Aultman St., 775/289-4112, inside

Collins Court across from the Hotel Nevada. They serve heaping portions of Mexican dishes such as enchiladas, tacos, and rellenos. The chips are served warm and the salsa is fresh.

If you're hankering for a frothy coffee beverage, the **Flower Basket Espresso Depot**, 445 E. 11th St. (located near the train depot), 775/289-2828, serves cappuccinos and all the coffee drinks. You can pick up a latte and a flowering begonia on the same trip.

Steptoe Drug, 504 Aultman St., 775/289-2671, has a soda fountain where you can get a Coca-Cola made the old-fashioned way. While sipping the syrupy concoction, you can sit at the counter or browse the gifts. The shop also serves sandwiches.

As for casinos, the **Copper Queen** has Evah's Restaurant, 701 Ave. I, 775/289-4884, and the **Hotel Nevada**, 501 Aultman St., 775/289-6665, has a coffee shop, both of which are suitable for prime rib, hamburgers, and pancakes. The **Holiday Inn's Prospector Casino**, 1501 Ave. F, 775/289-8900, also has a restaurant. The **Orient Express**, 562 Aultman St., 775/289-3313, and **Good Friends Chinese**, 1455 Aultman St., 775/289-4888, both serve respectable Chinese cuisine.

In Baker, the **Outlaw Bar and Restaurant**, five miles east of Great Basin National Park at Baker Street and Elko Avenue, 775/234-7302, is worth a stop—the steaks are good, the conversation is lively, and the clientele ranges from ranchers to hikers. At Great Basin National Park itself, **Lehman Caves Cafe**, inside the gift shop, 775/234-7221, has surprisingly good sandwiches and snacks—try a slice of fresh pie a la mode before your tour of the caves.

LODGING

For train lovers the best place to bed down for the night is the **Steptoe Valley Inn**, 220 E. 11th St., 775/289-8687, just a stone's throw from the train depot. The two-story house, which once housed a grocery store and meat market and had rooms upstairs for railroad workers, today has five rooms with private baths and verandas as well as a dining room, library, and rose garden. Each room is named for a prominent Ely citizen—rates range from $68 to $90 depending on the room. (The B&B is open from June through September.)

The grand old **Hotel Nevada**, 501 Aultman St., 775/289-6665 or 888/406-3055, was built in the 1920s and was recently restored. The charm of its age is still there—old-fashioned faucets in the rooms and a squeaky elevator are a reminder of its heyday when it hosted such entertainers as Wayne Newton and Vikki Carr. No room is the same—each has its own furniture style and decor. The **Ramada Inn-Copper Queen**, 701 Ave. I, 775/289-4884 or

SIDE TRIP: McGILL

McGill, 12 miles northeast of Ely, was established as a copper company town to house workers at McGill's smelter. The mines eventually shut down, but a few hardy residents make their home in this quiet bedroom community. Visitors who pause here will find friendly folks and worthwhile attractions. The best is the **McGill pool,** *an old-fashioned community swimming hole that was built by Kennecott copper company several decades ago. The pool, fed by a hot spring, has sandy beaches, shade trees, a high dive, volleyball courts, barbecue grills, lap swimming, and even water-aerobics classes. A swim will cost you $1.25 (75 cents for kids 14 and under), and the pool is open in the summer from 11 to 8.*

After you've washed off the road grime, you can head for a watering hole of a different sort—the **McGill Club.** *This saloon has a lot of character—and characters—and on some weekends you might stumble upon a jam session comprised of local musicians. At the entrance, the wall is covered with photographs of 145 McGill residents who served in World War II.*

Across the street, the **McGill Drug Store** *has been frozen in time. When it closed in the 1960s, all the shelves and merchandise were left intact. The drug store was reopened as a museum where visitors can peruse the 1950s appliances and items that were for sale, including Dippity-Do and Milk of Magnesia. The museum also has a functioning soda fountain where you can order a Coke from a soda jerk.*

800/851-9526, has one of Nevada's most unique features amid the slot machines in the casino—a swimming pool. Guests can go straight from their rooms, stop to empty their pockets at the slots, and take a dip in the pool—all in the same trip.

Also downtown, the **Jailhouse Motel**, 211 Fifth St., 775/289-3033 or 800/541-5430, has an exercise room and hot tub.

The newest hotel in Ely is the **Holiday Inn and Prospector Casino**, 1501 Ave. F, 775/289-8900, on the east end of town. Other chains include the **Best Western-Main Motel**, 1101 Aultman St., 775/289-4529 or 800-528-1234, and the **Best Western Park-Vue Motel**, 930 Aultman, 775/289-4497 or 800/528-1234, which, you guessed it, has a view of the park and pond filled with geese and ducks.

A couple of other good motels include the **Bristlecone Motel**, 700 Ave. I, 775/289-8838, and the **El Rancho Motel**, 1400 Aultman St., 775/289-3644.

Baker, five miles east of Great Basin National Park, has two small motels: the **Silver Jack**, 10 Main St., 775/234-7323, and the **Hidden Canyon Guest Ranch**, 15 miles southeast of Baker via Big Wash Canyon Road, 775/234-7267.

CAMPING

Campers will find numerous places to pitch a tent or park an RV in the Ely area. **Great Basin National Park** has four campgrounds. Lower Lehman has 11 sites, Wheeler Peak (situated at 10,000 feet) has 37 sites, Upper Lehman has 24, and Baker Creek has 33. Camping at Great Basin costs $5 per night and all the campgrounds have restrooms, fire rings, and tent pads. Lower Lehman campground is open year-round, the other three are open June through August, weather and snow melt permitting. The **Humboldt National Forest**, 775/289-3031, which surrounds Ely to the east and west, offers a number of campgrounds for tents and RVs. **Ward Mountain Campground**, six miles southwest of Ely on U.S. 6, has 22 sites.

Cave Lake State Park, 775/728-4467, 15 miles southeast of Ely on the Success Summit Road, has two small campgrounds: Elk Flat Campground, which has showers and flush toilets, and Lake View Campground, which is more rustic but is next to Cave Lake.

NIGHTLIFE

Even small towns in Nevada have an active nightlife thanks to the 24-hour casinos. The Hotel Nevada has Ely's only live-action table games as well as a rare penny slot machine and live entertainment in the lounge on weekends. The Jailhouse Casino and the Prospector Casino also have slot machines.

The Central Theater, 145 W. 15th St., 775/289-2202, could easily hold two or three of today's multiplex rooms. The room is trimmed in authentic 1950s art deco design, and a huge red-velvet curtain covers the screen. The sound is so-so (they didn't have Surround-Sound back then), but the ambiance makes the movie-watching experience worth it. Tickets are $5 for adults and $3 for children ages 3 to 11.

Scenic Route: Success Summit Loop

The meandering Success Summit Loop is a classic Sunday drive. You can begin the 35-mile dirt road at Cave Lake State Park, just south of Ely. From there the terrain becomes a changing canvas painted by Mother Nature—grassy meadows with aspen groves give way to sagebrush and limestone cliffs. Cattle graze along the roadways (watch out for darting cows), and deer, elk, snakes, hawks, and chipmunks are plentiful along the route. My favorite time to take the drive is fall afternoons. That's when the air is crisp and the sun strikes the aspens in their various shades of red and gold just right. The drive is best tackled with a high-clearance vehicle, but the road is well maintained and most obstacles (rocks and branches) are easily surmountable in a passenger car during good weather. The Success Summit Loop ends on U.S. 93 just north of McGill.

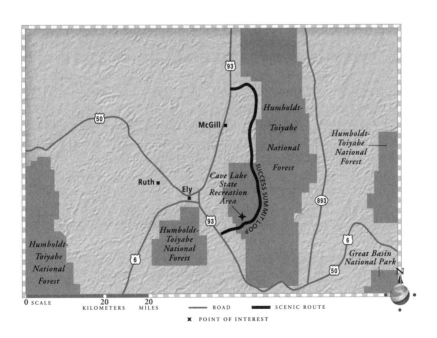

14
THE WILD AND WEIRD

This attractive little corner of the state is often referred to as Nevada's backyard due to the high concentration of state parks and recreation areas that beckon visitors to hike, fish, and camp. It's also an isolated area, largely unspoiled and unpopulated, making it a good place to stretch out when the aches of civilization have set in. This area encompasses three major (although still small) communities: Rachel, Caliente, and Pioche.

Rachel is one of Nevada's newest communities. It is mostly comprised of workers at the nearby Nevada Test Site and a few other independent spirits who like the desolation of the desert and the freedom to sprawl out on large tracts of land. Named for the first resident born there, Rachel is mostly trailers, mailboxes, and a few ranches, but the rumors of alien and secret aircraft attract skywatchers from all over the world. Rachel sits near the boundary of Area 51, the super-secret military base where high-tech airplanes and weaponry are tested—locals have seen strange lights shoot across the skies for years. Another rumor is that the hangars at Area 51 store spaceships that have crash-landed on Earth. Whatever your beliefs, the alien phenomenon is alive and well in Rachel, making it a fascinating place in which to ponder whether the truth is out there.

Caliente is more about alien landscapes—the formations at Cathedral Gorge State Park look as if they could have been transplanted from Mars. Caliente began as a railroad town, and you can still see the row of government housing that lines the main street. The depot is a stark reminder of the town's more prolific days, although its history doesn't rival that of Pioche, its sister town farther north.

Pioche is a classic Old West town, and miners who toiled deep in the earth during the day celebrated heartily in the town's saloons. Today it's much quieter, and its colorful history make the town worth taking the time to explore. Both towns are a stone's throw from several state parks, forming a pocket of recreation amid the history of eastern Nevada.

A PERFECT DAY AMONG THE WILD AND WEIRD

Begin with a walking tour of Pioche. Its wild and woolly past is still evident in the old storefronts. A stop at the Lincoln County Historical Museum will provide an educational backdrop to seeing the town's Boot Hill, where the earliest residents are buried, as well as the Million Dollar Courthouse. Then it's off to Caliente with a stop along the way at Cathedral Gorge State Park where you can enjoy a picnic lunch beneath the Fred Flintstone–style cabanas. The exotic formations and hiking trails can provide endless hours of exploration. In Caliente, take the time to tour the Union Pacific Train Depot and other historic attractions. Evening should be saved for an Alien Burger and UFO hunting at the Little A 'Le' Inn. There you can strike up conversations with friendly locals and hear their tales of UFO encounters in the area.

SIGHTSEEING HIGHLIGHTS: PIOCHE

★★★★ LINCOLN COUNTY HISTORICAL MUSEUM
69 Main St., Pioche, 775/962-5207

A tour of the raucous mining town of Pioche should begin at the Lincoln County Historical Museum. It is jam-packed with local artifacts. Naturally you will find mining exhibits, but you'll also be surprised to find a collection of the musical saws of James Wheeler, a local musician who plied his talents on the utilitarian hardware. Music lovers also can take note of the instruments that once belonged to the members of the Pioche Brass Band as well as the collection of old player pianos that covers one wall of the museum. The guides are friendly locals who enjoy chatting about their town's history.

Details: Open daily 10–1, 2–4. Donation. (1 hour)

★★★★ MILLION DOLLAR COURTHOUSE
Lacour St., Pioche, 775/962-5182

A tour of this creaky old building will reveal Pioche's wild days as a booming mining town filled with lawless roustabouts. As the name

THE WILD AND WEIRD REGION

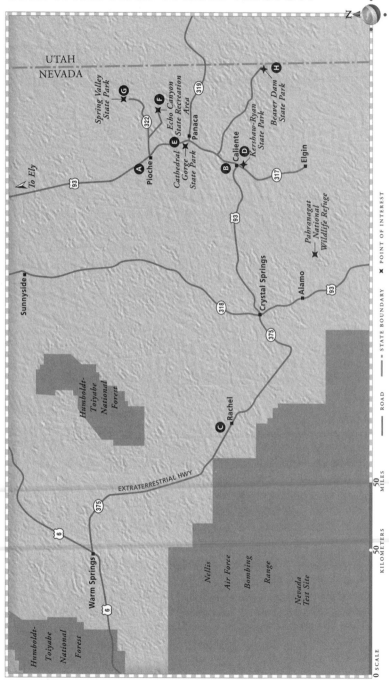

UTAH
NEVADA

Spring Valley
State Park

G

Echo Canyon
State Recreation
Area

F

322

Beaver Dam
State Park

H

319

Kershaw-Ryan
State Park

Catbedral
Gorge
State Park

E Panaca

Caliente

D

A

Pioche

B

317

Elgin

To Ely

93

93

Pahranagat
National
Wildlife Refuge

Sunnyside

Crystal Springs

Alamo

93

318

375

Humboldt-
Toiyabe
National
Forest

Rachel

C

EXTRATERRESTRIAL HWY

375

6

Warm Springs

6

Nellis
Air Force
Bombing
Range

Nevada
Test Site

Humboldt-
Toiyabe
National
Forest

ROAD ——— STATE BOUNDARY ■ ■ ■ POINT OF INTEREST ✶

50 MILES

50 KILOMETERS

0 SCALE

would imply, construction of the two-story courthouse in the 1870s encountered some major cost overruns that put the county heavily into debt. Construction costs shot from $16,000 to $26,000. By 1890 the principal and interest had accrued to about $400,000. The debt had climbed to $650,000 by 1907. It was refinanced and finally paid off in 1938—four years after the building had been condemned and the same year that a new courthouse had been built. But the story of the high-priced courthouse has a happy ending—the building was renovated and converted to a museum housing some intriguing displays that depict the courthouse's—and the town's—glory days. In one room you'll find a huge collection of old typewriters. Another room houses the clerk's office, and the district attorney's office has a law library packed with old volumes. On another wall you'll find a list of Pioche murder victims from 1870 to 1878. The courtroom is set up with mannequins of jurors, witnesses, and a judge whose gavel is activated by infrared sensors. Visitors can take their places in the jury box. The most chilling exhibit is the old jail cell out back, which still has an original leg iron.

Details: *Open Apr–Oct daily 10–12, 1–4. Donation. (30 minutes–1 hour)*

★ BOOT HILL
Comstock St., Pioche

The headstones here tell quite a story—several of the cemetery's

---

SIGHTS
- Ⓐ Boot Hill
- Ⓑ Intellectual Cowboy Bookstore
- Ⓐ Lincoln County Historical Museum
- Ⓒ Little A 'Le' Inn and the E.T. Highway
- Ⓐ Million Dollar Courthouse
- Ⓓ Rainbow Canyon
- Ⓑ Union Pacific Railroad Station

FOOD
- Ⓑ Brandin' Iron Restaurant
- Ⓑ Carl's
- Ⓐ Grub Steak
- Ⓑ Knotty Pine Restaurant
- Ⓒ Little A 'Le' Inn
- Ⓐ Overland Hotel and Saloon
- Ⓐ Pioche Cafe
- Ⓐ Silver Cafe

LODGING
- Ⓑ Hot Springs Motel
- Ⓐ Hutchings Motel

LODGING (continued)
- Ⓒ Little A 'Le' Inn
- Ⓐ Motel Pioche
- Ⓐ Overland Hotel
- Ⓑ Shady Motel

CAMPING
- Ⓔ Cathedral Gorge
- Ⓕ Eagle Valley Resort
- Ⓖ Echo Canyon
- Ⓕ Horsethief Gulch Campground
- Ⓖ Spring Valley
- Ⓗ Beaver Dam

Note: Items with the same letter are located in the same area.

early pioneers were laid to rest from gunshot wounds. Local legend boasts that 75 people were killed here before anyone died of natural causes. The faded wooden gravemarkers date back to the 1860s and 1870s, when the town was known for its wild and woolly miners who caroused and fought in its streets and saloons. **Details:** *Just off Main St. at the end of Comstock St. Free. (30 minutes)*

SIGHTSEEING HIGHLIGHTS: CALIENTE

★★★ INTELLECTUAL COWBOY BOOKSTORE
U.S. 93, Caliente, 775/726-3823

Caliente is beginning to see glimmers of new retail shops opening in town. An intriguing little nook on the main drag is the Intellectual Cowboy Bookstore, which opened in August 1998. This cozy little shop is packed with tomes on topics ranging from ghost-town hunting to children's books, and there's an extensive collection of Nevada books. The shop owners are good sources for tourist information—and in the winter you can usually find a pot of hot cider brewing. **Details:** *Open Mon–Sat 9–7. Free. (30 minutes)*

★★★ RAINBOW CANYON
SR 317, Caliente, 775/726-8100

Travelers should pick up the Rainbow Canyon driving tour brochure and take in the history and sights of this colorful area. The sheer walls of the canyon are made from volcanic tuff and have been colored over the past 34 million years by hot water that deposited such minerals as iron (which created reds and yellows) and copper (which stained some areas blue and green). The 20-mile drive leads past Kershaw-Ryan State Park, which offers scenic picnicking and hiking. Three more miles down the road is Etna Cave, where a short walk under a train trestle leads to a series of petroglyphs left by early Native Americans. The road continues past more train trestles, tunnels, and areas to look for petroglyphs. The drive ends at the End of the Rainbow Ranch, established in the 1880s and owned by the Bradshaw family. In the fall, visitors can stop at the ranch and pick the prolific winesap, golden delicious, and other varieties of apples for $5 a bucket. **Details:** *Just south of Kershaw-Ryan State Park and Caliente on SR 317. Free. (1 hour minimum)*

★★ UNION PACIFIC RAILROAD STATION
100 Depot St., Caliente, 775/726-3129

Built in 1923, the stark white depot dominates Caliente and belies its roots as a railroad town. The building, with its red tile roof and arched entryways, is a striking example of Mission-style architecture. Originally the Union Pacific train depot, the building has been a hotel, restaurant, and telegraph office. Today it has been adapted to serve as Town Hall, a library, an art museum, and an Amtrak passenger waiting room. The entryway is decorated with a mural, painted by a couple of talented locals, that depicts the history of the area and southern Nevada. Mary Ellen Sadovich operates a little railroad museum inside a boxcar next to the museum.

Details: *Mon–Fri 10–2. Free. Boxcar Museum $1. (30 minutes)*

SIGHTSEEING HIGHLIGHTS: RACHEL

★★★★ LITTLE A 'LE' INN AND THE E.T. HIGHWAY
Hwy. 375, Rachel, 775/729-2515

UFO watchers should grab their binoculars and head for the Extraterrestrial Highway, a lonely, 62-mile stretch on NV 375. You're not likely to be abducted—the area's reputation for having UFOs is due to its proximity to Area 51, the super-secret air force base where Stealth airplanes were tested. There are also rumors that the alien spaceship that crashed in Roswell, New Mexico, is stored in the hangars at Area 51. No civilians can confirm the report, and the military is not divulging any secrets. The alien lore is alive and well in Rachel at the Little A 'Le' Inn. Here you can enjoy an alien burger and shop for alien-themed merchandise. Some visitors try to get close to the perimeters of Area 51, but be sure you ask at the A 'Le' Inn for careful instructions or hire a guide for a tour—the government is strict about trespassers, and guards are authorized to use deadly force.

Details: *Open daily 8–10. Free. (1–2 hours)*

FITNESS AND RECREATION

Pahranagat National Wildlife Refuge, about 60 miles west of Caliente on U.S. 93 near Alamo, 775/725-3417, is a perpetual hangout for bird-watchers. Pahranagat, a Paiute Indian word for "place of many waters," is a series of lush marshes, ponds, and three major spring-fed bodies of water—the Upper Lake, Middle

Nevada Commission on Tourism

Pond, and Lower Lake. The place tends to sneak up on you—visitors traveling from Las Vegas will pass 80 miles of parched sagebrush desert before the refuge seems to pop up out of nowhere. But the area is a crucial resting and nesting spot for several species of migratory birds as well as a few permanent residents. Established as a national wildlife refuge in 1964, Pahranagat is on the Pacific Flyway, so spring and fall are often the best times for the binocular set. Grebes, pelicans, double-crested cormorants, Canada geese, several types of ducks, red-tailed hawks, American kestrels, hummingbirds, larks, and warblers are known to visit Pahranagat during specified seasons. Hunting and fishing are allowed at the refuge. Anglers can fish for largemouth bass, black bullheads, and carp. Camping is allowed on the shores of the Upper Lake.

The sandstone spires and other-worldly formations at Cathedral Gorge State Park in Panaca, 775/728-4460, can cause hikers, campers, and picnickers to feel as though they've landed on another planet. Established in 1935 as one of Nevada's first state parks, Cathedral Gorge has a bizarre landscape that lured thespians even in the 1920s to use the canyons and spires as a backdrop to their vaudeville acts and plays. About a million years ago Cathedral Gorge was covered by a lake, which receded and eroded, leaving behind the Martianesque formations. The narrow canyons and odd shapes make for a great game of hide-and-seek. The area also has 22 campsites as well as attractive picnic sites with ramadas, some of which were built by the Civilian Conservation

Corps in the 1930s. Hikers can explore the four-mile trail that leads to over-looks of the bluffs. The visitors center is architecturally striking and is a good place to stock up on information, watch the videotaped programs about the area, look at the taxidermied wildlife, and scope out the books and other items at the gift shop.

Several state parks that offer fishing, boating, camping, and hiking are clustered in this far eastern edge of Nevada. Echo Canyon State Park, 12 miles east of Pioche via State Routes 322 and 323, 775/962-5103, is a pleasant oasis amid alfalfa fields, and it has a reservoir, boat launch, and a hiking trail. Spring Valley State Park is 16 miles east of Pioche, 775/962-5102. It offers similar facilities as well as a couple of preserved historic ranch houses. The Millet Ranch is used as park headquarters, and hikers can explore the trails near the historic stone cabin, which is being renovated.

Beaver Dam State Park, 34 miles east of Caliente on the Nevada-Utah border, 775/728-4467, is a remote and rustic recreation area accessible by a dirt road. The 15-acre Schroeder Reservoir, steep canyon walls, and lush juniper trees also make it one of the state's most scenic places. The park has picture-perfect hiking trails, picnic areas, three campgrounds, and an abundance of wildlife, including beaver, deer, frogs, bats, and lizards.

Another scenic picnicking and hiking area is Kershaw Ryan State Park, three miles south of Caliente, 775/728-4467. The park recently reopened after a flood a few years ago wiped out and closed it. But it's back now better than ever. Tucked into the northern end of Rainbow Canyon, the park has a rugged landscape as well as grassy areas with lots of trees. Early settlers cultivated grapevines here, and they still cling to the canyon walls. The park has two picnic areas, a pond, and hiking trails.

FOOD

While you won't find Le Cirque or Spago in this—or any—area of rural Nevada, you will be in some of the country's best coffee-shop territory. In most cases the decor isn't fancy, but the coffee is always strong, the burgers fresh, and the folks eager to hear tales from your travels.

The conversation is especially colorful along the E.T. Highway at the **Little A 'Le' Inn** in Rachel, 775/729-2515. The restaurant-bar is plastered with pho-tographs of UFOs from all over the world. In Caliente you'll find a rustic assort-ment of eateries, including the **Brandin' Iron Restaurant**, 190 Clover St., 775/726-3164, **Carl's**, 146 Front St., 775/726-3138, and the **Knotty Pine Restaurant**, 690 Front St., 775/726-3194, all of which offer coffee-shop fare.

On Main Street in Pioche, the **Silver Cafe**, 775/962-5124, and the **Pioche**

Cafe, 775/962-5507, are recommended for burgers and sandwiches. The **Grub Steak**, 82 Main St., 775/962-5527, is a steak house with a mining theme. One of the most happening spots in town is the **Overland Hotel and Saloon**, 85 Main St. The fabulous Brunswick back bar, originally transported from England in 1863 to a bar in a nearby mining camp, is the focal point of the saloon. Live music and other performances are also featured at the saloon. During a recent visit, owners Ron and Candice Mortenson were hosting a revue of male dancers. The hotel has a new restaurant (that opened in winter 1998), slot machines, and a mounted buffalo head.

LODGING

In Caliente you can also rest your weary bones at the **Hot Springs Motel** on U.S. 93, 775/726-3777 or 888/726-3777, where the waters are soothing although the rooms are somewhat sparse and rustic. The **Shady Motel**, 450 Front St., 775/726-3106, is the newest and nicest in town, but it's close to the railroad tracks on which the Union Pacific Railroad still rumbles through town. Both charge between $30 and $40, which includes a soak in the hot springs at the Caliente Hot Springs Motel.

In Pioche, the **Overland Hotel**, 85 Main St., 775/962-5895, has spacious, clean rooms. At the **Hutchings Motel** on Mill Street, 775/962-5404, and the **Motel Pioche** on Lacour Street near the Million Dollar Courthouse, 775/962-5551, rates range from $30 to $40 per night.

If you really want to soak up the rural Nevada—and alien-watching—ambiance, you can check into the **Little A 'Le' Inn**, 775/729-2515, in Rachel. The accommodations are far from glamorous—you share a bathroom in a single-wide trailer—but the characters can make the stay worth the sacrifice in creature comforts.

CAMPING

Since this area has one of Nevada's highest concentrations of state parks, you can expect to find plenty of excellent camping here. **Cathedral Gorge**, 775/728-4460, **Echo Canyon**, 775/962-5103, **Spring Valley**, 775/962-5102, and **Beaver Dam**, 775/728-4467, state parks all have well-maintained campgrounds. For visitors who like a little more civilized camping, the **Horsethief Gulch Campground** at Spring Valley State Park has some of the area's most modern facilities with flush toilets and showers. All the parks can accommodate tents or RVs. Another popular campground near Spring Valley State Park is the **Eagle Valley Resort**, 775/962-5293, which has a 40-space

RV park (36 with full hookups), a store, and a bar with a pool table. Fees range from $11.50 to $15 for RVs and $7.50 for tents.

Alien watchers can call the Little A 'Le' Inn to find out when the next Friendship Campout will be held in Rachel. During these gatherings, folks stay up late around the campfire to hear stories about alien encounters and to scan the skies for UFOs.

Scenic Route: U.S. 93 to U.S. 50

Nature lovers will find that this remote route is one of the best ways to get to Great Basin National Park, 74 miles east of Ely. Beginning at Crystal Springs, this highway hugs the eastern edge of Nevada, traversing some of the state's wildest and most unspoiled scenery. A state-designated scenic byway, U.S. 93 takes travelers through a variety of vegetation and geologic zones.

The initial eastward stretch is sagebrush desert, but at Caliente the highway takes a sharp elbow northward, where red and purple canyons dominate the scenery. Along the way, the spires and narrow canyons of Cathedral Gorge State Park lure visitors off the highway. The terrain becomes more mountainous at Pioche, which sits at 6,064 feet in elevation. For the next 81 miles, the road slips through foothills, valleys, and alongside towering peaks before it terminates on U.S. 50 at Majors Place, 39 miles west of Great Basin National Park.

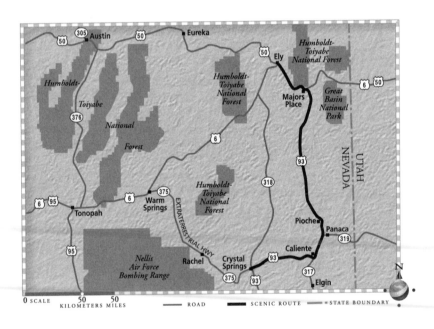

APPENDIX

Consider this appendix your travel tool box. Use it along with the material in the Planning Your Trip chapter to craft the trip you want. Here are the tools you'll find inside:

1. **Planning Map.** Make copies of this map and plot out various trip possibilities. Once you've decided on your route, you can write it on the original map and refer to it as you're traveling.

2. **Mileage Chart.** This chart shows the driving distances (in miles) between various destinations throughout the state. Use it in conjunction with the Planning Map.

3. **Special Interest Tours.** If you'd like to plan a trip around a certain theme—such as nature, sports, or art—one of these tours may work for you.

4. **Calendar of Events.** Here you'll find a month-by-month listing of major area events.

5. **Resources.** This guide lists various regional chambers of commerce and visitors bureaus, state offices, bed-and-breakfast registries, and other useful sources of information.

PLANNING MAP: Nevada

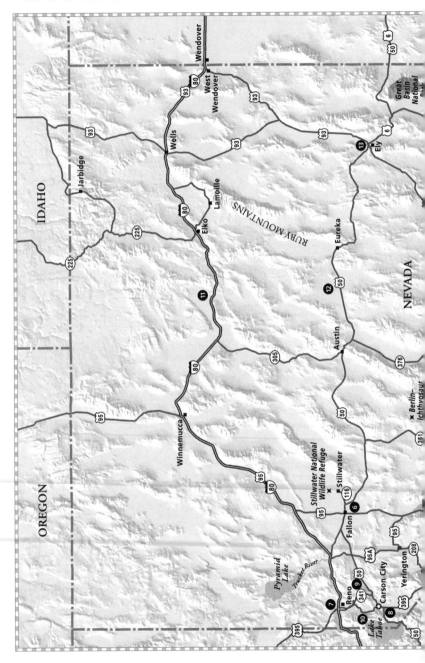

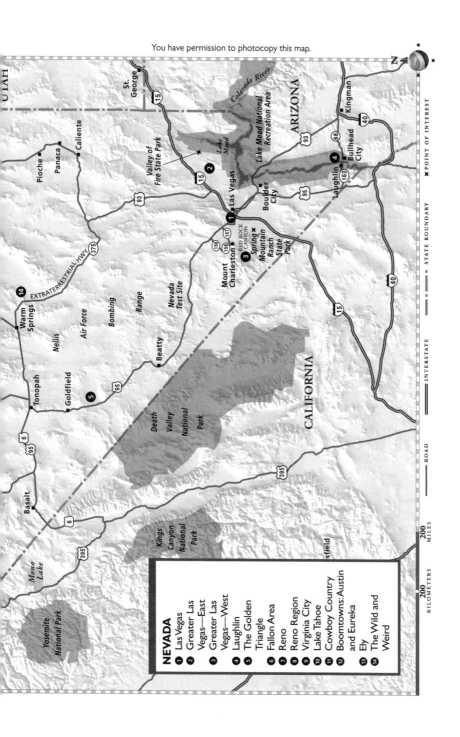

N

UTAH

St. George

Caliente

Pioche · Panaca

Colorado River

15

Valley of Fire State Park

15

93

2

Lake Mead

Lake Mead National Recreation Area

ARIZONA

93

68

Kingman

40

4

Bullhead City

Laughlin

163

95

Boulder City

1 Las Vegas

157

RED ROCK CANYON

156 158

3 Spring Mountain Ranch State Park

Mount Charleston

375

EXTRATERRESTRIAL HWY

Nevada Test Site

Bombing

Range

Air Force

Nellis

Beatty

40

15

14

Warm Springs

95

Tonopah

Goldfield

5

Death Valley National Park

CALIFORNIA

6

95

Basalt

6

395

Mono Lake

Kings Canyon National Park

395

Yosemite National Park

sfield

NEVADA

1 Las Vegas
2 Greater Las Vegas—East
3 Greater Las Vegas—West
4 Laughlin
5 The Golden Triangle
6 Fallon Area
7 Reno
8 Reno Region
9 Virginia City
10 Lake Tahoe
11 Cowboy Country
12 Boomtowns: Austin and Eureka
13 Ely
14 The Wild and Weird

200 KILOMETERS

200 MILES

ROAD

INTERSTATE

STATE BOUNDARY

POINT OF INTEREST

NEVADA MILEAGE CHART

	Las Vegas	Laughlin	Tonopah	Fallon	Reno	Carson City	Virginia City	Elko	Austin	Ely
Laughlin	95									
Tonopah	209	304								
Fallon	385	480	175							
Reno	446	541	236	61						
Carson City	435	555	229	61	32					
Virginia City	436	531	227	61	24					
Elko	430	525	270	255	288	306	303			
Austin	326	421	117	111	172	170	172	159		
Ely	242	337	169	259	320	318	319	188	148	
Pioche	174	269	215	367	428	428	428	296	256	108

SPECIAL INTEREST TOURS

With Nevada Travel•Smart you can plan a trip of any length—a one-day excursion, a getaway weekend, or a three-week vacation—around any special interest. To get you started, the following pages contain six special interest itineraries geared toward a variety of interests. For more information, refer to the chapters listed—chapter names are in boldface, and chapter numbers appear inside black bullets. You can follow a suggested itinerary in its entirety, or shorten, lengthen, or combine parts of each, depending on your starting and ending points.

Discuss alternative routes and schedules with your travel companions—it's a great way to have fun even before you leave home. And remember: Don't hesitate to change your itinerary once you're on the road. Careful study and planning ahead will help you make informed decision as you go, but spontaneity is the extra ingredient that will make your trip memorable.

BEST OF NEVADA TOUR

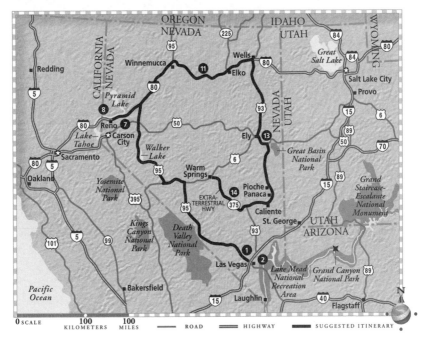

Nevada encompasses 110,000 square miles and an eclectic mix of terrain—everything from ranch country and pristine lakes to high-wattage boulevards. After you've traversed Nevada from north to south and east to west, you may truly feel as though you've seen it all.

❶ Las Vegas
❷ Greater Las Vegas—East
❼ Reno
❽ Reno Region
⓫ Cowboy Country
⓭ Ely
⓮ Wild and Weird

Time needed: 3 to 4 weeks

NATURE LOVER'S TOUR

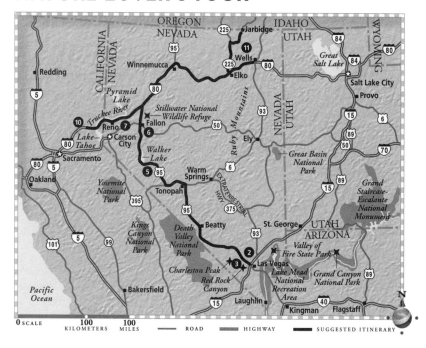

Although Nevada is mostly desert, the state also has more than 300 mountain ranges. For a dry state, Nevada also has surprisingly good lakes, rivers, and marshes. The wildlife reflects the diverse geography.

❷ Greater Las Vegas—East (Valley of Fire State Park)
❸ Greater Las Vegas—West (Mount Charleston, Red Rock Canyon National Conservation Area)
❺ Golden Triangle (Walker Lake, Death Valley National Park)
❻ Fallon Area (Stillwater National Wildlife Refuge)
❼ Reno (Truckee River)
❿ Lake Tahoe (Tahoe Rim Trail)
⑪ Cowboy Country (Ruby Mountains, Lamoille, East Humboldt Mountains, Jarbidge)

Time needed: 2 to 3 weeks

ARTS AND CULTURE TOUR

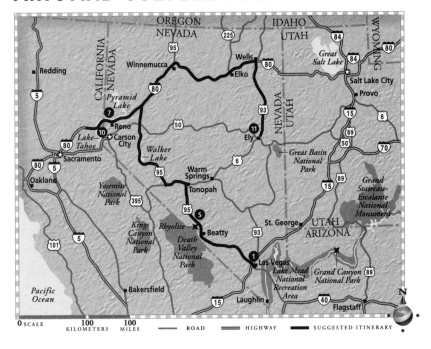

From the Bard on the beach at Lake Tahoe to van Gogh at the Bellagio on the Strip, the state's arts offerings are varied. You'll even find outdoor art in the desert.

- ❶ **Las Vegas** (Bellagio, Las Vegas Art Museum)
- ❺ **Golden Triangle** (Rhyolite)
- ❼ **Reno** (Nevada Museum of Art)
- ❿ **Lake Tahoe** (Shakespeare at Sand Harbor)
- ⓫ **Cowboy Country** (Cowboy Poetry Gathering, Western Folklife Center)

Time needed: 1 to 2 weeks

FAMILY FUN TOUR

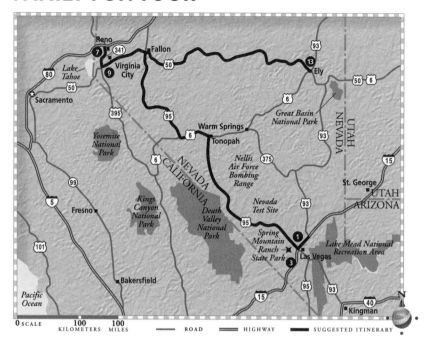

Although often considered an adult playground, Nevada reaches out to families and offers superb attractions that are both thrilling and educational.

- ❶ **Las Vegas** (Circus Circus, New York-New York, Lied Children's Discovery Museum, Liberace Museum, Southern Nevada Zoological-Botanical Park)
- ❸ **Greater Las Vegas—West** (Spring Mountain Ranch State Park, Bonnie Springs)
- ❼ **Reno** (Animal Ark, Sierra Safari Zoo, Wilbur D. May Museum and Arboretum, Circus Circus)
- ❾ **Virginia City** (Virginia and Truckee Railroad, old-fashioned saloons)
- ❸ **Ely** (Great Basin National Park)

Time needed: 2 weeks

HISTORY TOUR

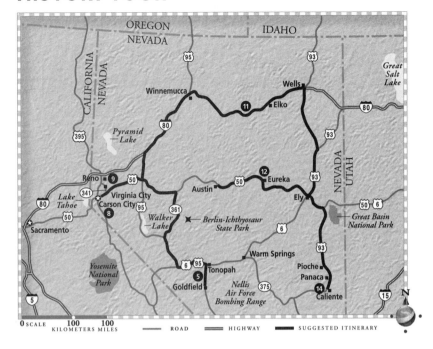

Nevada is dotted by ghost towns as well as mining towns that have managed to cling to life. Nevada's history is close to the surface and is easy to find throughout the state.

❺ Golden Triangle (Central Nevada Museum, Berlin-Ichthyosaur State Park, Goldfield, Mineral County Museum, Belmont, Tonopah Mining Park)
❽ Reno Region (Carson City)
❾ Virginia City (Way It Was Museum, boardwalk, saloons, churches)
⓫ Cowboy Country (Northeastern Nevada Museum, Humboldt Historical Museum)
⓬ Boomtowns (Austin churches, Stoke's Castle, Eureka Opera House, Eureka Sentinel Museum)
⓮ Wild and Weird (Boot Hill, Lincoln County Historical Museum, Million Dollar Courthouse)

Time needed: 2 weeks

GOLF LOVER'S TOUR

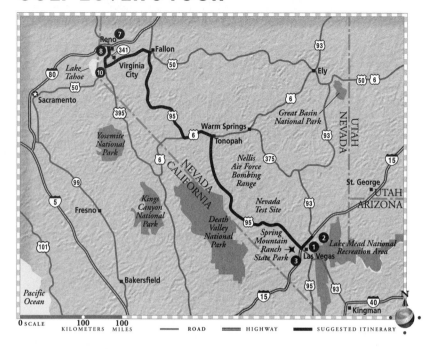

Golfers will find a course in nearly every town in Nevada.

❶ Las Vegas (Desert Inn, Angel Park, Royal Links)
❷ Greater Las Vegas—East (Lake Las Vegas Resort, Rio Secco)
❸ Greater Las Vegas—West (Shadow Creek, Las Vegas Paiute, Calvada Valley)
❼ Reno (Lakeridge, Wildcreek, Rosewood Lakes)
❽ Reno Region (Dayton Valley, Genoa Lakes, Sierra Nevada, Eagle Valley)
❿ Lake Tahoe (Edgewood Tahoe, Incline)

Time needed: 2 to 4 weeks

CALENDAR OF EVENTS

January

Martin Luther King Jr. Birthday Celebration, Las Vegas and Reno
Art exhibits, musical performances, and tribute dinners in honor of the slain civil rights leader
Elko Cowboy Poetry Gathering
Aspiring poets spin heartfelt rhymes about the range. Other events include a gift show and jam sessions. Hotel rooms and tickets sell out fast, so make reservations no later than November. 775/738-7508

February

Las Vegas International Marathon and Half-Marathon
Besides the main races, events include a 5K run and others. 702/240-2722
Walker Lake Fishing Derby, Hawthorne
Anglers earn cash prizes for catching big fish that have been specially tagged for the event. 775/945-5896

March

Snowfest Winter Carnival, North Lake Tahoe
A parade, polar bear swim, dress-up-your-dog contest, and ski races are part of this annual, weeklong celebration. 775/832-7625
Mountain Oyster Cook-Off, Virginia City
Adventurous diners can sample this distinctly Western dish prepared numerous ways. 775-847-0311
St. Patrick's Day Parade, Virginia City
Even the road stripe down C Street is painted green for this boisterous bash. 775/847-0311
Shooting the West, Winnemucca
High-caliber photographers from National Geographic and other publications present images and the stories behind their work. There's also a photo contest. 775/623-5071

April

Loon Festival, Walker Lake, Hawthorne
Walker Lake is a stopover for the birds, which are celebrated with lectures and loon-watching expeditions. 775/945-5896

Laughlin River Run
Harley-Davidson riders roar into the Colorado River town for show 'n' shines, concerts, and poker runs. 800/357-8223

May

Pioche Heritage Days
The town celebrates its mining heritage with plays, melodramas, and other activities. 775/962-5308

Comstock Historic Preservation Week, Virginia City
An 1880s ball and other events help Virginia City honor its silver- and gold-mining past. 775/847-0311

Armed Forces Day, Hawthorne
Veterans and current military personnel arrive for patriotic events and a parade. 775/645-5896

Snow Mountain Powwow, Las Vegas
Native Americans from tribes throughout the country gather for competitive dancing and fancy dancing, singing, and food. 702/386-0758

Fallon Air Show
Precision flying teams such as the Blue Angels perform aerobatics. The free show includes plenty of airplane souvenirs. 775/423-4556

June

Carson City Rendezvous
Mountain men encampments, Old West and modern crafts, Indian tacos, and live music are part of the celebration in Mills Park. 775/687-7410

Carson Valley Days, Gardnerville
You'll find a multitude of crafts, food, and entertainment at this small-town gathering. 775/265-2021

Gridley Days and Rock and Bottle Show, Austin
Using a flour sack, Austinite Reuel Gridley raised money for Civil War victims. Visitors will find flour-sack races, and rock hounds and bottle collectors can scour the booths. 775/964-2200

Reno Rodeo
The "Richest and Wildest Rodeo in the West" includes a cattle drive. 775/329-3877

Celebrity Golf Tournament, Lake Tahoe
Stars like Michael Jordan and Matt Lauer tee up for this PGA-style tournament at Edgewood Golf Course. 530/544-5050

July

Elko National Basque Festival
Basque families celebrate their homeland with a Catholic mass, dancing, games of strength and endurance, and a sheepherder's bread auction. 775/738-7135

Uptown Downtown ARTown, Reno
A monthlong schedule of dance performances, concerts, and art shows at locations throughout Reno. 775/329-1324

Lake Tahoe Shakespeare Festival
Performances on the beach at Sand Harbor with Lake Tahoe as a backdrop. 775/832-7625

Jim Butler Days, Tonopah
Tonopah celebrates its founder, who discovered gold here in the early 1900s, with a parade and party. 775/482-3558

August

Hot August Nights, Reno
Vintage automobiles, show 'n' shines, a parade, sock hops, and concerts featuring performers from the 1950s and '60s. 775/353-2291

Nevada State Fair, Reno
Carnival rides and games, livestock shows and auctions, art shows, food booths, concerts, and other events. 775/688-5767

Outhouse Races, Virginia City
Competitors in all forms of privies race to see whose is the fastest. 775/847-0311

Storey County Fair and Carnival, Virginia City
Camel rides, carnival games and rides, animals, and food. 775/847-0311

White Pine County Fair and Horse Races, Ely
Jam and quilt competitions, horse racing, and other events. 775/289-8877

September

Elko County Fair
Tomato growers and 4-H cow and pig raisers gather to show their wares at this old-fashioned, small-town fair. 775/738-3616

Best in the West Nugget Rib Cook-Off, Sparks
The cook-off includes rib tasting, lots of other food, free headliner concerts, and crafts. 775/353-2291

Virginia City International Camel Races
Participants bounce and jostle their way to the finish line atop sometimes

uncooperative camels. You'll also find ostrich races and a Camel Hump
Ball. 775/847-0311
Great Reno Balloon Race
The race attracts more than 100 balloonists. The most spectacular event
is the Dawn Patrol. 775/826-1181
National Championship Air Races, Reno
The country's largest air races include four classes: AT-6, Unlimited,
Formula One, and Biplane. The event includes airplane memorabilia and
other displays. 775/972-6663
Genoa Candy Dance
Includes crafts and plays in addition to a dance and candy sale.
775/782-TOWN
Hearts o' Gold Cantaloupe Festival, Fallon
Cantaloupe-eating contests and other events. Be sure to sample the can-
taloupe-flavored ice cream and take a camel ride. 775/423-4556

October

Great Italian Festival, Reno
Visitors can nosh on spaghetti and other Italian delights. You'll also find a
grape-stomping competition and plenty of accordions and Italian music.
775/786-5700
Art in the Park, Boulder City
Nevada's largest craft fair has more than 300 booths filled with everything
from quilts to artwork. 702/294-1611
Las Vegas Invitational Golf Tournament
Top PGA players converge on three courses in Las Vegas for five days of
tournament play. 702/242-3000
Celtic New Year's Celebration, Reno
Bagpipe music, Celtic dancing, and other entertainment. 775/332-3333
Nevada Day Celebration, Carson City
Nevada's statehood—October 31, 1864—is celebrated with the state's
longest parade, a chili cook-off, fireworks, a period-costume dance, and
historic home tours. 775/687-4680
Bonneville World Finals, Wendover
Drivers attempt to set new world land-speed records on a 10-mile track.
805/526-1805

November

Rhymer's Rodeer Cowboy Poetry, Minden
  Cowboy poets regale listeners with tales and rhymes that reflect the buckaroo spirit and lifestyle. 775/782-9711
Veterans Day Parade, Virginia City
  The parade honors all those who've served in the armed forces. 775/847-0311

December

National Finals Rodeo, Las Vegas
  Top bronc and bull riders saddle up for more than $2.5 million in prize money. Hotels book country performers during the event. Make reservations several months in advance. 702/260-8605
National Finals Rodeo Christmas Gift Show, Las Vegas
  You'll find all things cowboy—from saddles and silver conchos to Western shirts and cowboy music—at this show held in conjunction with the National Finals Rodeo. 702/260-8605
Lake Mead Parade of Lights, Henderson
  Boaters deck out their watercraft with elaborate Christmas-light displays and parade around Lake Mead. 702/457-2797
Sparks Hometowne Christmas
  A parade (with grand marshall St. Nick), tree-lighting, music, and crafts. 775/353-2291
Buck 'n Ball, Reno
  Ring in the new year with a rodeo and dancing. 800/FOR-RENO

RESOURCES

Austin Chamber of Commerce: Box 212, Austin, NV 89310, 775/964-2200

Battle Mountain Chamber of Commerce: Box 333, Battle Mountain, NV 89820, 775/635-8245

Beatty Chamber of Commerce: Box 956, Beatty, NV 89003, 775/553-2424

Boulder City Visitor Center: 100 Nevada Hwy., Boulder City, NV 89005, 702/294-1252

Bureau of Land Management: Main: 1340 Financial Blvd., Reno, NV 89520, www.nv.blm.gov, 775/861-6400

Caliente Chamber of Commerce: Depot Building, Box 553, Caliente, NV 89008, 775/726-3129

Carson City Convention and Visitors Bureau: 1900 S. Carson St., Suite 200, Carson City, NV 89701, www.carson-city.org, 775/687-7410 or 800/NEVADA-1

Carson Valley Chamber of Commerce and Visitors Authority: 1512 Hwy. 395, No. 1, Gardnerville, NV 89410-5283, www.carsonvalleynv.org, 775/782-8144 or 800/727-7677 in U.S.

Dayton Area Chamber of Commerce: 15 Main St., Box 2408, Dayton, NV 89403, 775/246-7909

Elko Convention and Visitors Authority: 700 Moren Way, Elko, NV 89801, 775/738-4091 or 800/248-3556

Ely's Bristlecone Convention Center: 150 Sixth St., Box 958, Ely, NV 89301, 775/289-3720

Eureka County Chamber of Commerce: Box 14, Eureka, NV 89316; 775/237-5484

Fallon Convention and Tourism Authority: 100 Campus Way, Fallon, NV 89406, www.fallon.net, 775/423-4556 or 800/874-0903

Fernley Chamber of Commerce: 70 N. West St., Box 1606, Fernley, NV 89408, fernleynevada.com, 775/575-4459

Goldfield Chamber of Commerce: Box 219, Goldfield, NV 89013, members.xcom.com/gfldchamber, 775/485-3560

Great Basin Business and Tourism Council: Box 166, Baker, NV 89311, 775/234-7323

Great Basin National Park: Baker, NV 89311, www.nps.gov/grba, 775/234-7331

Hoover Dam Visitors Services: Box 60400, Boulder City, NV 89006, www.hooverdam.com, 702/294-3523

Humboldt National Forest: 2035 Last Chance Rd., Elko, NV 89801, 775/738-5171

Jarbidge Community Association: c/o Trading Post, Box 260072, Jarbidge, NV 89826, e-mail Jarbidge@aol.com, 775/488-2315

Jean Visitor Center: I-15 S., Exit 12, Jean, NV 89019, 702/874-1360

Lake Mead National Recreation Area: 601 Nevada Hwy., Boulder City, NV 89005, www.nps/gov/lame, 702/293-8907

Lake Tahoe, Incline Village/Crystal Bay Visitors and Convention Bureau: 969 Tahoe Blvd., Incline Village, NV 89451, www.gotahoe.com, 775/832-1606 or 800/GO-TAHOE

Lake Tahoe Visitors Authority: 1156 Ski Run Blvd., South Lake Tahoe, CA 96150, www.virtualtahoe.com, 530/544-5050 or 800/AT-TAHOE

Las Vegas Convention and Visitors Authority: 3150 Paradise, Las Vegas, NV 89109, www.lasvegas24hours.com, 702/892-0711

Laughlin Visitor Center: 1555 Casino Dr., Laughlin, NV 89029, www.visit-laughlin.com, 702/298-3321 or 800/4LAUGHLIN

Mason Valley Chamber of Commerce: 227 S. Main St., Yerington, NV 89447-2536, www.tele-net.net/lceda, 775/463-2245

Mesquite Visitor Center: I-15, Exit 122, 460 Sandhill Blvd., Mesquite, NV 89027, 702/346-2702 or 877/MESQUITE

Mineral County Chamber of Commerce: 932 E. Street, Box 1635, Hawthorne, NV 89415, e-mail info@mcchamber.hawthorne.nv.us, 775/945-5896

Nevada Commission on Tourism: Capitol Complex, Carson City, NV 89710, www.travelnevada.com, 775/687-4322 or 800/NEVADA-8

Nevada Division of State Parks: 1300 South Curry St., Carson City, NV 89710, 775/687-4370

Pahrump Valley Chamber of Commerce: Box 42, Pahrump, NV 89041, 775/727-5800 or 800/633-WEST

Pioche Chamber of Commerce: Box 127, Pioche, NV 89043, www.pioche.com/chamber.htm, 775/962-5544

Red Rock Canyon National Conservation Area: HCR 33, Box 5500, Las Vegas, NV 89124, 702/363-1921

Reno-Sparks Convention and Visitors Authority: 4590 S. Virginia St., Reno, NV 89502, www.playreno.com, 775/827-7600 or 800/FOR-RENO

Toiyabe National Forest: 1200 Franklin Way, Sparks, NV 89431, 775/331-6444, 2881 S. Valley View, Suite 16, Las Vegas, NV 89102, www.fs.fed.us/htnf/, 702/873-8800

Tonopah Convention Center: Box 408, Tonopah, NV 89049, www.tonopah-miningpark.org, 775/482-3558

Virginia City Chamber of Commerce: V&T Railroad Car, C St., Virginia City, NV 89440, 775/847-0311

Wendover USA Chamber/Visitors Bureau: Box 2468, West Wendover, NV 89883, www.wendover-usa.org, 775/664-3414 or 800/426-6862

Winnemucca Convention and Visitors Bureau: 50 W. Winnemucca Blvd., Winnemucca, NV 89445, www.winnemucca.nv.us, 775/623-5071 or 800/WMCA-NEV

INDEX

Map Index

Guidebooks that really *guide*

City•Smart™ Guidebooks

Pick one for your favorite city: *Albuquerque, Anchorage, Austin, Calgary, Charlotte, Chicago, Cincinnati, Cleveland, Denver, Indianapolis, Kansas City, Memphis, Milwaukee, Minneapolis/St. Paul, Nashville, Pittsburgh, Portland, Richmond, Salt Lake City, San Antonio, San Francisco, St. Louis, Tampa/St. Petersburg, Tucson.* US $12.95 to 15.95

Retirement & Relocation Guidebooks

The World's Top Retirement Havens, Live Well in Honduras, Live Well in Ireland, Live Well in Mexico. US $15.95 to $16.95

Travel•Smart® Guidebooks

Trip planners with select recommendations to *Alaska, American Southwest, Arizona, Carolinas, Colorado, Deep South, Eastern Canada, Florida, Florida Gulf Coast, Hawaii, Illinois/Indiana, Kentucky/Tennessee, Maryland/Delaware, Michigan, Minnesota/Wisconsin, Montana/Wyoming/Idaho, New England, New Mexico, New York State, Northern California, Ohio, Pacific Northwest, Pennsylvania/New Jersey, South Florida and the Keys, Southern California, Texas, Utah, Virginias, Western Canada.* US $14.95 to $17.95

Rick Steves' Guides

See *Europe Through the Back Door* and take along guides to *France, Belgium & the Netherlands; Germany, Austria & Switzerland; Great Britain & Ireland; Italy; Scandinavia; Spain & Portugal; London; Paris;* or *Best of Europe.* US $12.95 to $21.95

Adventures in Nature

Plan your next adventure in *Alaska, Belize, Caribbean, Costa Rica, Guatemala, Hawaii, Honduras, Mexico.* US $17.95 to $18.95

Into the Heart of Jerusalem

A traveler's guide to visits, celebrations, and sojourns. US $17.95

The People's Guide to Mexico

This is so much more than a guidebook—it's a trip to Mexico in and of itself, complete with the flavor of the country and its sights, sounds, and people. US $22.95

John Muir Publications
5855 Beaudry Street • Emeryville, CA 94608

Available at your favorite bookstore.

CAROLYN GRAHAM

Jay Aldrich

ABOUT THE AUTHOR

Carolyn Graham earned a journalism degree from New Mexico State University before moving to Nevada in 1989. She has written for several Nevada publications, including the *Nevada Appeal*, the *Comstock Chronicle*, and *Nevada Magazine*, where she serves as associate editor.

Carolyn is a member of the Society of American Travel Writers and has contributed to guidebooks on Costa Rica and Belize. She lives in Carson City with her husband, Steve, and their border collie, Bongo.